PRAISE FOR
HEROIC LEADERSHIP

"In this day of Enrons and Tycos, there is a need to reexamine
corporate values. *Heroic Leadership* gives the leader food for thought.
The sections on love and heroism are truly energizing."

—JOHN F. GALBRAITH, PRESIDENT AND CEO,
CATHOLIC MEDICAL MISSION BOARD

"With our renewed focus on sustainable growth, Lowney's book comes at
the right time, not providing recipes for becoming a leader but
guiding us along the Jesuit principles to turn us into leaders."

—PETER WOICKE, EXECUTIVE VICE PRESIDENT,
INTERNATIONAL FINANCE CORPORATION

"Lowney demonstrates how today's organizations need to scrap
the traditional and narrow vision of leadership and adopt
the Jesuit model of 'everyone is a leader.'"

—DURANT "ANDY" HUNTER, PRESIDENT, U.S., WHITEHEAD MANN

"*Heroic Leadership* advances a leadership unafraid to put love at
the center. This is a lively, witty book about profound matters."

—JAMES N. LOUGHRAN, S.J., PRESIDENT, SAINT PETER'S COLLEGE

"Lowney brings together extensive experience in international banking, a
solid grasp of Jesuit spirituality and history, and a good acquaintance
with recent leadership literature to produce a book
that is at once challenging and compelling."

—THE REVEREND HAROLD RIDLEY, S.J.,
PRESIDENT, LOYOLA COLLEGE IN MARYLAND

"The Jesuits have something unique and profound to offer . . . [to] those of us trying to operate a business that is both successful and true to our deepest values and convictions."

—GREGORY F. A. PIERCE, AUTHOR, *SPIRITUALITY AT WORK*; PRESIDENT AND COPUBLISHER, ACTA PUBLICATIONS; COFOUNDER, BUSINESS LEADERS FOR EXCELLENCE, ETHICS, AND JUSTICE

———————

"I am confident that I would have been a far more effective leader if I had read *Heroic Leadership* years ago, Highly recommended!"

—RON BURKARD, FORMER EXECUTIVE DIRECTOR, WORLD NEIGHBORS

———————

"These are stories of great heroism . . . Lowney offers a spirituality of work here that needs to be listened to."

—NATIONAL CATHOLIC REPORTER

———————

"With a light touch and fine writing, Chris Lowney brings the sixteenth century into the twenty-first. Presidents of both colleges and corporations can apply this text extensively to their own worlds with great profit."

—CHARLES J. BEIRNE, S.J., PRESIDENT, LE MOYNE COLLEGE

———————

"As Asia surges forward, its managers are realizing that shallow leadership checklists and flashy management slogans from the West do not always work. *Heroic Leadership* sets out four key principles that . . . can be applied across cultures and geographies."

—JACKSON TAI, CEO, DEVELOPMENT BANK OF SINGAPORE

———————

"A wonderfully stimulating book for those interested in forging closer links between their Christian faith and a business vocation."

—WILLIAM BYRON, S.J., AUTHOR, *JESUIT SATURDAYS*

———————

"Lowney's examination of the principles of Jesuit leadership . . . makes for fascinating reading. Jesuits and lay alike will find much to celebrate and emulate."

—BRADLEY M. SCHAEFFER, S.J., PRESIDENT, JESUIT CONFERENCE

———————

HEROIC LEADERSHIP

BEST PRACTICES FROM A 450-YEAR-OLD COMPANY THAT CHANGED THE WORLD

CHRIS LOWNEY

LOYOLA PRESS.
A JESUIT MINISTRY
Chicago

LOYOLA PRESS.
A JESUIT MINISTRY

3441 N. Ashland Avenue
Chicago, Illinois 60657
(800) 621-1008
www.loyolapress.com

The photo of Ignatius Loyola (p. 41) is from the Curia Generalizi of the Society of Jesus. The photo of the Jesuits at the Mughal court (p. 66) is reproduced by permission of the Trustees of Chester Beatty Library, Dublin. The photo of Matteo Ricci (p. 75) is from *Generation of Giants: The Story of the Jesuits in China in the Last Decades of the Ming Dynasty* by George H. Dunne, S.J. The photo of Christopher Clavius (p. 82) is from the Mary Evans Picture Library. The photo of Francis Xavier (p. 131) is from the collection of Gonzaga University's Jundt Art Museum. The photo of Roberto de Nobili (p. 150) is from *The First Scholar* by S. Rajamanickam, S.J., copyright © 1972. The photos of Guaraní art and architecture (p. 187) are from José Maria Blanch, S.J. The photo of Johann Adam Schall von Bell (p. 259) is from *Adam Schall: A Jesuit at the Court of China, 1592–1666* by Rachel Attwater, originally from *China* by Athanasius Kircher, published in 1667.

Jacket and interior design by Megan Duffy Rostan

Library of Congress Cataloging-in-Publication Data
Lowney, Chris.
   Heroic leadership : best practices from a 450-year-old company that changed the world / Chris Lowney.
         p. cm.
Includes bibliographical references and index.
   ISBN-10: 0-8294-1816-4, ISBN-13: 978-0-8294-1816-3
   1. Leadership. 2. Jesuits—History. I. Title.
   HD57.7.L69 2003
   658.4'092—dc21

                                                          2003004774

First paperback printing, January 2005
paperback ISBN-10: 0-8294-2115-7, ISBN-13: 978-0-8294-2115-6

Printed in the United States of America
08 09 10 11 12 13 14 Bang 10 9 8

CONTENTS

CHAPTER 1

Of Jesuits and J. P. Morgan

After living for seven years as a Jesuit seminarian, practicing vows of poverty, chastity, and obedience to the Jesuit general in Rome, I morphed into corporate man. On Friday afternoon, my role model was the Jesuit founder, St. Ignatius Loyola, whose writings reminded us seminarians that "poverty, as the strong wall of the religious life, should be loved." The following Monday brought a new career in investment banking—and new role models. One managing director lured talented would-be recruits with the tantalizing prospect of becoming "hog-whimperingly rich." I never quite got the image, but I did get the point.

At first I kept a low profile. My head was often spinning, and even casual conversation left me acutely aware that my background was, to say the least, a bit different from that of my new peers. When fellow new hires regaled colleagues with tales of amorous scores that summer, what was I going to talk about—making my final weeklong silent retreat or purchasing my first non-black suit?

It was my great fortune and privilege to have left the best company in one "business" only to land at the best company in another. J. P. Morgan headed *Fortune* magazine's list of most-admired banking companies every year but two of the seventeen I worked there—two facts that, I hasten to add, are coincidentally rather than causally related.

A LEADERSHIP CHALLENGE

Mighty though the House of Morgan was, we struggled with a long list of challenges, none of them unique to either J. P. Morgan or the investment banking business. One core issue cropped up again and again: eliciting the leadership from our teams that would enable J. P. Morgan to emerge a winner in a highly competitive industry. I served Morgan as a managing director in Tokyo, Singapore, London, and New York, discovering that our leadership challenge knew no geographic boundaries. I was also fortunate enough to serve successively on the firm's Asia-Pacific, Europe, and Investment Banking Management Committees, where I, who apprenticed in a seminary, and Management Committee colleagues, who apprenticed in the world's best business schools, all grappled with the same challenge of recruiting and molding winning teams.

We hired those supersmart, ambitious, and strong-willed people whom Tom Wolfe famously tagged "masters of the universe" in *The Bonfire of the Vanities*. And like Wolfe's protagonist, our masters of the universe frequently suffered tragic downfalls. Raw talent and sheer ambition didn't always translate into long-term success. Many up-and-comers blazed meteoric paths through Morgan skies: first shining brightly in the number-crunching roles assigned to junior "cannon fodder," then flaming out spectacularly when challenged with the "grown-up" tasks integral to company leadership. Some were terrified of making major decisions; others terrorized anyone who dared make a decision without them. Some were great managers so long as they managed only numbers; their management repertoire didn't extend to thinking, feeling human beings, who are less easily manipulated than spreadsheets. Ironically, many were uncomfortable with change and with taking personal risks—even though investment banking's fast pace had lured them to the business in the first place (in addition, of course, to the prospect of hog-whimpering wealth). Not only was the industry

highly cyclical, but it was roiled by sweeping fundamental realign-
ment: by the time I left Morgan, every one of the ten largest U.S.
banks had been through a transforming merger.

It was clear that only a handful of banks would emerge as winners in our changing, consolidating industry. And the winners
likely would be those whose employees could take risks and innovate, who could work smoothly on teams and motivate colleagues,
and who could not only cope with change but also spur change. In
short, *leadership* would separate the winners from the losers.

At Morgan, we took whatever initiatives we could to elicit the
mindset and behavior we needed. In the course of one such initiative, I experienced a small epiphany. J. P. Morgan was in the
process of instituting "360-degree feedback," a then cutting-edge
practice. Annual performance assessments would incorporate
input not only from one's direct manager but from subordinates
and peers as well. We proudly thumped our chests as one of the
first companies to implement this "best practice" on a broad scale.

Really?

Hadn't I seen this somewhere before? I vaguely recalled a long-
ago time in a galaxy far away, when I often dressed in black and
when I loved poverty as the "strong wall of the religious life." The
Jesuit company also had a 360-degree feedback system of sorts. In
fact, its 360-degree feedback process had been launched approximately 435 years before it caught on at *Fortune*'s perennially most-
admired bank and in the rest of corporate America.

A CENTURIES-OLD COMPANY

Come to think of it, the Jesuits had also grappled—quite successfully—with other vital challenges that confronted J. P. Morgan
and still test great companies today: forging seamless multinational teams, motivating inspired performance, remaining
"change ready" and strategically adaptable.

Moreover, the Jesuits were launched into an environment that, though four centuries removed, had telling analogies to our own. New world markets were opening as voyages of discovery established permanent European links to the Americas and Asia. Media technology was evolving: Gutenberg's printing press had transformed books from luxury goods into more widely accessible media. Traditional approaches and belief systems were questioned or discarded as Protestant reformers mounted the first widespread and permanent "competition" to the Roman Catholic Church. Because the Jesuit company was cast into this increasingly complex and constantly changing world, it's no great surprise that its organizational architects prized the same mindset and behaviors that modern companies value in today's similarly tumultuous environments: the abilities to innovate, to remain flexible and adapt constantly, to set ambitious goals, to think globally, to move quickly, to take risks.

> I was intrigued by what sixteenth-century priests might teach us twenty-first-century sophisticates about leadership and about coping with complex, changing environments.

As I started to look beyond the obvious fact that an investment bank has a different mission than a religious order, these equally obvious parallels fell into focus. And as I considered Ignatius Loyola and his early Jesuit colleagues in this context, I became convinced that their approach to molding innovative, risk-taking, ambitious, flexible global thinkers *worked*. In some ways—dare I say it—it worked better than many modern corporate efforts to do the same.

My epiphany provided the impetus for this book. I began this project fascinated by the parallels between two very different moments in history. I was intrigued by the challenge of exploring what sixteenth-century priests might teach us twenty-first-century sophisticates about leadership and about coping with complex, changing environments. I finished the project completely convinced of the value and timeliness of what the early Jesuits have to offer.

REVOLUTIONARY LEADERSHIP

Some elements of the Jesuit approach are increasingly finding validation in recent research—for example, the link between self-awareness and leadership. I'm sure Loyola would be pleased that the research is finally catching up with his intuitions. But we haven't completely caught up with him, and some aspects of Jesuit-style leadership carry the uncomfortable and even kooky ring common to provocative new ideas. For example, Loyola and his colleagues were convinced that we perform our best in supportive, encouraging, and positively charged environments (so far so good), and so he exhorted his managers to create environments filled with—I say it with trepidation, picturing my hard-charging Morgan ex-colleagues—"greater *love* than fear." But after living with the idea of a loving work environment for a while, it seems to me more wise than kooky, and I hope readers will find similar wisdom in Loyola's ideas after living with them for a while.

What has been most revolutionary and most refreshing for me personally is that these principles address one's whole life and not merely one's work life. The Jesuits' principles made the company better because they made individual Jesuits better. Their principles are rooted in the notions that we're *all* leaders and that our whole lives are filled with leadership opportunities. Leadership is not reserved for a few Pooh-Bahs sitting atop large companies, nor do leadership opportunities arise only "on stage" at work. We can be leaders in everything we do—in our work and in our daily lives, when teaching others or learning from others. And most of us do all those things in the course of any given day.

I've been fortunate to work with some great leaders, and I'm convinced that Ignatius Loyola and his team were great ones as well. That's the only reason for paying attention to the ideas they offer about leadership. Loyola also happened to be a saint, and he and his Jesuit colleagues were Catholics, priests, and, thus, all men. I've tried to refrain from basing judgments on these facts in order to measure them by one criterion only: how well they led themselves and others. Similarly, I ask the reader to shake off whatever positive or negative feelings that he or she may harbor about Loyola's particular religious beliefs or males-only organization. Whenever possible I've stripped overtly religious imagery and phrasings from quotes; Jesuits did not become successful leaders simply by adhering to particular religious beliefs but by the way they lived and worked. And their way of living holds value for everyone, whatever his or her creed.

In the end, Loyola's latter-day colleagues may be more rankled by the religious content that's *missing* from this book than some others will be by the religious content that remains. But Loyola himself established the Jesuit success formula of attacking real-world opportunities with real-world leadership strategies, and colleagues observing him coined the Jesuit maxim "Work as if success depended on your own efforts—but trust as if all depended on God."[1] Loyola's successor, Diego Laínez, echoed the sentiment in blunter terms: "While it is true that God could speak by the mouth of an ass, this would be considered a miracle. We are tempting God when we expect miracles. This would certainly be the case in a man who lacks common sense but who hopes to be a success merely by praying for it."[2]

In the end, I'm confident that readers will give Loyola and his team their due. After all, the "leadership lessons" genre has proven flexible enough to embrace such unlikely gurus as Attila the Hun, Winnie the Pooh, the Mafia Manager, the Founding Fathers, and W. C. Fields. Surely any tent big enough to fit such a cross section of leaders also has room for a sixteenth-century priest and his colleagues!

WHY THE JESUITS?

Founded in 1540 by ten men with no capital and no business plan, the Jesuits built, within little more than a generation, the world's most influential company of its kind. As confidants to European monarchs, China's Ming emperor, the Japanese shogun, and the Mughal emperor in India, they boasted a Rolodex unmatched by that of any commercial, religious, or government entity. Yet, infused with restless energy, Jesuits seemed less content at imperial courts than out testing imperial frontiers. Though their journeys deposited them at the very ends of the world as then known to Europeans, they invariably probed each boundary to understand what lay beyond it. Jesuit explorers were among the first Europeans to cross the Himalayas and enter Tibet, to paddle to the headwaters of the Blue Nile, and to chart the Upper Mississippi River.

Their colleagues back in Europe focused the same will to achieve and intense energy on building what would become the world's largest higher-education network. With exactly no experience running schools, they somehow managed to have more than thirty colleges up and running within a decade. By the late eighteenth century, seven hundred secondary schools and colleges sprawled across five continents. By one estimate, Jesuits were educating nearly 20 percent of all Europeans pursuing a classical higher education.

> As confidants to European monarchs, China's Ming emperor, the Japanese shogun, and the Mughal emperor in India, the Jesuits boasted a Rolodex unmatched by that of any commercial, religious, or government entity.

Jesuits in Europe and their colleagues farther afield leveraged one another's efforts in a richly symbiotic relationship. Jesuit astronomers and mathematicians in Rome supplied Jesuits in

China with the technical know-how to win unprecedented prestige and influence in that country—as heads of the astronomical bureau, reformers of the calendar, and personal advisers to the emperor. Jesuits in remote outposts more than repaid any favors of their European colleagues by enabling them to burnish their corporate mystique as scholars and pioneers who were plugged in all over the world. French Jesuits proudly presented King Louis XV with a copper-plated edition of the first comprehensive atlas of China, prepared by French colleagues in China at the emperor's behest. Educated Europeans eagerly learned about Asia, Africa, and the Americas through nearly a thousand works of natural history and geography penned by Jesuits all over the globe.

Their coups were by no means only academic. Though religious strife bitterly divided Protestants and Catholics in Counter-Reformation Europe, fever sufferers of all religious persuasions gratefully used the quinine distilled from what widely became known as Jesuit's bark, while benzoin-based Jesuit's drops soothed those afflicted with skin irritations. Jesuits had learned of both herbal medicines from indigenous new world populations.

This innovative, wide-ranging Jesuit company still exists. Once dwarfed by larger religious orders, it has long since become the world's largest religious order.[3] Its twenty-one thousand professionals run two thousand institutions in more than a hundred countries.[4] More than 450 years have passed since its founding; this longevity alone is a remarkable testament to success in the Darwinian corporate environment. The Jesuits are marching inexorably toward their five hundredth anniversary; by comparison, a mere sixteen of the hundred largest American companies of the year 1900 survived long enough to celebrate a centennial.

Why were, and why are, these Jesuits successful? What spurred their creativity, energy, and innovation? How have they succeeded while so many other companies and organizations have long since fallen by the wayside?

FOUR PILLARS OF SUCCESS

What often passes for leadership today is a shallow substitution of technique for substance. Jesuits eschewed a flashy leadership style to focus instead on engendering four unique values that created leadership substance:

- self-awareness

- ingenuity

- love

- heroism

In other words, Jesuits equipped their recruits to succeed by molding them into leaders who

- understood their strengths, weaknesses, values, and worldview

- confidently innovated and adapted to embrace a changing world

- engaged others with a positive, loving attitude

- energized themselves and others through heroic ambitions

Moreover, Jesuits trained every recruit to lead, convinced that all leadership begins with *self*-leadership.

This four-pillared formula still molds Jesuit leaders today. And the formula can mold leaders in all areas of life and work.

This book examines not only what made sixteenth-century Jesuits successful but also who leaders are and how they are molded in every generation—including our own. The Jesuit founders launched their company into a complex world that had probably changed as much in fifty years as it had over the previous thousand. Sound familiar? They speak to us not as experts in dealing with an antiquated sixteenth-century landscape but as experts in eliciting confident performance despite uncomfortably shifting landscapes—in whatever century.

This book looks closely at what made the early Jesuits successful and then relates that wisdom to the person or organization today who wants to learn and to practice effective, whole-person leadership.

Succeeding chapters explore the four Jesuit principles in greater detail, illustrating each with anecdotes drawn from Jesuit history. Some stories fit familiar perceptions of what priests do for a living; others certainly don't. Nor does every story show the Jesuits at their best; equally illuminative are the instances when they failed their own leadership principles. Even great companies stumble, and Jesuit stumbles proved particularly spectacular. Their high-profile tactics and successes regularly won them almost as many enemies as admirers. An exasperated John Adams once vented to Thomas Jefferson, "If ever any congregation of men could merit perdition on earth and in hell, it is the company of Loyola. Our system however of religious liberty must afford them an asylum."[5] Not every nation proved as tolerant as "the land of the free." By 1773, the Jesuits' growing ranks of detractors caught up with them, winning papal approval for their total global suppression. Hundreds of Jesuits were jailed or executed; others were deported to wander Europe as refugees. (The story of the great suppression is detailed in chapter 10.)

Most readers already know that this disastrous suppression did not end Jesuit history. Indeed, if ever there was a striking display of leadership, it was the company's phoenixlike resurgence after a forty-year suspended animation. Our Jesuit leadership story will draw anecdotes from the two-hundred-odd years from their

> They speak to us not as experts in dealing with an antiquated sixteenth-century landscape but as experts in eliciting confident performance despite uncomfortably shifting landscapes.

founding through the suppression, a period I'll arbitrarily call early Jesuit history.

The very last thing these early Jesuits would have considered themselves to be was leadership pundits. They rarely if ever used the word *leadership* as management consultants might employ that term today. Instead of talking about leadership, they lived it. The following chapter outlines their unique leadership values in greater detail, values that differ starkly from what's bandied about in today's crowded field of leadership gurudom. The next chapter also explores the dire need for greater personal leadership throughout our society, and contrasts three popular contemporary leadership stereotypes with the countercultural Jesuit vision of effective leadership.

CHAPTER 2

What Leaders Do

Bookstore shelves today groan with what sometimes resemble indoctrination manuals for some bewildering talismanic cult. Want to become a better leader? Consult any of the current works unlocking the mysteries of the leadership and management arts by revealing "7 miracles," "12 simple secrets," "13 fatal errors," "14 powerful techniques," "21 irrefutable laws," "30 truths," "101 biggest mistakes," and "1001 ways."

We've long known what "outputs" we want leaders to deliver. Harvard Business School professor John Kotter, for more than thirty years a leading commentator on corporate management practices, offers as good and concise a working summary as any of what we think of as a leader's duties:

- Establishing direction: developing a vision of the future—often the distant future—and strategies for producing the changes needed to achieve that vision
- Aligning people: communicating direction in words and deeds to all those whose cooperation may be needed so as to influence the creation of teams and coalitions that understand the vision and strategies and that accept their validity
- Motivating and inspiring: energizing people to overcome major political, bureaucratic, and resource barriers to

change by satisfying basic, but often unfulfilled, human needs.

- [And largely as a result of these first three roles:] Produc[ing] change, often to a dramatic degree[1]

In other words, the leader figures out where we need to go, points us in the right direction, gets us to agree that we need to get there, and rallies us through the inevitable obstacles that separate us from the promised land.

So we're pretty sure we know what leadership looks like, and we can pretty easily compile a thousand-item checklist of "secrets," "irrefutable laws," and assorted pointers that promise to turn any one of us into effective leaders. Yet oddly enough, given all we think we know, no one seems to believe that our society has the broad leadership it needs. Again Kotter, offering a sorry indictment: "I am completely convinced that most organizations today lack the leadership they need. And the shortfall is often large. I'm not talking about a deficit of 10% but of 200%, 400%, or more in positions up and down the hierarchy."[2] Four hundred percent is *a lot*. Still, no critics derided Kotter for hyperbolism. No pundit has yet won prominence arguing the contrary, "don't worry be happy" vision that our companies and organizations are brimming with all the leadership they will ever need. The leadership deficit is widely accepted as real, not hype, and probably with good reason.

> We know what we think leaders should do, and we know that we have been experiencing a leadership deficit for more than two decades.

So what do we know? We know what we think leaders should do, we know that we have been experiencing a leadership deficit for more than two decades, and we know that a steady stream of leadership prescriptions flows from a wide-open spigot. Yet we're still a tad shy—try 400 percent shy—of the leadership we need.

The Jesuit Contribution to Leadership Wisdom

What does a collection of sixteenth-century priests possibly bring to this party?

The Jesuit team doesn't tell us much we don't already know about what leaders *do*. Nor do they teach us anything about what leaders achieve.

But they have a lot to say about who leaders *are*, how leaders live, and how they *become* leaders in the first place. In so doing, the Jesuits offer a leadership model that flows against the tide of most contemporary leadership models. It rejects quick-fix approaches that equate leadership with mere technique and tactics. Their approach scraps "command and control" models that rely on one great person to lead the rest. It finds leadership opportunities not just at work but also in the ordinary activities of everyday life. The Jesuit approach examines leadership through a very different prism, and refracted through that prism, leadership emerges in a very different light. Four differences stand out:

- We're all leaders, and we're leading all the time, well or poorly.

- Leadership springs from *within*. It's about *who I am* as much as what I do.

- Leadership is not an act. It is my *life*, a way of living.

- I never complete the task of becoming a leader. It's an ongoing process.

We're all leaders, and we're leading all the time

Harry Truman called leadership "the art of persuading people to do what they should have done in the first place." Good for Harry.

But the early Jesuits do him one better. The job of Jesuit managers was not to persuade recruits what to do but to equip them with the skills to discern *on their own* what needed to be done.

The Jesuit vision that each person possesses untapped leadership potential cuts against the grain of the corporate top-down model that continues to dominate thinking about who leaders are. Although corporate America is experiencing a leadership dearth, its leadership model has slowly insinuated itself into most notions of who leaders are. The stereotypical role models are those in charge: company presidents, generals, and coaches. The leader is the one who whips subordinates into the motivated frenzy that propelled Henry V's inspired, outnumbered soldiers "once more into the breach" for a glorious victory at Harfleur. Dramatic though such depictions may be, they are a bit insidious. They foster what might be called a "1 percent" model of leadership: 1 percent of the team, only 1 percent of the time. Yet the narrow focus on 1 percent of the team, the general, overlooks the challenges facing the other 99 percent, the troops. The even narrower focus on the 1 percent of the time the leader supposedly leads—the peak opportunity at battle's eve—ignores the other 99 percent of the opportunities he or she has every day to make a leadership impact. That's 1 percent of the chances to lead enjoyed by 1 percent of the potential leaders, or 1/10,000 of the leadership pie. Think of what's lost, and imagine the power of capturing that potential.

> The stereotypical role models are those in charge: company presidents, generals, and coaches.

The early Jesuits were a little greedier and a little hungrier when leadership pie was served. Throwing aside the blinders that forced people to focus only on those in command as leaders, they developed *every* recruit to lead. They shunned "one great man" theories of leadership in order to focus on the other 99 percent of the potential leaders.

Everyone is a leader, and everyone is leading all the time—sometimes in immediate, dramatic, and obvious ways, more often in subtle, hard-to-measure ways, but leading nonetheless.

All well and good for the Jesuits, but isn't "We're all leaders" mere feel-good sloganeering that conveniently defines away the very essence of leadership? After all, if everyone leads, no one follows, and without lots of followers there are no real leaders. "One great man" leadership theories may not be egalitarian, but they reflect the reality of leadership in the real world. Or do they? Most would agree that leaders influence others and produce change. But what kind of influence or change defines leadership? The company president's bold decision to merge will inevitably be praised as corporate leadership, as will his efforts to identify and develop his company's promising future leaders. Yet these are two completely different kinds of behavior. The merger creates immediate, material, and obvious impact, while developing subordinates is a subtle initiative that may not pay off for years. Yet few would have trouble recognizing both as displays of leadership, at least when it's the company president undertaking such initiatives.

But if the president nurturing the company's future management is a leader, aren't they also leaders who years earlier taught these same rising corporate stars to read and write and think?

If the general rallying hundreds of troops for a decisive engagement is a leader, aren't the parents who molded these same troops into conscientious, self-confident adults leaders as well?

If the manager navigating colleagues through a work crisis is a leader, isn't the person who encourages a friend to tackle a difficult personal problem also a leader?

In sum, who invented the yardstick that measures some as leaders and others as merely teachers, parents, friends, or colleagues? And what are the dividing lines? Does one have to influence at least a hundred people at a time to be a leader? Or will fifty do? And if fifty, what about twenty, ten, or even a single person?

And does a leader's impact have to become apparent within the hour? Or within a year? Are there not also leaders whose impact is barely perceptible within their own lifetimes but manifests itself a generation later through those they raised, taught, mentored, or coached?

The confusion stems from an inappropriately narrow vision of leaders as only those who are in charge of others *and* who are making a transforming impact *and* who are doing it in short order. And the faster they do it, the more transforming it is, and the more people it affects, the hotter they register on the leadership thermometer.

But the stereotype of top-down, immediate, all-transforming leadership is not the solution; it's the problem. If only those positioned to direct large teams are leaders, all the rest must be followers. And those labeled followers will inevitably act like followers, sapped of the energy and drive to seize their own leadership chances.

The Jesuit model explodes the "one great man" model for the simple reason that everyone has influence, and everyone projects influence—good or bad, large or small—all the time. A leader seizes all of the available opportunities to influence and make an impact. Circumstances will present a few people with world-changing, defining-moment opportunities; most will enjoy no such bigtime opportunities in their lifetimes. *Still, leadership is defined not by the scale of the opportunity but by the quality of the response.* One cannot control all of one's circumstances, only one's responses to those circumstances.

> Those labeled followers will inevitably act like followers, sapped of the energy and drive to seize their own leadership chances.

Leadership springs from within; it's about who I am as much as what I do

Instead of rehashing well-worn tactical lists of what leaders do, the Jesuit approach focuses on who leaders are. No one ever became an effective leader by reading an instruction book, much less by parroting one-size-fits-all rules or maxims.

Rather, a leader's most compelling leadership tool is who he or she is: a person who understands what he or she values and wants, who is anchored by certain principles, and who faces the world with a consistent outlook. Leadership behavior develops naturally once this internal foundation has been laid. If it hasn't been, mere technique can never compensate.

A leader's greatest power is his or her personal vision, communicated by the example of his or her daily life. *Vision* in this sense refers not to vague messages and mottoes adopted from the corporate lexicon—"bringing good things to life" or being "the supermarket to the world"; instead, vision is intensely personal, the hard-won product of self-reflection: *What do I care about? What do I want? How do I fit into the world?*

To the chagrin of public relations gurus, company mission statements don't take root simply because they've been elegantly worded. They take root when subordinates see managers take a personal interest in the mission. Beating the competition comes alive for me not when I hear my manager parrot the goal but when I see his or her passionate commitment to winning. More simply, what springs from within makes the difference between talking the talk and walking the walk. Technique—how to spellbind a team, how to fashion long-term goals, how to establish objectives and win buy-in—can amplify vision, but it can never substitute for it.

> Leadership is defined not by the scale of the opportunity but by the quality of the response.

Leadership is not an act; it's a way of living

Leadership is not a job, not a role one plays at work and then puts aside during the commute home in order to relax and enjoy real life. Rather, leadership *is* the leader's real life.

Technique—how to spellbind a team, how to fashion long-term goals, how to establish objectives and win buy-in—can amplify vision, but it can never substitute for it.

The early Jesuits referred often to *nuestro modo de proceder*, "our way of proceeding," or in Americanese, "the way we do things." Certain behaviors fit *nuestro modo*; others didn't. No one ever tried to capture *nuestro modo* in writing, because no one could have and no one needed to. "Our way of proceeding" flowed from a worldview and priorities shared by all members of the Jesuit team. Their way of proceeding was a compass, not a checklist. If you know where you're heading, the compass is an infinitely more valuable instrument. And so it was for the Jesuits. Thrown into China's unfamiliar cultural terrain, a Jesuit found that the checklist of tactics that worked in Europe was useless to him in this foreign land. But his "compass"—his way of proceeding—served him well. By knowing what he valued and wanted to achieve, he oriented himself to the new environment, adapting confidently to unfamiliar circumstances.

Becoming a leader is an ongoing process of self-development

The beguiling but misleading promise implicit in "seven steps to becoming a leader" is that one will actually become a leader by completing the steps. Anyone who has tried to lead oneself or a team knows that nothing could be less true. Personal leadership is a never-ending work in progress that draws on continually maturing self-understanding. The external environment evolves and personal circumstances change, as do personal priorities. Some personal strengths erode, even as opportunities arise to develop others. All these changes demand consistent balanced growth and evolution as a leader. For the weak leader, the ongoing process becomes a threat or a chore; a more attractive prospect is to arrive at some imaginary leadership plateau where one coasts and enjoys one's leadership status. In contrast, the strong leader relishes the opportunity to continue learning about self and the world and looks forward to new discoveries and interests.

AN ODD LEADERSHIP DEFINITION COMPARED WITH OTHERS

All the above makes Ignatius Loyola and his colleagues strange additions to the leadership bookshelf. They certainly *look like* those we call leaders today. And they do the things we expect leaders to do: innovate, take risks, and produce major change. They would have little trouble establishing their leadership bona fides.

Still, they set themselves apart from the mainstream—sometimes uncomfortably so—by offering a unique vision of who leaders are and how they're molded. In our instant-gratification culture, there is something alluring about the prospect of buying a book before you board a plane in Chicago and arriving in New York a better leader. The Jesuit team offers no such handy promise. Their vision can't be distilled to mere technique; it comes with no ready-made list of tactics. They offer us direction but send us away with questions in place of pat, practical, and easily implemented answers. If all leadership is first *self*-leadership that springs from personal beliefs and attitudes, then each person must first decide what personal leadership legacy he or she wants to leave behind. If our leadership role is continually unfolding, we'll be making that decision more than once. And if we're influencing those around us all the time whether we realize it or not, we're usually not choosing our opportunities to lead; they're thrust upon us willy-nilly. Our only options are to respond well or to do a lousy job.

But if these early Jesuits are leadership contrarians, they may also be better role models than what's usually served up to us—for the simple reason that their model was built for real people living real life in the real world. Consider, on the other hand, some of the gurus we've consulted for enlightened leadership advice as we embark on the third millennium.

The general

Attila the Hun, a.k.a. the "Scourge of God," has been celebrated in at least two leadership guides. No doubt, Attila deserves credit as a leader of sorts. He cobbled together a united Hun enterprise from disparate tribes roaming central Europe around A.D. 440. Moreover, he definitely "clarified" the Hun leadership structure by murdering his brother and coleader, Bleda. Secure in his authority, Attila articulated and pursued a clear strategic vision. His Hun horde rampaged Europe from the Rhine to the Caspian Sea, extorting tribute from hapless states in exchange for peace treaties terminating the pillage. He was probably the first entrepreneur to build a successful business on the principle that customers would pay him to *stop* providing his service.

Attila's motivational powers must have been impressive, given what he asked his followers to endure. He drove the Huns against larger, better-equipped, technologically superior armies. If his team won, the spoils went largely to Attila and his inner circle. But if he lost, the bottom-rung Huns suffered the consequences disproportionately. When Romans, Franks, and Visigoths joined together to trounce the Huns at the Catalaunian Plains, Attila simply turned his horse around and headed home, leaving behind more than a hundred thousand dead Huns, proportionately one of the most horrifying death tolls in military history.

Attila took this "heads, I win; tails, you lose" management phi-losophy to the grave: according to legend, those who buried him with his treasure hoard were summarily executed so that the gravesite would never be revealed and looted.

Impressive though Attila's early extortionate forays may have been, one can hardly cite his Hun organization as a model of sus-tained excellence. After eight years of largely successful rampage, Attila lost his last two major campaigns, and the Hun dynasty began to slowly drift into eclipse even before his death.

The insider turned management consultant

Ignatius Loyola's historical contemporary Niccolò Machiavelli (1469–1527) has been lionized in at least half a dozen leadership books.

Six books. What did Machiavelli have that poor Loyola didn't? Certainly not leadership experience. True, Machiavelli's career started with promise. By age twenty-nine he was already a top bureaucrat in Florence; Loyola was *forty-nine* when he launched the Jesuits. But Machiavelli's inner-circle experience was embarrass-ingly short-lived. He was "downsized" while still in his early forties as soon as the famed Medici family reclaimed power in Florence. A year later he was briefly imprisoned under the probably unfounded suspicion that he was conspiring to overthrow them.

Marginalized and unemployed, Machiavelli had plenty of time to draft *The Prince*, his primer for would-be leaders intent on gaining, holding, or using power and the reason for our seemingly insatiable fascination with Machiavelli as a leadership consultant. Though he dedicated *The Prince* to Lorenzo de Medici in a trans-parent but unsuccessful attempt to ingratiate himself with the powerful family and reenter politics, the real inspiration for the work was Cesare Borgia. The wunderkind Borgia had been anointed a cardinal at the tender age of seventeen. Was this a remarkable recognition of his budding saintliness? Well, not quite. It turns out that the pope who elevated him also happened to be his father. Like many adolescents who abandon high school jobs upon reaching adulthood, Borgia soon hung up his cardinal's hat and robes. He got married and then succeeded his murdered older brother as captain general of the papal army. No culprit was ever prosecuted for his brother's tragic death, although Cesare has been historians' favorite suspect.

Machiavelli approvingly notes how the cruel, treacherous, and ruthlessly opportunistic Cesare double-crossed a loyal lieutenant, having him murdered and "placed on the public square of Cesena one morning, in two pieces." A page later Machiavelli says, "Looking over all the duke's actions, then, I find nothing with which to reproach him; rather, I think I'm right in proposing him . . . as a model."[3]

While the reticent Attila spoke little and wrote nothing, Machiavelli left behind numerous choice nuggets of his leadership wisdom:

"If you have to make a choice, to be feared is much safer than to be loved. For it is a good general rule about men, that they are ungrateful, fickle, liars and deceivers, fearful of danger and greedy for gain."[4]

"Those princes have accomplished most who paid little heed to keeping their promises, but who knew how to manipulate the minds of men craftily. In the end, they won out over those who tried to act honestly."[5]

"You must be a great liar and a hypocrite. Men are so simple of mind, and so much dominated by their immediate needs, that a deceitful man will always find plenty who are ready to be deceived."[6]

Well, at least we know where Machiavelli stands on the issue. But is it really where we want our leaders to stand? Is it where you want to stand?

The coach

Sports coaches may have become our culture's most prominent leadership role models. A trip to any average-sized bookstore will be rewarded with at least a dozen invitations to purchase management advice from active or retired coaches. Given this tidal wave of sporting wisdom, it would seem that the challenges faced by coaches must be highly analogous to the challenges we all face in life.

Are they? How many of us live and work in an environment that even remotely resembles professional basketball? The rules of that game rarely change, and then only marginally. Three people with whistles ensure that everyone obeys the rules, stopping play to deliver immediate justice for even miniscule trespasses. Those dissatisfied with or overwhelmed by the course of events can stop things with a time-out, regroup, and head back onto the court.

Every coach is restricted to producing only one product: a championship basketball team. So no one has to worry about being outflanked by competitors introducing new products. (Imagine how relaxed life would have been for record player manufacturers had there been similar prohibitions against cassette tapes or compact discs.) Nor, in this little world, need anyone agonize over optimal staffing levels for the company; the optimal staffing level is twelve employees (not eleven, not thirteen—always twelve). The twelve employees always work together in the same location; they work on only one project at a time, and it's always the same project: beat team X.

The leader's defining mark is his ability to motivate these twelve employees to work together toward the common goal of winning a basketball game. He draws mightily on his experience, wisdom, and knowledge of the game. But he also employs one other motivational tool: the approximately $80 million he has to spread among the twelve people on his payroll. He provides his *least* valuable players with approximately $280,000 apiece—as dictated by the NBA's "minimum wage"—to motivate them to practice and to work hard during each of the eighty-odd games they play a season. This typically leaves him enough to pay better players between $5 million and $10 million apiece to encourage them to dedicate themselves to company success.

Would it be presumptuous to assert that the work environments and life challenges of the overwhelming majority of the 135 million people employed in the civilian labor force in the United States don't very much resemble the working environment of the professional basketball player?

The Jesuits

Although the Jesuits aren't popularly known as leadership experts, their methods, vision, and longevity make them superior leadership role models to the aforementioned crowd. Unlike Attila's flash-in-the-pan Huns, the Jesuit team boasts a 450-year legacy of success. While Machiavelli pinned his hopes on one great prince's ability to lead hapless subjects, the Jesuit team lodged its hopes in the talents of its entire team. And the Jesuits saw these hopes fulfilled in the heroic, innovative performance of their members over centuries and all over the globe. They were as fiercely committed to winning as Attila, but unlike Attila or Machiavelli, they didn't deem deceit or murder acceptable strategies for winning or holding influence. And unlike professional basketball players, the early Jesuits operated in a rapidly changing world without rules.

A CLOSER LOOK
AT THE FOUR PILLARS

What *are* the Jesuit leadership secrets? How did individual Jesuits become leaders and why were their corporate efforts successful?

Four principles stand out. Jesuits became leaders by

- understanding their strengths, weaknesses, values, and worldview
- confidently innovating and adapting to embrace a changing world
- engaging others with a positive, loving attitude
- energizing themselves and others through heroic ambitions

These four principles don't come from a Jesuit rule book or leadership instruction manual. It's pretty certain that no early Jesuits—and no one else in the sixteenth century, for that matter—ever used the word *leadership* as we understand it today. Nor did they speak explicitly of self-awareness, ingenuity, love, and heroism as four core principles driving their organization. Instead, their leadership principles emerge only as we sift through their words and actions to find those themes that animated them at their most successful. In the early Jesuits' case, one could do the sifting with a pitchfork: these four themes infused their work and achievements, leap from their writings, and dominated their carefully mapped training program.

These four leadership principles guided individual Jesuits, and the same four formed the basis of Jesuit corporate culture.

Self-awareness: "To order one's life"

Leaders thrive by understanding who they are and what they value, by becoming aware of unhealthy blind spots or weaknesses that can derail them, and by cultivating the habit of continuous self-reflection and learning.

Only the person who knows what he or she wants can pursue

The early Jesuits invented an array of tools and practices to mold self-aware recruits.

it energetically and inspire others to do so. Only those who have pinpointed their weaknesses can conquer them. Obvious principles, but rarely heeded in practice.

The early Jesuits invented an array of tools and practices to mold self-aware recruits. Cut off for a month from work, friends, news, and even casual conversation, Jesuit trainees dedicated all their energy to a searching self-assessment. Engaging in the Spiritual Exercises was the peak developmental moment of a training regimen that encompassed everything from scutwork to begging for food and lodging on a solitary long-distance pilgrimage. Recruits emerged from training knowing what they wanted in life, how to get it, and what weaknesses could trip them up.

Self-awareness is never a finished product. Granted, some guiding life values are usually adopted early on and thereafter remain nonnegotiable. But our already complex world keeps changing. Leaders must keep changing as well. Every early Jesuit dedicated an intensively focused week each year to revitalizing his core commitment and assessing his performance during the previous year. Moreover, Jesuit self-awareness techniques accommodated change by instilling in recruits the habit of continuous learning, of daily reflection on activities. These techniques remain relevant today precisely because they were designed to allow busy people to "reflect on the run." Most religious prior to the Jesuits counted on the cloister walls to help them remain focused and re-collected each day. But Loyola essentially tore down the monastery walls to immerse his Jesuits in the maelstrom of daily life. Once those walls came down, Jesuits had to employ techniques to remain re-collected while all hell was breaking loose around them—just as everyone else has to today.

> These techniques remain relevant today precisely because they were designed to allow busy people to "reflect on the run."

Centuries later, academic studies are finally catching up to Loyola's vision and are validating his emphasis on self-awareness. Though executives frequently rise through the ranks on the strength of their technical expertise, raw intelligence, and/or sheer ambition, these traits alone rarely translate into successful long-term leadership performance. Research increasingly suggests that IQ and technical skills are far less crucial to leadership success than is mature self-awareness. In other words, the hard evidence points to the critical soft skills that are encompassed by knowing oneself.

Ingenuity: "The whole world will become our house"

Leaders make themselves and others comfortable in a changing world. They eagerly explore new ideas, approaches, and cultures rather than shrink defensively from what lurks around life's next corner. Anchored by nonnegotiable principles and values, they cultivate the "indifference" that allows them to adapt confidently.

Loyola described the ideal Jesuit as "living with one foot raised"—always ready to respond to emerging opportunities.

Self-awareness is key to successfully living with one foot raised. A leader must rid him- or herself of ingrained habits, prejudices, cultural preferences, and the "we've always done it this way" attitude—the baggage that blocks rapid adaptive responses. Of course, not *everything* is discardable baggage. Core beliefs and values are nonnegotiable, the centering anchor that allows for purposeful change as opposed to aimless drifting on shifting currents. The leader adapts confidently by knowing what's negotiable and what isn't.

Our generation has been dizzied by seemingly unending change. Within the last fifty years, a handful of humans has stood on the moon; the Earth-bound majority learned to e-mail friends. The early Jesuits faced equally profound changes. Voyages of discovery had more than tripled the size of the settled world then known to

Europeans. Asia and the Americas had begun to appear on the world map—the *European* version of the world map, that is—first in sketchy outline but with increasing definition over the early decades of the sixteenth century. In Europe, a Protestant reformation sparked by Martin Luther had in one generation ended Roman Catholicism's monolithic domination of Christendom, winning broad support for new religious ideas and practices. The reformers helped spur the world's first media revolution. It's been estimated that Martin Luther alone was responsible for composing one-quarter of all the titles published in Germany over a ten-year period. As Luther and others exploited the full power of the printing press for the first time in its short history, publishers inundated Europe with more books in a fifty-year period than had been published in the previous millennium.

In those troubled times, the Vatican hierarchy vacillated between deer-in-the-headlights paralysis and defensive overreaction to the roiling environment.[7] Distracted by other priorities or wallowing in denial, church authorities first allowed Martin Luther's challenge to fester; then, by summarily excommunicating the dissident monk, they handed him a platform with which he could rally support. While Luther and others swamped Europe with books and pamphlets outlining their reform message, Vatican authorities got busy publishing their first index of banned books.

While the Vatican sputtered in its efforts to halt unwelcome changes, Loyola's Jesuits plunged headlong into this changing world. In Europe, Vatican officials were condemning the vernacular Bibles and prayer books used in Protestant worship; outside Europe, Jesuits were compiling groundbreaking translating dictionaries for Tamil, Japanese, Vietnamese, and a host of other languages so that they could present their message in local languages through local culture. While a lumbering institutional church squandered nearly a decade in preparations for the Council of Trent—where they would galvanize strategic responses to the Protestant threat—nimbler Jesuits pursued their strategic agenda with greater speed and urgency. Within a decade of identifying higher education as a key priority in the 1540s, they had opened more than thirty colleges around the world.

How did the early Jesuits make themselves so immediately and totally comfortable in a world that had probably changed as much in their lifetimes as it had over the previous thousand years? Jesuits prized personal and corporate agility. They were quick, flexible, open to new ideas. The same set of tools and practices that fostered self-awareness, Loyola's Spiritual Exercises, also instilled "indifference," freedom from attachments to places and possessions, which could result in inappropriate resistance to movement or change. The "living with one foot raised" message was reinforced constantly: Loyola's chief lieutenant barnstormed Europe reminding Jesuits that for men open to new and ever changing missions, "the whole world will become [their] house."[8] He meant it literally, urging them to speed, mobility, and rapid response. But he was also describing a mindset for each Jesuit to cultivate.

> Loyola's Spiritual Exercises also instilled "indifference," freedom from attachments to places and possessions, which could result in inappropriate resistance to movement or change.

Love: "With greater love than fear"

Leaders face the world with a confident, healthy sense of themselves as endowed with talent, dignity, and the potential to lead. They find exactly these same attributes in others and passionately commit to honoring and unlocking the potential they find in themselves and in others. They create environments bound and energized by loyalty, affection, and mutual support.

Machiavelli counseled leaders that "to be feared is safer than to be loved." Unsurprising advice from a man convinced that humanity was "ungrateful, fickle, liars and deceivers, fearful of danger and greedy for gain."

Ignatius Loyola was his polar opposite, counseling Jesuit managers to govern using "all the love and modesty and charity possible" so that teams could thrive in environments of "greater love than fear."[9]

This starkly contrasting Jesuit approach stemmed from their starkly contrasting worldview. Whereas Machiavelli beheld a world peopled with fearful, ungrateful deceivers, Jesuits viewed the world through a very different lens: they saw each person as uniquely endowed with talent and dignity. The Jesuits' behavior flowed from their vision, as Machiavelli's advice did from his. Love-driven Jesuits worked with passion and courage, whether teaching teenagers or confronting colonialists who abused indigenous peoples in Latin America.

Jesuits remained committed to this vision because it *worked*. They were energized by working with and for colleagues who valued, trusted, and supported them. Teams were bound by loyalty and affection, not riddled with backstabbing and second-guessing. The company's pioneer in Asia, Francis Xavier, eloquently exemplified the depth and far-reaching power of these ties. Crisscrossing Asia, thousands of miles and some years removed from his cofounder colleagues, he drew energy from mere scraps of paper he carried bearing each one's signature. Why? Their signatures alone reminded him of "the great love which [colleagues] always showed and are still showing toward me."[10] It's hard to imagine today's corporate road warriors snapping open briefcases to draw similar energy from the latest memo from headquarters.

> They were energized by working with and for colleagues who valued, trusted, and supported them. Teams were bound by loyalty and affection, not riddled with backstabbing and second-guessing.

Their egalitarian, world-embracing vision enabled Jesuits

to create teams that seamlessly blended recruits from European nobility, the world's poorest families, and most everything in between. Jesuits working in China included nationals from half a dozen countries, all this centuries before the term *multinational teams* entered the corporate lexicon.

Everyone knows that organizations, armies, sports teams, and companies perform best when team members respect, value, and trust one another and sacrifice narrow self-interest to support team goals and their colleagues' success. Individuals perform best when they are respected, valued, and trusted by someone who genuinely cares for their well-being. Loyola was unafraid to call this bundle of winning attitudes "love" and to tap its energizing, unifying power for his Jesuit team. Effective leaders tap its power today as well.

Heroism: "Eliciting great desires"

Leaders imagine an inspiring future and strive to shape it rather than passively watching the future happen around them. Heroes extract gold from the opportunities at hand rather than waiting for golden opportunities to be handed to them.

Management consultants endlessly search for the elusive sure-fire formula to elicit motivated, committed performance from individuals and teams. As much as managerial America would like to throw a switch or push a button to ignite a corps of charged-up workers, it doesn't work that way. There is no on switch for motivation. Or, more accurately, there is a switch of sorts, but it is on the *inside*. Ultimately, only each individual can motivate him- or herself.

> There is no on switch for motivation. Or, more accurately, there is a switch of sorts, but it is on the *inside*.

Loyola once encouraged a Jesuit team in Ferrara, Italy, by saying that they should "endeavor to conceive great resolves and elicit equally great desires."[11] It was not an isolated sentiment. Jesuit culture spurred Jesuits to "elicit great desires" by envisioning heroic objectives. Outstanding personal and team performance resulted, just as it does when athletes, musicians, or managers focus unrelentingly on ambitious goals. Jesuits were also driven by a restless energy, encapsulated in a simple company motto, *magis*, always something *more*, something greater. For Jesuit explorers all over the world, *magis* inspired them to make the first European forays into Tibet, to the headwaters of the Blue Nile, and to the upper reaches of the Mississippi River. For Jesuit teachers in hundreds of colleges, *magis* focused them on providing what was consistently the world's highest-quality secondary education available—one student at a time, one day at a time. Regardless of what they were doing, they were rooted in the belief that above-and-beyond performance occurred when teams and individuals aimed high.

The Jesuits built their company on this conviction. They looked to enlist total team effort in something that was larger than any one Jesuit. Yet team commitment followed individual commitment. Each recruit first went through the process of *personally* shaping and owning the team's goals, of eliciting his own "great desires" and motivating himself.

How did the Jesuits build the most successful religious company in history? And how do individuals become leaders today? By knowing themselves. By innovating to embrace a changing world. By loving self and others. By aiming high.

Self-awareness, ingenuity, love, and heroism. Not four techniques, but four principles forming one way of living, one *modo de proceder*. No early Jesuit succeeded by adopting three and ignoring the fourth. To understand Jesuit leadership, we must first dissect it to study its four core elements and then conclude by reassembling them to bring Jesuit leadership to life. For its real power lies not in the mere sum of its parts but in what results when these four principles reinforce one another in an integrated life.

Later chapters explore each pillar in further detail. But the Jesuit leadership story must begin with the man most responsible for inspiring it: Ignatius Loyola. Loyola's story, of military man turned public leader, is a familiar archetype, as venerable as George Washington and as fresh as Colin Powell. But Ignatius Loyola's journey from soldier to company leader defies all stereotypes of how such human transformations happen. His journey to company leadership provokes reflection on the attributes that distinguish true leadership. The following chapter also revisits the unlikely origins of the Jesuit company, founded by a team who had no product, brand, or business plan—but who perceived clearly what they valued and how they wanted those values reflected in their work.

CHAPTER 3

The Jesuits

An Accidental Company with a Purposeful Vision

Jesuits enjoy enviable brand-name recognition. But while everyone knows why Coca-Cola is famous, the Jesuit brand often summons only a vague jumble of disconnected facts, anecdotes, and images: a handy epithet to hurl at a cunning adversary in a negotiation ("Jesuitical"), the image of a priest packed into a police van at a Vietnam War protest, or of another one retiring from Congress at the behest of a disapproving pope, or of still others slaughtered by armed forces in El Salvador. *Jesuit* also brings to mind quality educational institutions, with an alumni roster including Bill Clinton, François Mitterrand, Antonin Scalia, and Fidel Castro; and quality college basketball teams, with a deep bench of perennial NCAA championship contenders, including Georgetown, Gonzaga, Boston College, Marquette, and the University of Detroit Mercy.

The ten Jesuit founders were an unlikely group, a vastly more diverse team than headed most sixteenth-century companies and organizations. Twenty-four years separated the youngest from the oldest of a motley group of Spaniards, French, and a Portuguese. Their family and socioeconomic backgrounds created an equally wide gulf. Pierre Favre was the son of poor French subsistence farmers. Francis Xavier was a Basque noble from Navarre, raised in his family's castle and well placed to inherit a hefty benefice later in life. Like Xavier, the Castilian Diego Laínez was also wealthy. But unlike Xavier or any of the others, Laínez also happened to be the great-grandson of a Jew and therefore a "New Christian" in the rabidly anti-Semitic code of Inquisition-era Spain. New Christians were not even permitted to join major religious orders, so it was ironic that Laínez helped found one, and more ironic still that he succeeded Loyola to become the Jesuits' second general.

The core group slowly coalesced while studying for advanced degrees at the University of Paris, then the world's most prestigious university system. Though most of them distinguished themselves even in that selective academic circle, their intellectual gifts varied no less widely than their backgrounds. One of them recalled Diego Laínez as being "endowed with a singular, almost divine, intellect, well nigh miraculously informed in the subtleties of various branches of learning."[1] On the other hand, Laínez himself couldn't help but note Ignatius Loyola's "limited endowments of eloquence and learning."[2]

Still, the one with the "limited endowments" of eloquence and learning became the group's focal point. On the face of it, this handful of Europe's top talent had chosen to rally around a most unlikely character utterly lacking in conventional leadership credentials. At the age of thirty-eight, well into the twilight of an average sixteenth-century lifetime, Loyola's track record hardly suggested leadership potential—two failed careers, two arrests, multiple run-ins with the

> At the age of thirty-eight, well into the twilight of an average sixteenth-century lifetime, Loyola's track record hardly suggested leadership potential—two failed careers, two arrests, multiple run-ins with the Spanish Inquisition and other authorities, and no money.

Spanish Inquisition and other authorities, and no money. He had no notable accomplishments, no clear prospects, no followers, and no plan.

Would you sign up with this man?

A LEADER TWICE BORN

Harvard Business School professor emeritus Abraham Zaleznik once observed that "leaders are 'twice born' individuals who endure major events that lead to a sense of separateness, or perhaps estrangement, from their environments. As a result, they turn inward in order to reemerge with a created rather than an inherited sense of identity."[3] Ignatius Loyola may have had a skimpy resumé, but he certainly qualified as twice born. Birth number one was in Azpeitia, a tiny Basque village not far from the French border in a remote area of northern Spain. The Loyolas were minor nobles, and while nobility hardly entailed a life of luxury in isolated Azpeitia, it did bring political connections that provided Loyola's ticket out of the hinterland. The teenage Loyola served as a page to the chief treasurer of the royal court. It was his apprenticeship for a military and courtly career; little time was wasted on less critical skills like reading and writing, and plenty of time was devoted to swordsmanship and the code of chivalry that so animated Cervantes's *Don Quixote*.

Loyola's autobiography and later biographies offer only the most superficial glimpse of his early years, probably with good reason. Hagiographers tend to airbrush away the more embarrassing details of a saint's portrait, and some of Loyola's biographers were no exception. Loyola had his flaws. The Jesuit Juan Polanco, who served as Loyola's executive assistant, had occasion to hear the stories that slipped out at unguarded moments, and Polanco paints enough of a picture of "preconversion" Loyola for readers to imagine the rest: "Although much attached to the faith,

[Loyola] did not live in accordance with his belief, and he did not keep himself from sin. He was especially out of order in regard to gambling, matters pertaining to women, and duelling."[4] He was arrested at least once for misdemeanors that the local magistrate avoided detailing in deference to the Loyola family but nonetheless called "most outrageous." Another early acquaintance recalled the testosterone-charged Loyola in action: "[Loyola] drew his sword and chased them down the street. If someone had not restrained him, either he would have killed one of them, or they would have killed him."[5] What grave offense had prompted this unrestrained rage? Two passersby had bumped into him in a narrow passageway.

His first career, that of military officer, didn't last very long. It ended with the battle that started it. Loyola and his garrison had the misfortune to be guarding the Spanish citadel at Pamplona when a far superior French army came calling. The heroic if misguided Basque rallied his compatriots for a certainly futile defensive stand. It only delayed the inevitable, at the cost of his career, his self-image, and very nearly his life, thanks to a French cannonball that shattered his right leg.

A dashing rake—as Loyola fancied himself—doesn't dash as convincingly with one leg hobbled by a battle injury. Nor do the tight-fitting leggings favored at medieval courts make for very flattering attire when a clumsily set bone leaves an ugly, pronounced protrusion below the knee. Still, the stubborn Loyola refused to surrender his military and courtly aspirations immediately, instead subjecting himself to the sixteenth-century equivalent of reconstructive cosmetic surgery. One imagines a largely self-taught "surgeon" gamely hacking away at the offending tibia with the sharpest available local excuse for a saw, and it's safe to assume that there was no anesthesiologist on hand. It's hard to decide what's more remarkable: that Loyola survived his battle injury or that he survived the subsequent surgery to repair the damage. In any event, he survived both. And while the surgery resulted in

The Jesuits' pioneering leader

This posthumous portrait of Ignatius Loyola was painted by the Renaissance master Jacopino del Conte in 1556. It is displayed in the international headquarters of the Society of Jesus in Rome.

some improvement, it left him with a slight limp—and without a military career.

Loyola's story unfolds with unfortunate storybook predictability: the dissolute youth, the personal crisis, the intense conversion experience. The familiar, often romanticized plot line whitewashes what must have been a much more complicated internal struggle to reconstruct some sense of self and purpose. As gruesome as it was, his leg surgery might have been the easier part of this personal reconstruction. The surgery lasted only a few hours. But what Zaleznik would call Loyola's second birth dragged on for the better part of a decade. A profound and permanent religious conversion during his convalescence gave him a spiritual destination, but translating that goal into mature, sensible engagement in the everyday world proved a long, drawn-out, torturous process.

At first taken with fantasies of imitating the heroic deprivations he read about in popularized legends of the saints, "he thought of

going to Jerusalem barefoot, and of eating nothing but plain vege-
tables and of practicing all [the saints'] other rigors."[6] Though his
fantasies were particular enough to encompass footwear and diet
for the trip, other details were apparently of less concern to him—
like what he would actually *do* once he reached Jerusalem. His
family were as appalled by the ill-conceived plan as any other
family would be and did what they could to talk him out of it, "His
brother took to one room and then another, and with much feeling begged him not to throw himself away."[7]

To no avail. And thus began career two. Loyola traveled more
than two thousand miles in an era when few Europeans ever
strayed more than ten miles from their birthplaces. He begged for
food and lodging, frequently sleeping in open fields or huddled in
doorways. Once so vain as to submit to a life-threatening leg operation in a desperate attempt to restore his appearance, he now
swung wildly to the opposite extreme, as he related in his autobiography (always referring to himself in the third person): "He
decided to let [his hair] go its way according to nature without
combing or cutting it or covering it with anything by night or day.
For the same reason he let the nails grow on toes and fingers
because he had been fastidious in this too."[8] Though Loyola was
far from the first European to undertake a pilgrimage to the Holy
Land, he must have made for a particularly pitiful sight.
Devastating outbreaks of bubonic plague still swept European
cities periodically, leaving urban dwellers permanently vigilant
and acutely anxious. Some towns refused entry entirely to vagrants
such as Loyola who were unable to provide "passports" verifying
good health. It isn't surprising that Loyola recalled bumping into
a man in Venice who took one look at the pilgrim and "fled in hor-
ror . . . presumably because he saw him so very pale."[9]

Against the odds, Loyola landed in Jerusalem in the fall of 1523
after an eighteen-month odyssey—and was promptly deported
after three weeks. Jerusalem was a dangerous place for the few solo

travelers who managed to find their way there, and the religious order overseeing pilgrim visitors was growing exasperated and impoverished from having to ransom all the Europeans taken hostage. Thus, Loyola's second career, that of spending his life in Jerusalem imitating the heroics of the saints, evaporated as quickly, if not as violently, as his first.

The discouraged deportee backtracked from Jerusalem. After near shipwreck he reached Venice. Six more months and six hundred miles later he was in Barcelona, where at age thirty-three a resilient Loyola launched his third career: studying basic Latin grammar with a class of preteen boys. He devoted only one sentence of his autobiography to explaining this sudden shift in direction to what many might call the first sensible thing he had done with his life: "He continually pondered within himself what he ought to do; and eventually he was rather inclined to study for some time so he would be able to help souls."[10] He crawled forward, from grammar studies in Barcelona, through college studies in Alcalá and Salamanca, and finally to Paris, where he made the acquaintance of those who would become his Jesuit cofounders. The future "CEO" of the Jesuit company had finally landed at what most would consider the *starting point* of his life's calling, yet he was nearly forty years old, in the twilight years of an average sixteenth-century lifespan.

THE PERSONAL APPEAL
OF A TWICE-BORN MAN

How did anyone, much less a cross section of Europe's best talent, ever allow himself to fall in with this guy? *Eccentric* seems too mild a word to describe Loyola's life before reaching Paris.

Granted, his wasn't the most straightforward way to build a resumé. Nor was his career progression the sort that impresses search committees: no painstaking climb up the corporate ladder, no assiduously cultivated network of power brokers, no succession of ever more accountable management positions, no track record of results as a rainmaker.

But omitted from the above itinerary of Loyola's seven-year journey from Pamplona to Paris was a life-altering detour into the tiny Spanish town of Manresa. Intending to rest there a few days, he stayed a year. Words failed his later attempts to describe with precision what happened there. But he left no doubt about the impact of the mystical experiences that overwhelmed him. One afternoon spent on the banks of the river Cardoner "left his understanding so very enlightened that he felt as if he were another man with another mind." If he added together everything he had ever learned in his lifetime, he continued, "he does not think he had got as much as at that one time."[11]

Mystical though this experience may have been, *magic* it was not. Though in one spiritual gulp he apparently learned more about himself and the world than he had absorbed throughout his whole previous life, the profound revelation didn't bring insight about more mundane matters, such as "What *job* would I be good at?" Well, conventional wisdom notwithstanding, life is like that: there are dimensions to self-understanding beyond merely choosing a career path. Loyola left Manresa with no clearer career plan than what he had when he arrived and found himself back on the road, pursuing his vague, unrealistic plan to spend his life in Jerusalem.

But what he *had* gained proved far more important and durable than divine career counseling—and is far more important to an understanding of lasting leadership. He walked away with deep self-understanding, able to pinpoint his flaws with greater maturity and accuracy than ever before, yet at the same time able to appreciate himself as a uniquely dignified and gifted person in a world that seemed far more positive than it did when he entered Manresa. Though his personal pilgrimage continued, his self-punishment stopped. He determined, for example, that it was no great sin to comb one's hair. Well, minor accomplishments precede great ones. If he didn't know what job to do, his greater sense of purpose and direction now served as a personal compass of sorts. Finally, he had developed a worldview. Or in less grandiose terms, he understood how he fit into the world and that it was not a hostile place.

The self-awareness he had won was ultimately what drew others, even Europe's finest, to him. Of course, they must have been attracted in part by his natural leadership gifts, which even his eccentric history could not totally obscure—the heroism he displayed as the soldier rallying the defense of compatriots at Pamplona; the commitment and toughness he possessed as a pilgrim undeterred from his goal of reaching Jerusalem; and the resilient adaptability manifest in his transformation from soldier to pilgrim to remedial grammar student to university scholar. But Loyola's core appeal was not his *own* leadership traits—it was his ability to identify and unlock *others'* latent leadership potential. Each member of the founding team tells a similar story of undertaking a systematic self-examination under Loyola's personal guidance and emerging energized, focused, and able to articulate life goals and personal weaknesses. Here was supercharged mentoring from a man who modeled this poorly understood and drastically underutilized life tool. Loyola not only grasped his own strengths and weaknesses but also was generous, dedicated, and straightforward enough to guide others through their own self-assessment.

Loyola's second birth lasted years and saw him wandering a penniless beggar for thousands of miles. But he had discovered a way to spare others the trauma and lost years of his second birth while delivering the fruits of self-awareness that were borne of it. He had translated his own experiences into an accessible program of meditations and practices he called the Spiritual Exercises. The members of his multinational, socioeconomically diverse team had little in common with one another upon arriving in Paris beyond their ambitions for the highest-quality education then attainable. Their unifying team bond became the common experience of undertaking these self-revelatory Exercises.

Each member of the founding team tells a similar story of undertaking a systematic self-examination under Loyola's personal guidance and emerging energized, focused, and able to articulate life goals and personal weaknesses.

As their mutual friendship developed, they banded together in a loose association to help souls. To help souls? What did *that* mean? What were their occupations? What were their products? They couldn't have answered those questions with much precision, and it showed in early endeavors. They first resurrected Loyola's quixotic early ambition to work in the Holy Land, making their way to Italy to obtain papal approval for the pilgrimage. As often happens with ambitious but poorly conceived strategies, neither they nor their plan went anywhere. No ships were sailing for Jerusalem; rising political tensions put ships venturing into the Mediterranean at unacceptably high risk of raids from Ottoman Turkish fleets. So, to their great disappointment—but, as it turned out, to their own and the world's great fortune—the ten were effectively stranded in Italy, occupying themselves by preaching on street corners, working in hospitals, and doing whatever else fit their own broad conception of helping souls. Not all of them were equally talented at street religion. Colleagues remembered Loyola in Italian town squares, gamely preaching away in some nearly unintelligible pidgin of Spanish, Latin, and Italian, ridiculed by children who pelted the balding, limping Basque with apples.

THE FORMATION OF A COMPANY

Deeply self-aware or not, the Jesuits had, by superficial appearances, failed. In fact, however, the only thing they really failed at was escaping notice. Their drive, creativity, and resilience attracted attention to even these haphazard early efforts. As so often happens, quality was proving to be its own best advertisement, and Loyola's bungled attempts at street preaching were the only exception to the team's overall performance excellence. The pope and other church officials began to pick the group for scattered missions to preach or lecture. Soon two were destined for Parma, two for Siena, and one for Naples. "Talent will out," as the saying goes, and the Catholic Church's need for talent had rarely been greater. Martin Luther and other reformers had made extraordinary gains in Europe in little more than a generation. For more than a millennium the church had enjoyed near unchallenged hegemony in European spiritual and moral affairs, yet after a twenty-year onslaught by the reformers, the Vatican could count on secure allegiance from only a handful of countries rimming the Mediterranean. The institutional Catholic Church was an easy target: corrupt bureaucrats filled its hierarchy, and the rank and file was riddled with poorly educated, demoralized clerics. Against this backdrop, the energy, integrity, and raw intellectual horsepower of the new arrivals from Paris combined into rare and badly needed tonic.

But like many of today's rising-star start-ups, the friends rapidly became victims of their own success and reputation. After a few years in Italy, it became obvious that Loyola's little team was on the verge of disintegrating. Already pulled in different directions, the team had amassed a backlog of projects that would have occupied "four times their number." And the centripetal force was accelerating. Within a few years the same ten would be scattered not only across Italy but across Europe and beyond: Portugal, Ireland, Germany, Austria, Switzerland, and India.

The prospect of inevitable dispersion spurred their first serious debates about their long-term joint future. Should they incorporate as a new religious order and elect a superior general? Or should they continue with their looser association, accepting that their far-flung assignments could mean its eventual dissolution? They discussed the issue intermittently over the course of a summer, work demands allowing. In the end they decided to incorporate. Why?

Heroism and mutual affection. Hardly what drives most companies today—big, lumbering, bureaucratic, unimaginative, competitive, anonymous modern companies. What holds most companies together today? The critical mass, scale, capital, global reach, and broad capabilities to pulverize opponents, yes. Limited liability? Of course. The chance to become rich by going public? Naturally. But heroism and mutual affection? Not usually.

The team accepted that work opportunities would separate them physically; indeed, they relished the chances to flex their talent and imagination in uncharted territory. Shunning wide-ranging, far-flung opportunities merely to remain in close contact was out of the question. Still, they seemed convinced that there was a way to preserve the spirit that unified them even as diverse missions separated them physically. The question they asked themselves makes clear that what they got out of their company is not quite what most of us get out of our companies: "Should we have a mutual understanding so that those who are sent from our midst will still be the object of our affectionate concern as we will be of theirs?"[12] After all, why else does anyone form or join a company? Otherwise, why not go it alone?

> They seemed convinced that there was a way to preserve the spirit that unified them even as diverse missions separated them physically.

Still, the decision to incorporate wasn't straightforward. There were drawbacks to consider. Sixteenth-century religious orders were not highly esteemed, and one cofounder argued that formal incorporation would only damage the team's hard-won reputation for integrity: "It seems this term 'religious obedience' has fallen into disfavor and has been discredited among Christian people."[13] Moreover, they envisioned an order that would have wide-open flexibility to pursue emerging opportunities, and they feared the pope might saddle them with an already existing religious rule that would hem them in and "not provide ample opportunity and scope" for carrying out their broad vision. They wanted to protect their ability to mobilize, adapt, and innovate.

One argument convincingly trumped these negatives: "Obedience issues in an uninterrupted life of heroic deeds and heroic virtues. For one who truly lives under obedience is fully disposed to execute instantly and unhesitatingly whatever is enjoined him, no matter to him whether it be very hard to do."[14]

An uninterrupted life of heroic deeds and heroic virtues. Something else we don't typically associate with most companies. But Loyola's team did. Incorporation was the path to heroism and the best way to preserve mutual "affectionate concern." They resolved to formalize their association and sought papal approval to found a new religious order to be called the *Compañía de Jesus*.

THE MERGER THAT MIGHT HAVE HAPPENED

Unfortunately, as they had feared, Vatican bureaucrats did try to fold Loyola's small team into an existing, well-established religious company, the Theatines. It would have made complete sense. The Theatines had everything Loyola's group lacked. They were well connected, founded by a powerful cardinal destined to become pope. They had financial resources and a growing membership, whereas the small Jesuit team was an undercapitalized upstart. But the Jesuits were determined to pursue their own revolutionary approach to religious life, and after some back-channel diplomatic maneuvering that turned a future pope into an enemy, the Jesuits won approval for their own company with its own charter. Still, there were official doubts about their long-term viability. A wary pope initially limited their membership to a maximum of sixty.

Today more than twenty thousand Jesuits work in more than a hundred countries. There are approximately two hundred Theatines.

THE LEADERSHIP SUCCESS OF IGNATIUS LOYOLA

Somehow the story of Loyola the saint works better than that of Loyola the budding corporate leader. One wants to sand away the rough edges before featuring him in a leadership book. Sure, he was a battle hero, but the stuff about the unkempt hair has to go. And one wants to make the early Jesuit team a bit more focused in their aspirations, a bit more *corporate*. After all, they built the world's greatest education network. Why not start with their fierce determination to do so and jettison the "mutual affection" stuff?

How does one become a successful leader today? If Loyola's suggested route involves a wrecked leg, a yearlong pilgrimage, a year of intense meditation, and a couple of arrests, most sane people would say no thank you and opt instead for the old-fashioned way to the top: get an MBA and hitch yourself to a powerful mentor.

As remarkable as the Jesuits' achievements were during Loyola's final fifteen years, even those sympathetic to his story might be tempted to wonder how much more they might have accomplished had Loyola gotten his act together at twenty-nine instead of forty-nine.

Maybe they would have accomplished *less*.

Rather than recasting Loyola's story into a conventionally acceptable mold, it's worth pondering what his actual life and his team's evolution say about leadership. One is tempted to scan Jesuit prehistory as one scans resumés: looking for tangible accomplishments and dismissing the rest. Loyola had virtually no *tangible* accomplishments to show for almost two-thirds of his life. But what he and his team did accomplish might have been just as or even more important than the classic resumé builders. The Jesuits knew themselves; they emerged from their corporate prehistory with clear ideas about how they wanted to work as a team—driven by heroism, open to new opportunities, and tightly bound by mutual support. When they finally jumped from the corporate starting block, they did so with an explosive momentum rarely seen in their era or any other. Isn't it possible that these facts are more than just coincidental? In other words, the Jesuits' immediate and sustained corporate success just might have had something to do with the self-understanding and team values forged during their prehistory. And such intangibles just might, in the end, be more critical to personal and corporate success than the tangibles we prize when scanning resumés or plotting our own futures.

Put differently, but for his military mishap at Pamplona, Loyola might well have continued his climb through the military and courtly ranks without ever taking profound stock of his strengths, weaknesses, values, and life goals. Without this self-awareness, it's very possible, even likely, that he would have accomplished less in *that* career than he did as the founder and leader of the Jesuit company, even though his Jesuit career started late in life, after a circuitous, ten-year detour. Loyola the military man might have steadily moved up whatever passed for a corporate ladder in sixteenth-century Spain. Yet without the setbacks, crises, and challenges that punctuated his *real* life he might never have grappled with who he was, what he wanted, what personal resources he had, and why he had failed along the way. Only by asking and answering those questions does one develop personal leadership capacity.

A Religious Order among Many

The question that frames this chapter—What is a Jesuit?—remains only half-answered. It's clear what the Jesuits founded their company to do: nothing specifically. Or, to give them their due, anything and everything that fit a mission statement that was hardly confining: helping souls and doing it heroically. But as broad a strategic playing field as they left themselves, it wasn't *completely* wide open. They had, after all, formed a religious order, whatever that meant.

Not all Vatican opposition to the Jesuits' desire to form their own company had reflected animosity toward Loyola and his ideas. Many church bureaucrats had a more basic objection: there were already too many religious orders roaming Europe. Then as now, the great majority of clergy were *not* members of religious orders but instead tended parishes under the sponsorship and control of a local bishop. But from early in the church's history, groups of clerics or laypeople had banded together outside this network of local dioceses into so-called religious orders. Each order had slightly different rules, different traditions, and different outfits; it was confusing. Because the orders sprawled across diocesan boundaries, they were harder for bishops to supervise, and some bureaucrats feared this was exacerbating the corruption problems plaguing the church.

Some of these orders had sprouted under the charismatic leadership of a saintly founder. St. Francis of Assisi, for example, who expressed no ambition to lead a large company, nonetheless exerted a magnetism that drew more than three thousand followers within his lifetime. Other orders had been launched for no other reason than to satisfy the sheer monomania of a legacy-building ecclesiastical higher-up. Still others carved out an occupational niche: the warrior monks of the Knights Templar vowed to protect Christian pilgrims traveling to the Holy Land and manned a string of fortifications along popular pilgrimage routes.

But the Knights Templar were exotic departures in a tradition that spawned more contemplatives than warriors. Most orders followed monastic traditions of one sort or another. The psalmist of the Old Testament had written, "Seven times a day I praised you, and in the middle of the night I arose to confess to you." St. Benedict took the psalmist's words to heart, codifying in the sixth century a famous monastic rule that has governed many religious orders right up to the present. Benedictines pray communally at seven set times each day—including once *in the middle of the night.* They pass the balance of each day in quiet study, domestic labor, and contemplation. Some monks went further still in pursuit of a contemplative life. St. Bruno led six companions high into the Alps, as far as possible from the distractions of urban life. Both Bruno's order and the sweetish liqueur his monks churned out to support themselves took their name from their remote Alpine cloister site of Chartreuse. The austere Carthusians lived (and still do today) a hermitlike existence. Each cooked his own food in a private cell within a larger communal compound, joining colleagues only for common prayer and a rare recreation period.

Hundreds of religious orders came into existence, and hundreds survive. Some are well-known, with global memberships exceeding ten thousand: the Jesuits, Dominicans, and Franciscans, for example. Others are much smaller, lesser-known groups boasting mysterious, almost cabalistic names: Scalabrinians, Eudists, Somascans, Rogationists, Rosminians, Premonstratensians, the Order of St. Paul the First Hermit, the Stigmatine Priests and Brothers, the Lebanese Maronite Order, the Camaldolese Order of Monte Corona, the Hospitaller Brothers of St. John of God, and so on.

AN IDENTITY OF THEIR OWN

How does one distinguish among the bewildering array? What makes them alike, and what makes them different? And how do the Jesuits fit in?

First, while each religious order may emphasize certain traditions or practices, all share membership in the Catholic Church and adherence to its core beliefs. That holds even for the Jesuits, though their enemies within the Catholic Church—and perhaps even an exasperated pope or two—have had their doubts. There is no religion of Jesuitism, nor do Jesuits exclusively dedicate themselves to a specific occupation, as did the Knights Templar. Though higher education has from early on absorbed a large majority of Jesuit manpower, the founders prepared their members to engage in any occupation that would "help souls." Finally, the Jesuits do not distinguish themselves by unique team colors. Few cappuccino lovers, for example, consider that their beloved stimulant takes its name from the color of the habit of a Capuchin friar; and few pedestrians crossing London's Whitefriars Street spare a thought for the monastery of white-robed Carmelites that once stood there. The Jesuits? Nothing so distinctive in their wardrobe. They were always plain old "black robes" until, as we shall see, some early Jesuits began adapting to Asian cultures in which the priestly classes wore anything but black.

Jesuits, like all religious order members, pronounce vows of poverty, chastity, and obedience. These vows mean exactly what one would suppose: no (material) personal possessions, no spouse, no sex, and when the boss says they need you in Timbuktu, you go. As if poverty, chastity, and obedience don't offer enough challenge, in rare cases religious orders have set themselves apart by professing some additional vow. Each member of the centuries-old Order of Merced—the romantically nicknamed Brothers of Ransom or Order of Captives—vowed to exchange himself as a ransom for captives. The Jesuits are another of these rare cases; most members pronounce a special fourth vow to mobilize immediately for any mission requested by the pope. Granted, it's a bit more prosaic than what the Brothers of Ransom came up with, but it's a Jesuit hallmark nonetheless.

Religious orders may comprise men or women, clerics or laypeople. Sometimes an order is divided into two or three smaller
orders. There is, for example, a Dominican order of male clerics, a
separate Dominican order of women religious, and a so-called
third order of laypeople—all governed separately but following the
tradition and vision of St. Dominic. Unlike the Dominican order,
the Jesuit order is exclusively male.

Well, almost exclusively male. Mateo Sánchez would have had
something to say about *exclusively*. Mateo, a.k.a. *Juana* of Austria,
daughter of Holy Roman emperor Charles V, sister of King Philip II
of Spain, widow of the crown prince of Portugal, was obviously
very well connected, very much a woman—and just as much a
Jesuit. She was one of a long list of powerful, prestigious supporters cultivated by the early Jesuits. Loyola's contacts eventually
included key European power brokers such as the pope, the kings
of Spain and Portugal, the Holy Roman emperor, and countless
"lesser" cardinals, dukes, and princes. Jesuit membership increased
fifteenfold and their operations expanded accordingly within only
a few years of their founding; the rapid growth vitally depended on
opportunities and financial support doled out by patrons. King
John III of Portugal reportedly once gushed to an undoubtedly
alarmed member of his entourage that "he would like to have the
entire Society come to his kingdom, even if that were to cost him
part of his empire."[15]

Beyond providing the Jesuits with work opportunities and
financial support, well-connected or noble Europeans sometimes
went so far as to petition for admission into the society, despite the
fact that Loyola imposed the same rule of poverty on the well connected as on the "lesser" mortals. The company's membership roster soon boasted names that are familiar to any tourist who has
wandered Italian museums and palazzos: Borgia, Gonzaga,
Acquaviva, Bellarmine. While each left wealth behind to join the
Jesuits, none abandoned his family name or connections. And the

company benefited no less from those connections than any successful company would today from well-networked employees sporting a Rolodex of high-powered contacts.

But every once in a while, Jesuit cultivation of Europe's elite backfired. Loyola surely was delighted that someone as powerful as Juana of Austria had taken supportive interest in his Jesuits. His delight became dismay when an enthralled Juana announced her plan to join the Jesuits. That she was a woman who had every intention of continuing her royal lifestyle didn't seem an insurmountable obstacle to her, and she apparently didn't expect Loyola to be deterred by such minor considerations either. He was left with a no-win situation. To turn her down would be to risk the wrath of a spurned princess not much accustomed to being told no. To accept her would be to risk horrific embarrassment and the whiff of scandal should her royal brother, her royal father, or the general European public learn that the fledgling Jesuits had granted the unique favor of admission to a woman known to be personally friendly with Ignatius Loyola.

Juana got her wish but was admitted on the condition that her membership remain strictly confidential. She merrily pursued her royal affairs while secretly relishing her privileged status as the only woman member of the Jesuit company she so admired. To the immense relief of Loyola and his inner circle, no lower-ranking Jesuit clerk ever inquired about the mysterious Mateo Sánchez who never seemed to show up for meals, in chapel, or in the recreation room.

To be precise, then, the Jesuits are *now* an exclusively male order, as they always have been, with only one exception—or one exception that has so far come to light.

Virtually all religious orders have something else in common: they've fallen on hard times. Pity the poor recruiter peddling "poverty, chastity, and obedience" to the MTV generation. Membership in religious orders has gone into free fall. In 1965, there were nearly 230,000 religious-order priests around the world; today there are less than

150,000—even as the Catholic population they serve has continued to grow.[16] And the demographics don't presage a bright future: the average age of clerics in the United States is approximately sixty. The Jesuits have not been exempt from these trends. Worldwide membership reached 36,000 in the 1960s and today hovers around 21,000. Still, they've fared better than most. Throughout much of their common history, the Jesuit order was dwarfed by the Dominican and Franciscan orders; today the Jesuit order stands as the largest fully integrated religious order in the world.[17]

But Jesuit resiliency has been fired in far hotter crucibles than the inhospitable popular culture of the early twenty-first century, and the Jesuits' own tactics helped stoke the flames that threatened them. Loyola seemed well aware from the outset that his Jesuits' ambitious and sometimes brash operating style was dangerous. A Jesuit visiting the grand duchess of Tuscany's court railed against the excesses of wealthy women who adorned themselves with expensive baubles while the poor went without basic necessities. Loyola no doubt endorsed the sentiment, but he nonetheless rebuked the Jesuit for too bluntly hammering his hosts about their lifestyles: "We [already] have a reputation among some persons who do not trouble to find out the truth, especially here in Rome, that we would like to rule the world."[18]

Loyola's worries proved prescient. The Jesuits never learned to keep a low profile. They inevitably found themselves in the middle of controversies, too often because they had stirred them up in the first place—and they took righteous relish in rubbing their opponents' noses in it. Over the decades, their aggrieved enemies formed the oddest collection of bedfellows. Non-Jesuit missionaries in China condemned the progressive tactics of Matteo Ricci and his successors as heretical. Liberal Enlightenment thinkers such as Voltaire and Rousseau, many of them educated by the Jesuits, saw the company as the only group capable of intellectually rebutting their attacks on the Catholic Church. Politicians throughout Europe made the Jesuits a political dartboard in attempts to beat back Vatican power. Conservatives and liberals, politicians and priests, devout believers and atheists certainly could not have found anything at all to agree on, save one thing: wanting the Jesuits to go.

The Jesuits never learned to keep a low profile. They inevitably found themselves in the middle of controversies, too often because they had stirred them up in the first place.

By the mid-1700s, with the company reaching a membership of twenty-five thousand, the Jesuits' detractors caught up with them in spectacular fashion. Banished from one country after another, the Jesuits were entirely disbanded by the pope in 1773. The Jesuit general was jailed, their schools shut down, and their properties confiscated. Many of the suddenly ex-Jesuits were marched to deportation ports under armed guard and sent to wander Europe as outcasts. For nearly forty years the company remained shuttered.

Truth be told, the claim that the pope *entirely* suppressed the Jesuits is a slight exaggeration. Though more than 99 percent of the company was shut down, two hundred Jesuits hung on in an unlikely jurisdiction sheltered by an unlikely defender. Catherine the Great so valued the four Jesuit schools in Russia that she never allowed promulgation of the papal suppression decree on Russian soil. This rump group tenaciously exploited the loophole, electing a general from among their ranks and continuing their work. Over time, small knots of "suppressed" Jesuits crawled out of the woodwork to join this Russian Jesuit order, levering themselves back into tenuous existence. Georgetown University, alma mater of the forty-second American president, proudly boasts being the first of twenty-eight Jesuit-founded colleges in the United States. But Georgetown was founded in 1789, in the middle of the Jesuit suppression and therefore by *ex-Jesuits*. Moreover, these ex-Jesuits joined the Russian Jesuit order in 1805. The odd affiliation lasted only a few years, as the Georgetown team and others rejoined the global order upon its 1814 papal restoration. Those fond of history's wackier hypotheticals can while away a few hours pondering what might have become of this Georgetown University had the Russian Revolution come before the Jesuit restoration.

Luck, shrewd diplomacy, and the shifting geopolitical landscape all played a part in keeping the Jesuit company alive through their time of crisis. But vastly more critical was the scrappy tenacity of Jesuits in the field who refused to let their company and its vision die. It's the kind of story that plays itself out today on a smaller stage when sports teams believe in themselves enough to rally and overcome late-in-the-game deficits, when the employees at Harley-Davidson pitch in to pull their company back from the brink of collapse, or when parents sacrifice to get their families through seemingly overwhelming financial difficulties: success that flows from the undying commitment and persistence of many, not the isolated efforts of one.

THE MEANING OF *COMPANY*

The Jesuits are routinely called a company throughout this book, something that will grate equally on some Jesuits and non-Jesuits alike. Some Jesuits will resent the sullying of their noble, lofty enterprise by the implicit association with the crass pursuit of profit. Conversely, die-hard free marketers will reject the comparison—the Jesuit order isn't a for-profit enterprise, and it's disingenuous to present it as a company.

But there's a straightforward reason to call the Jesuits a company: that's what they called themselves. When the first handful banded together, they had no name at all. People took to calling them *Iñiguistas* or *Ignatiani*—the people following Ignatius Loyola. This type of nickname had plenty of precedents. After all, the Dominicans were the followers of St. Dominic, and the Franciscans followed St. Francis. But Loyola, perhaps appalled at the prospect of a personality cult, pressed his colleagues to come up with something different. They settled on *Compañía de Jesus*, the "Company of Jesus." In formal Latin documents the name was rendered as *Societas Iesu* ("Society of Jesus"), hence Jesuits' occasional references to themselves as "the Society."

Whatever the first team called themselves, it certainly wasn't "Jesuits." That nickname originated in the mid-1500s. For some it was simply shorthand, but for many more the word implied something more sinister. One Englishman complained about "the most dangerous infections, and . . . irremedilesse poyson of the Iesuiticall doctrine." Like other groups throughout history who have been labeled with offensive nicknames, the Jesuits eventually wrested control of theirs by using it themselves. Still, they never totally shook the negative connotation of *Jesuitical* that continues to appear in edition after edition of dictionaries.

So they founded a company. What kind of company did they think they were founding? What did they mean by the word? Today, *company* almost inevitably connotes a commercial enterprise. But sixteenth-century *compañías* were usually something quite different: religious organizations, military groups, or simply groups of friends. Though it may not seem like it to those laboring in obscurity within one of America's corporate behemoths, the words *company* and *companion* do, after all, share the same root. And that's exactly how the Jesuit founders understood their *compañía*: it was, first and foremost, a religious organization, made up of "companions of Jesus," in some spiritual sense. But equally they were companions and friends to one another, and they intended for that spirit to infuse their *compañía*. Recall that a key motivation behind their incorporation was their desire to work in a group in which "those who are sent from our midst will still be the object of our affectionate concern as we will be of theirs."

Calling the Jesuits a company highlights the parallels between their *compañía* and our modern-day companies. The more intriguing question is not whether it's legitimate to call the Jesuits a company but why the word's connotation has drifted so far afield of its early meanings. The Jesuit company was animated by the rich undercurrent of "friendly companionship," and drew talented recruits eager to pursue an "uninterrupted life of heroic deeds and heroic virtues." How many Fortune 500 companies feel that way? How many people join companies looking to prove their heroism in action? Why has the modern company so thoroughly ceased to be "a group of friends," and is such camaraderie irretrievably lost?

Later chapters detail how the Jesuits built such a company and how their four-pillared approach can still mold heroic leaders today in all walks of life. But this Jesuit leadership story first skips ahead seventy years after their founding, to a man dying alone in a remote corner of China.

> The more intriguing question is not whether it's legitimate to call the Jesuits a company but why the word's connotation has drifted so far afield of its early meanings.

CHAPTER 4

Leadership Role Models
Three Unlikely Case Studies

By any conventional standard, Benedetto de Goes, Matteo Ricci, and Christopher Clavius are three unlikely leadership specimens. None of them ever managed scores of subordinates; none of them rose far in the Jesuit hierarchy. They were neither the holiest, most prominent, nor most influential Jesuits in history. But they were leaders. And it's precisely because they don't fit our conventional leadership mold that their lives raise important questions about what it means to lead—whether as a seventeenth-century Jesuit or in any walk of life today

THE EXPLORER

Benedetto de Goes died a failure. Or so it would seem—he was broke, more or less alone, and well short of a goal he had doggedly pursued for nearly five years. No one knows where he was buried or even whether he was buried at all. No one informed his relatives, because no one knew if he had any. The cause of death remains a mystery. In all likelihood he simply drove himself to death, physically broken and exhausted after a three-thousand-mile trek through some of Asia's remotest and most forbidding terrain. But rumors of foul play also surfaced, suspicions that he had been poisoned by thieves or religious zealots.

He was not completely alone when he died in 1607. Plenty of curious locals in Xuzhou, China, must have gone out of their way for one last glimpse of the stranger who had lived in their town for well over a year. Goes was not a curiosity simply because he was a foreigner; the Chinese in Xuzhou had seen plenty of foreigners. To those living in China's coastal provinces, dusty Xuzhou, near the border of what is today Gansu province, might have seemed the middle of nowhere, one thousand miles from Beijing.[1] But for merchant caravans traveling from the opposite direction, Xuzhou signaled the end of a bone-wearying journey through Gobi Desert wilderness and a return to civilization. Many traders arrived after years on the road, their fortunes hitched to caravans that snaked along the Silk Road all the way from India or the Middle East. Buying and selling as they traveled, most traders either settled at oases along the way, turned back after completing part of the journey, or died en route. Of those who made it all the way to Xuzhou, some stayed for good, founding their own small communities of Muslim traders.

But Goes was something strange and unique even to those in Xuzhou who were well accustomed to foreign faces: he was the first European to enter their town during living memory, perhaps the first European *ever* to enter Xuzhou.

It wasn't the first time Goes had made a curious entrance. He was a twenty-year-old soldier an ocean away from his birthplace in the Azores when he showed up in Goa petitioning admission to the Jesuits. He may have been a man looking to sweep away an earlier life and start afresh on a new continent—a sort of legionnaire of the spiritual life, as it were.

If that was the case, perpetual poverty, chastity, and obedience may have been too much, too fast. Goes walked out after two years of Jesuit training, only to reappear four years later, begging reinstatement.

The second time around, Goes stayed—and prospered. He apparently was a gifted linguist, so he was included in a three-person Jesuit embassy to the Mughal emperor Akbar's court in Agra. The Persian-speaking Mughal conquerors of northern India controlled an empire that by that time sprawled over much of what today forms northern India, Pakistan, Afghanistan, and Bangladesh. Akbar's grandson conceived the architectural masterpiece that is the Taj Mahal, and Akbar's own vision was no less grandiose: he aimed to tidy up the confusing array of world religions by folding them into one perfect, all-encompassing faith. He had summoned the Jesuits to his imperial court to help him with his grand plan and listened to them defend their Christian religion alongside Muslim mullahs and Hindu Brahmins. The ex-soldier Goes did not shine in theological debate, unlike his more extensively educated Jesuit colleagues. But his mastery of Persian won him access to Akbar and eventually the emperor's trust as well. When Akbar determined to conclude a peace with the Portuguese viceroy of India, Goes was his emissary to the negotiations.

The mission that ended Goes's life began soon after word arrived that one of his Jesuit colleagues had won permission to reside in the Chinese imperial city of Beijing. No Jesuit—no *European*—had been tolerated in the imperial city for well over a century. Now one of their team was not only living there but apparently had cultivated contacts close to the emperor himself. The successes in India and China undoubtedly encouraged Jesuits to imagine these two great kingdoms as emerging hubs of what they hoped would become their spiritual empire in Asia, and that vision spurred them to pioneer an overland link between the two countries. A superior linguist and a resilient ex-soldier, Goes was an obvious choice for the mission.

Neither the Jesuits nor any other westerners had the vaguest idea of what lay between these countries. Their hosts offered no reliable maps of the vast Asian interior. And while ocean-borne

Interfaith dialogue, seventeenth-century style

This image of two Jesuits at the court of the Mughal emperor is taken from a 1605 Mughal-era miniature depicting the Jesuits engaged in a debate with Hindu and Muslim scholars on their respective faiths.

European explorers were slowly tracing Asia's coastal perimeter, the inland expanse remained largely unknown.

Trying to find a less-expensive way

Goes and his Jesuit colleagues had two vital reasons for wanting to create this overland route through the unknown. The first was a very literal matter of life and death. Their progress in Asia had not been without cost. Not least of the difficulties was the treacherous ocean voyage from Portugal to Asia. Jesuits set out on tiny wooden ships only slightly longer and far less watertight than modern subway cars. Celestial navigation techniques allowed pilots to judge their latitude with some accuracy, but estimates of longitude were utter guesswork and would remain so for another century. Simply put, explorers, traders, Jesuits, and others bobbed along on ocean journeys seldom knowing just where they were or how far they might still be from where they were going.

Not surprisingly, the journeys took a horrific toll. In some years, as many as a third of the Jesuits heading east died in shipwrecks or through disease. Even successful voyages could drag on for years. Becalmed ships sat in dreaded doldrums off the African coast. Storm-damaged vessels limped into Mozambique or other intermediate ports and lost months completing needed repairs. Ships sat off Goa waiting for the seasonal turn of trade winds to allow onward journey.

Those who survived the journey arrived weakened and malnourished in alien environments, often having lost years of their lives. Yet even those who survived hadn't seen the last of difficulties caused by the primitive transport network. They could communicate with their colleagues elsewhere in Asia or back home in Europe only through letters posted on those same few ships that plied the trade routes. One Jesuit in what is now Malaysia reminded impatient superiors in Rome to "consider that when you send an order . . . you will not be able to receive a reply to what you send us in less than three years and nine months."[2] Another in China poignantly shared a more personal anguish: "Often when I call to mind the number of lengthy letters that I have written about this place to those who were already dead, I lose the strength and the spirit to write any more."[3]

There had to be a better way, and that's what Goes attempted to find—a better, safer, faster overland route for travel and communications within Asia, which would mean fewer colleagues lost at sea and years shaved from an arduous trip. And if there was a land route within Asia, perhaps a link could also be pioneered from Asia all the way back to Europe.

The Jesuits had reason to believe that the route might already exist. Merchants who arrived at Akbar's court described their journeys to China along a "silk road." Their tales corroborated centuries-old reports that had tantalized European explorers and gave Goes a second reason for his mission: to find the great Cathay.

Trying to find an elusive asset

The Italian Marco Polo claimed to have visited in the 1200s a powerful, wealthy, and highly civilized empire in the East. When Christopher Columbus dropped anchor in the Caribbean in 1492, he was convinced that only a few more days of sailing separated him from this great kingdom. No such luck for Columbus, and no such luck for those who succeeded him on voyages of discovery. Indeed, as explorers slowly assembled the world jigsaw puzzle, a disconcerting problem arose: no Cathay—and fewer and fewer empty spaces on the world map. Mapmakers grasped at a handy solution. Few European explorers had been bold enough to leave behind the safety of coastal trading posts to venture far inland, so the Asian interior remained largely a mystery. No one quite knew, for example, where the Chinese kingdom ended and what countries—if any—might lie on the other side of China's Great Wall. European mapmakers took advantage of this question mark hanging over the Asian landmass and simply plopped Cathay into the unmapped, unexplored chunk of Asia north of India and northwest of China.

The Jesuits had their own reasons for wanting to resolve the mystery of Cathay. Marco Polo had written of Christian communities in this kingdom, and now Jesuits in India were hearing descriptions of what sounded like Christian rituals from merchants who had traveled the Silk Road. If there were long-lost Christian communities somewhere in Asia, the Jesuits wanted to find them. Thus Goes was charged with a second objective: to find the great kingdom of Cathay, *if* it existed, and Cathay's lost Christian tribes, *if* they existed.

Journeying into the unknown

In the fall of 1602, Goes set off from Agra. His passport was a safe-conduct letter from Akbar, though Goes hadn't even reached the outskirts of the Mughal empire before finding independent-minded territories for whom Akbar was "more a name than a reality."[4] Goes, accompanied by a single guide, fell in with a five-hundred-person caravan. Snaking along narrow mountain trails and gorges, the caravan would have stretched out to quite some length—a motley jumble of camels, horses, merchants, and mercenaries bearing merchandise, food, and sleeping gear for the many nights spent in the open.

To blend in with the other travelers, Goes dressed as a merchant, but of course his disguise fooled next to no one. As a European Christian, Goes was alternately a welcome curiosity and a blasphemous stranger in the remote mountain communities through which the caravan slowly wound its way. The king of Kashgar feted the foreigner and entertained himself with debates about Christianity and Islam. Farther on, the twelve-year-old king of Aksu, less interested in such lofty pursuits as religious debate, asked Goes to dance in the style of his native country. Goes obliged. Who can refuse a king?

The journey must have been exhilarating, mortally terrifying, and breathtakingly beautiful. Goes almost certainly was the first European to travel the route in hundreds of years, if not the first ever, and no other European would pass that way again for another two centuries. The caravan wound through parts of what now forms India, Pakistan, Afghanistan, Russia, and Mongolia. Two years into the journey, the caravan crossed the so-called roof of the world, where the Karakoram, Himalaya, and Hindu Kush mountain ranges collide to form the highest plateau on Earth. Goes had little opportunity for leisurely contemplation of the snowcapped peaks topping out above twenty-three thousand feet that later generations would pridefully call Lenin Peak and Stalin Peak (which revisionists later rechristened Communism Peak). But there was little time for sightseeing; rather, Goes was preoccupied with the sheer struggle to survive while trudging through snowy passes at altitudes that sometimes reached eighteen thousand feet. He reported that at least five of their packhorses "perished through the intense cold and the entire lack of fuel together with the uncongenial state of the atmosphere, which made it almost impossible for the animals to breathe."[5] Intense cold, no fuel, and air too thin for the horses to breathe: how did the *human* travelers survive? Latter-day expeditions struggle with conditions on the great Asian peaks despite the high-tech accouterments of modern mountaineering: canned oxygen and space-age fabrics and freeze-dried high-protein foods. But Goes and his companions relied on distinctly low-tech, centuries-old remedies for coping with cold and high altitudes: eating dried apples and onions and rubbing garlic on the gums of their horses.

Those who survived the climb up the mountains wound their way down the other side to the Tarim Basin, so barren and remote even centuries later that the Chinese government regarded it the ideal landscape for a nuclear testing program. From three miles above sea level, the Silk Road plunged down to hundreds of feet below sea level. Caravans left bitter mountain cold for equally oppressive desert heat; sandstorms replaced snowstorms, and the landscape of ice and snow gave way to waterless desert. All but the most foolhardy traveled the desert terrain in large groups and only at night. Tartar raiding parties enjoyed free rein to swoop down on passing caravans. Goes matter-of-factly reported the frequent result of these attacks: "One often comes across the dead bodies of Mohammedans who have attempted the journey unaccompanied."[6]

Goes survived the desert, just as he had survived the mountains and the whole grueling

> Goes survived the desert, just as he had survived the mountains and the whole grueling three-thousand-mile trek. A journey anticipated to take six months had stretched on for nearly four years.

three-thousand-mile trek. A journey anticipated to take six months had stretched on for nearly four years. Soon into his journey it became more than clear to him that the overland route was, if anything, even more treacherous than the sea journey. He left this understated, stoic assessment for his Jesuit superiors: "The journey is very long, full of difficulties and dangers. No one from the Society [of Jesus] should ever attempt to repeat it."[7]

Redefining the success or failure of a leader

Goes survived the worst of the journey only to die a thousand miles short of Beijing. He never found the kingdom of Cathay. Nor did he find the hoped-for shortcut from India to China.

Appearances sometimes deceive. Goes may have died broke and more or less alone, but he was not a failure. Though the romantic notion of Cathay continued to haunt a few die-hard explorers, Goes had essentially resolved the vexing historical question of Cathay's location by proving what some of his Jesuit colleagues had begun to suspect: China *was* Cathay. There was no other great kingdom; there were no lost Christian tribes. If Marco Polo made the journey he claimed to have made (and some recent scholars have questioned this), the great empire he called Cathay was the same empire that sixteenth-century Europeans were calling China. Instead of dissipating their energies on the hunt for some mythical empire, Goes's colleagues could now focus their full efforts on two empires that really did exist: India and China.

> Appearances sometimes deceive. Goes may have died broke and more or less alone, but he was not a failure.

Goes also settled speculation about a more efficient route between the two countries. That didn't exist either, and it wouldn't until centuries later, when technological advances allowed for a faster, safer land route.

Goes's story is not well known, even to Jesuits. There is at least one obvious reason why this is: he left behind a scanty historical record, and the few supposed facts concerning his life sometimes conflict. But there's another reason as well. History readily celebrates those who literally put places on the map—Columbus, Hudson, even Goes's Jesuit colleague Jacques Marquette, who navigated the Upper Mississippi River. But there's only a quick slide into oblivion for those who came away empty, or those like Goes who *removed* places like Cathay from the map. The difference is completely understandable in one way and curious in another. Columbus found something, all right, but not what he was looking for. And what these early explorers discovered—or didn't—was often a result of chance and luck. The measure of their personal greatness is less what they found at journey's end and more the depth of human character that carried them along the way: their imagination, will, perseverance, courage, resourcefulness, and willingness to bear the risk of failure.

> The measure of their personal greatness is less what they found at journey's end and more the depth of human character that carried them along the way: their imagination, will, perseverance, courage, resourcefulness, and willingness to bear the risk of failure.

These traits have often marked those explorers who found "what's out there." But they have also marked lesser-sung explorers like Goes who discovered what's *not* out there, just as they have marked unheralded medical researchers whose failed efforts pointed the path toward medical solutions, as well as countless other scientists, inventors, philosophers, and mathematicians who have contributed similarly in their own fields. Goes's story redefines leadership success by illustrating how one need not make a big, visible, self-aggrandizing "win" to be successful; sometimes success comes in the form of a contribution that helps the *team* to win. In Goes's case, leadership was proven by something as unremarkable—yet arduous—as exploring a blind alley so that future colleagues wouldn't have to.

Goes died all but alone in a remote Chinese outpost. No Jesuit colleagues had accompanied him on his journey, and none tended him at his death. So how did even the few details of his historic journey ever become known?

Every once in a while the postal service surprises you. This was one of those times. Once Goes's trading caravan finally reached Xuzhou, he entrusted merchants bound for Beijing with letters addressed to a Matteo Ricci. The odds of his letter reaching this Ricci were slim: Goes had no address for Ricci, nor was he capable of addressing his letter with Chinese characters; more than a thousand miles still lay between Goes and Beijing; and his postman was a merchant trader who might become wealthy trading his goods in the capital but stood to gain absolutely nothing by tracking down this Ricci.

> In Goes's case, leadership was proven by something as unremarkable—yet arduous—as exploring a blind alley so that future colleagues wouldn't have to.

But the odds were not even *that* good. Strictly speaking, there was no one named Matteo Ricci in Beijing at the time. The Italian Jesuit Goes knew as Matteo Ricci was known in China by another name: Li Ma-tou.

However unlikely, the letter reached Ricci. And perhaps it's not so extraordinary that it did. The roman script of the letter would have been indecipherable to Beijing residents, but it would have pointed to a non-Chinese as the intended recipient. And there was only one westerner legally residing in Beijing at the time, together with a handful of his colleagues. So the letter perhaps naturally found its way into Ricci's hands, and he immediately dispatched a young Chinese candidate for Jesuit membership to rendezvous with Goes in Xuzhou. The young man arrived barely in time to see Goes die and to retrieve a few scraps from his diary. He returned to Beijing with the diary accounts and in the company of the servant who had traveled with Goes throughout his trek.

THE LINGUIST, MAPMAKER, PHILOSOPHER, AND MULTICULTURALIST

Matteo Ricci had been on a journey of his own. Though less physically taxing than Goes's passage through three-mile-high mountain passes, it had stretched over many more years. In one very real if intangible sense, Matteo Ricci's journey to Beijing began in 1552, the year of his birth in Italy. In that same year, the first Jesuit attempt to enter China ended in failure on a remote island some thirty miles from what is now Hong Kong. A succession of Jesuits followed, building up a years-long track record of uninterrupted and unmitigated failure.

Early Jesuits attempting to reach China remained bottled up in the Portuguese trading post of Macao. Those few to venture onto the decidedly xenophobic Chinese mainland were promptly deported—frequently in cages and under armed guard.

Ricci changed all that by radically altering the Jesuit approach to China, and in the process he helped shape Jesuit strategy across Asia for generations. Early on, he had established himself as a man given to charting his own course. His family had proudly sent him from their hilltop hometown of Macerata in central Italy to Rome for a law degree. They must have been puzzled if not dismayed to learn soon after that he had instead decided to join the Jesuits at age eighteen.

Ten years later he was in Macao immersing himself in Chinese language studies. His language texts in that pre-Berlitz era were a few hand-scrawled notes and vocabulary lists that his colleagues

Jesuit ingenuity: A linguist, mapmaker, and priest

This portrait of Matteo Ricci was painted soon after his death by his Chinese colleague (Manuel) Yu Wen-hui, a convert to Christianity who later joined the Jesuits. The Jesuit Nicolas Trigault brought the portrait to Rome on the same bittersweet trip during which he recruited Jesuits to work in China, only to see most of them die during the grueling ocean journey to Asia.

had managed to puzzle out. Ricci couldn't possibly have imagined or prepared for life in China. Who would have prepared him? Even the most educated Europeans had never seen an Asian person, heard an Asian language, or seen Chinese characters. Ricci's letters to his colleagues capture the challenge of describing something still utterly new to Europe:

> I have applied myself to the Chinese language and can assure Your Reverence that it is a different thing from Greek or German. . . . The spoken tongue is prey to so many ambiguities that many sounds mean more than a thousand things, and sometimes there is no more difference between the one and the other than in pronouncing the sound with the voice raised or lowered in four kinds of tone. . . . As to the alphabet, it is a thing one would not believe in had one not seen and tried it as I have. . . . Their manner of writing more closely resembles painting, which is why they write with a brush in the manner of our painters.[8]

Ricci mastered the Chinese language as no westerner known to history had mastered it before him. Within a few years of setting foot in Macao, he had drafted and published a treatise in Chinese, *On Friendship*. He made greater progress with this one document than his predecessors had made over forty years. "This treatise has established our reputation as scholars of talent and virtue; and thus it is read and received with great applause and already has been published in two different places."[9]

Applying a radical strategy

On Friendship was a linguistic tour de force, but it was even more remarkable for the radical strategic reversals it signaled. After all, European missioners had rarely attempted to master fully the languages of the countries they visited. When they dabbled in local tongues, it was generally only to produce direct translations of Christian prayers or catechisms. This attitude toward language betrayed a not-so-concealed belief that it was indigenous populations who needed to do the changing, not the European missioners and colonialists. Converts were expected to Europeanize themselves, or, as most Europeans regarded it, *civilize* themselves. Converts on the Indian subcontinent might have wondered how clunky European boots and heavy Portuguese garments were connected to a Christian lifestyle, not to mention why anyone would favor such attire in a subtropical climate. But to Europeans in Asia, these were not matters of discussion. Civilized people dressed themselves as Europeans did—or so most Europeans were convinced.

Enter Ricci. *On Friendship* fit comfortably; it didn't chafe like a European boot. For Ricci had not only mastered the Chinese language; he had also honed a style familiar to his readers. He wrote not in the dry, scholastic approach that he had studied in Rome but with the literary forms that a Confucian scholar might use. His ideas, grounded in Judeo-Christian values, were certainly new to his audience. But literate Chinese were familiar with his topic; he had purposely chosen not to translate some work of European literature but to address a core human relation discussed in Confucian texts.

Ricci had turned the tables *on himself.* Instead of dragging potential converts into an alien European culture, he was pioneering a radical strategy of "inculturation," a term coined by later Jesuits to describe their strategy of assimilating themselves to their host cultures. *He* did the changing, accommodating himself to the culture, values, and norms of his Chinese hosts. This time it wasn't the converts who were forced into unfamiliar dress; it was Ricci and his team who donned new robes. "We have let our beards grow and our hair down to our ears; at the same time we have adopted the special dress that the literati wear . . . which is of purple silk, and the hem of the robe and collar and the edges are bordered with a band of blue silk a little less than a palm wide."[10] What would they have thought back in Macerata, Italy?

> Instead of dragging potential converts into an alien European culture, he was pioneering a radical strategy of "inculturation," a term coined by later Jesuits to describe their strategy of assimilating themselves to their host cultures.

Taking the door that's open

Needless to say, no one mistook Ricci for a Chinese Confucian scholar, despite his new attire. But the symbolism of his gesture was instantly apparent. Priestly black robes may have been an immediately recognizable symbol on the streets of Rome, but black robes meant nothing in China and only reinforced the separateness of these strange visitors from the West. Ricci's newly adopted attire, on the other hand, was as well understood in China as his black cassock had been in Rome: he was presuming to present himself as a scholar possessed of ideas worthy of respect and attention.

Ricci soon found ways to back up his claims to be a man with unique wisdom to share. China had turned increasingly inward during the closing decades of the Ming dynasty. The country's applied sciences, once far superior to European technology, had long since ebbed. China's misfortune became Ricci's great opportunity. Not knowing what artifacts of western science and culture would interest his hosts, he had lugged along from Europe a most unusual bag of tricks. His residence soon became a cross between a curiosity shop, a museum, a university, and a salon for intellectual debate. Mathematicians discussed Euclidean geometry texts that Ricci had translated into Chinese. Educated visitors examined books, prisms, clocks, and sextants. Astronomers learned how the astrolabe could aid in calculating planetary and stellar motion. A world map particularly intrigued his visitors, because

> the Chinese, who had practically no commerce with foreign peoples, were grossly ignorant of the other parts of the world. Their own cosmographic tables bore the title of universal description of the whole world [but] reduced the extent of the earth to their own fifteen provinces; and on the seas painted around they set a few small islands, adding the names of the few kingdoms of which they might have heard, all of which kingdoms taken together would scarcely equal the smallest province of the Chinese Empire.[11]

Ricci had not entered China to make maps, but he jumped at another opportunity to burnish his image—and that of the West. After all, Chinese world maps not only reflected poor understanding of world geography but also implicitly conveyed their prejudice that there wasn't much worth knowing beyond Chinese borders. Ricci drafted a new world map with country names written in Chinese characters. A botched first effort demonstrated the difficulty of shaking off a European mindset and successfully acculturating. He had represented the world the way Europeans envisioned it: Europe proudly dominated the center of the map; Asia was on the right, with China pushed into the periphery. It was an affront. While his Chinese counterparts admitted some ignorance of world geography, they knew this much: China, which meant "middle kingdom" in Chinese, was the *center* of the world. Ricci's map was wrong.

Aiming high from the very beginning

The resourceful Italian quickly bounced back with the simplest of solutions. Reorienting his perspective as one might do by turning a globe, he soon came up with a new map. This effort situated China squarely in the center of the world, exactly where his hosts knew their country should be. Ricci went further, annotating his map with explanatory descriptions—though not exactly the kind of information one usually expects from a map. His annotation for the Roman states, for example, read, "The Holy Father, who is celibate, and concerns himself only with the Catholic religion, residing in Rome. All the Europeans who are in the Roman Empire revere him."[12] *All* the Europeans revere him? Protestant followers of the Lutheran and Calvinist traditions might have had something to say about that, but one can forgive Ricci for judging this might not be the best moment to complicate his map tutorial by introducing the embarrassing drama of the Reformation that was unfolding at that moment back in Europe.

The mapmaker, astronomer, and author had an agenda. Opportunistic though his approach was, it was not scattershot. His ultimate goal was an audience with the Chinese emperor. He must have harbored hopes of a grand coup, of converting the emperor and using the ruler's gravitational pull to attract millions of his Chinese subjects into the Christian fold. As absurd as the idea might seem today, it would have seemed perfectly logical to Ricci. After all, he had sailed from a Europe that had been transformed in precisely the same top-down fashion. Catholic England had suddenly become Protestant England because Henry VIII had decided it would. The same pattern had played itself out across the European continent in one variation or another. To Ricci's mind, a top-down strategy might produce the same result in Asia.

Even if Ricci didn't manage to convert the emperor, he hoped to at least win formal approval or tacit tolerance of Jesuit work in China. Despite Ricci's growing renown among leading Chinese officials, Jesuit status remained tenuous at best. Xenophobic regional governors or bureaucrats could at any time deport the Europeans. Ricci instructed his colleagues to maintain a low profile. No bell ringing in the Chinese equivalent of the town square to attract crowds for fire-and-brimstone sermons, and no showy churches. Instead, Ricci and the handful of Jesuits who joined him built unostentatious chapels on the grounds of their private residences.

It took Ricci twenty years from his arrival in Macao to reach the imperial city of Beijing. He had been on the move constantly, patiently cultivating a network of well-placed Chinese officials, always looking to secure some powerful bureaucrat's sponsorship for an imperial introduction.

Court officials eventually agreed to present the emperor with Ricci's gifts: statues of the Madonna and Christ, two clocks, a world map, a spinet (a harpsichord-like musical instrument), and two prisms. The gifts were accompanied by a message from Ricci introducing himself, "a religious without wife or children and therefore seeking no favor; that, having studied astronomy, geography, calculus, and mathematics, . . . would be happy to be of service to the emperor."[13]

The gifts were well chosen. The emperor was especially fascinated with a clock that chimed the hours. When it malfunctioned, Ricci was summoned to the imperial palace to teach the emperor's eunuchs how to repair it. It was the closest Ricci ever came to the imperial audience he craved. Still, reaching Beijing had been an impressive achievement in its own right. A Portuguese ambassador had traveled there almost a century prior to Ricci's arrival; the ambassador had been promptly escorted back to Hong Kong in a cage and expelled from China. There is no record of any other westerner arriving in between. In his final days, Ricci reportedly told his colleagues that they were "standing before an open door."

Ricci died three years after Goes's death in Xuzhou. No one really knows where Goes was interred. Visitors to Beijing can still find Ricci's grave; he was the first westerner granted a burial plot in the imperial precincts. The governor of Beijing commissioned a gravestone and had it inscribed with the names of Ricci's prestigious acquaintances in China—the minister of rites, the minister of finance, and various other ministerial officials and bureaucrats. His passing was marked by the gathering of the two-thousand-strong Christian community he had established and nurtured in Beijing. If any crowd commemorated Goes's passing, it was only the one hovering near his deathbed to loot his few belongings.

Ricci's unlikely life and accomplishments raise a number of questions. How did he make the imaginative, improbable strategic leaps from teaching astronomy to translating geometry to attempting to convert China? What inspired the decision, then the flexibility and self-confidence, to cast aside priestly habit and European habits to adopt a Chinese lifestyle? These questions and others like them take us to the very essence of Jesuit leadership and form the heart of later chapters.

Developing "brilliant and eminent men"

Jesuit scholar Christopher Clavius, who befriended Galileo and helped develop the Gregorian calendar still in use throughout the world today, is pictured here with the "cutting edge" tools of a Renaissance astronomer and mathematician.

THE MATHEMATICIAN AND ASTRONOMER

Christopher Clavius sticks out like a sore thumb alongside Benedetto de Goes and Matteo Ricci. During their lifetime, only the tiniest minority of Europeans ever ventured beyond the continent. Goes and Ricci had even done this adventurous minority one better. When years-long ocean voyages finally deposited grateful and fearful travelers at colonial outposts, most were more than happy to call it journey's end—all but the likes of Goes and Ricci. They kept on going, traveling routes no European had ever explored. They logged thousands of miles even after reaching Asia, leading peripatetic lifestyles that seldom left them in any one place for longer than a year or two.

The German Clavius is a far different story. He worked in the same job as a university professor for forty-eight years, forty-six of them in the same institution—the Collegio Romano run by the Jesuits. Most sixteenth-century Europeans didn't *live* to age

forty-eight, much less work for
that many years. The thought
of doing any one job for so
many years conjures up certain
images, most of them unflat-
tering—and few of them consistent with the adventure-ready
likes of Goes and Ricci.

He worked in the same job
as a university professor
for forty-eight years,
forty-six of them
in the same institution.

But images of a stuffy, tired professor recycling yellowing lecture
notes year after year are badly misplaced in Clavius's case. A drastically different image captures his life more effectively: that of a man
marveling before a solar eclipse. It is said that Clavius witnessed an
eclipse in 1560 as a twenty-three-year-old Jesuit trainee and
resolved on his life's work that afternoon. He relentlessly pursued
his passion for astronomy throughout his remaining years, bequeath-
ing that passion to men such as Ricci. Indeed, one of Ricci's Jesuit
successors accurately predicted a solar eclipse that darkened Beijing
skies one afternoon in 1629, a coup that won the Jesuits an unprecedented appointment within the imperial observatory.

Training recruits for a changing world

Clavius couldn't possibly have known that astronomy might someday hold the key to Jesuit success in China. He had started his
teaching career in a young Jesuit company that was enjoying phe-
nomenal growth while still shaping its practices and strategies.
With approximately a hundred colleges open globally, Jesuits were
well on their way to building the world's largest privately organized
school system. In the forty years since its founding, the Jesuit company itself had boomed from ten members to five thousand.

Senior Jesuits gathered in Rome to hash out a strategic direction for their rapidly growing company. The mathematician
Clavius ventured his own vision of the company they needed to
build. Jesuits should become experts not only in theology and

philosophy, the disciplines everyone expected priests to master, but also in languages, mathematics, and the sciences. The world was changing, and Jesuits needed to stay at the forefront by shining even in these minor but emerging disciplines. Clavius advocated master classes to position Jesuit trainees at the cutting edge of European scholarship. He argued that he and his colleagues needed to mold their recruits into

> brilliant and most eminent men, who, when they are distributed in various nations and kingdoms like sparkling gems, to the great honour of the Society [of Jesus], will be a source of great fear to all enemies, and an incredible incitement to make the youth flock to us from all parts of the world.[14]

Though his colleagues might have rolled their eyes at his bombastic rhetoric and tsked his lack of priestly modesty, most of them likely agreed. And those who didn't would have thought twice about tangling with Clavius's heavyweight intellect.

> Clavius advocated master classes to position Jesuit trainees at the cutting edge of European scholarship.

For more than forty years, Clavius applied his passion and vision to molding recruits into "brilliant and eminent men" at the Jesuits' Collegio Romano, teaching the teachers, as it were. The college gathered many of the Jesuits' most promising trainees from across Europe; Clavius plucked the best and brightest of these for master classes in mathematics and astronomy. Matteo Ricci was likely one of the chosen. When Ricci was studying astronomy under Clavius, he had no idea that he was destined to work in China; nor did anyone in Europe have the faintest inkling of the sorry state of Chinese applied sciences until Ricci traveled there.

Ricci wasn't studying astronomy as part of some elaborate plan to convert China, for Clavius's vision was at once simpler and even more extravagant than a quixotic plan to convert an Asian empire. Ricci, Clavius, and their Jesuit managers didn't stop to worry about what use higher math and astronomy would be to future priests. Like all teachers, Clavius believed that intellectual challenge in and of itself was turning his talented recruits into better people. As important as the facts learned was what was won through the very process of learning: discipline and dedication and willingness to see challenging problems through to their end; the wonder, curiosity, and creativity engendered by looking at the world through a different lens; and the confidence born of solving a problem that once seemed insoluble. Talented, well-trained recruits such as Ricci, once molded into "brilliant and eminent men," would find ways to make their own luck in the world.

Discarding long-cherished beliefs
for newly revealed truths

Clavius not only molded these brilliant and eminent men, he *was* one. When a young Italian scientist named Galileo Galilei first visited Rome in 1587, he made pilgrimage to seek the blessing of Clavius, one of Europe's leading mathematicians. Clavius was impressed enough to give Galileo the boost every young academic craves; a good word from the well-respected Jesuit helped Galileo secure his first teaching post. Clavius had offered support even though he and Galileo came from different worlds—different *universes*, to be precise. Clavius's astronomy texts quite naturally defended the Catholic Church–approved Ptolemaic system, which had the sun, moon, stars, and planets revolving around an Earth that God had honored by fixing it at the center of the universe.

But Galileo was slowly drifting away from this astronomical system that Clavius and every other loyal cleric accepted without question. By the early 1600s, Galileo had fashioned Europe's first modern telescope. Crude though the instrument was, it was powerful enough to reveal that Venus was exhibiting phases much like

those of the moon. It was a universe-shattering observation. It suggested that Venus revolved around the sun, not the Earth. If not,
how else to explain Venus's phases—that Venus revolved around
the sun, while the sun and other planets revolved around the
Earth in some bewilderingly complex solar system? It seemed that
an increasingly suspect theory of an Earth-centered universe could
be maintained only by twisting the planetary orbits into ever more
complicated knots.

Though Galileo tiptoed carefully, he was wandering into a mine-
field that would ultimately prove impossible to cross. Church
bureaucrats had too much invested in the idea of an Earth-centered
universe to retreat from the theory. No matter what Galileo saw
through his telescope, how plainly he saw it, or how naturally his
observations supported the conclusion of a sun-centered system,
the institutional church would have none of it.

Christopher Clavius was more than seventy when Galileo published these findings with their carefully hedged but unmistakable
challenge to Earth-centered theories. One could not have blamed
Clavius had he rested on his laurels at this point. Galileo's ideas
implicitly challenged Clavius's lifework, so the upstart Galileo
couldn't count on much support for his revolutionary, dangerous
ideas. It wouldn't have taken much effort for the well-regarded
Clavius to swat away the young upstart.

Instead, the old man led one last master class of Jesuit astronomy
students to the roof of the Collegio Romano. The Jesuits had by
now obtained their own telescopes, newer and more powerful
than the ones Clavius had used in his earlier astronomical work.
Clavius and his students attempted to duplicate the observations
Galileo claimed to have made. Soon after, Clavius published the
final edition of his own astronomy text. Many astronomers were
undoubtedly surprised—and many church officials outraged—to
read these words in Clavius's text: "Consult the reliable little
book by Galileo Galilei, printed at Venice in 1610 and called
Sidereus Nuncius."[15]

Clavius endorsed all of Galileo's findings and calculations. His verdict of "reliable" bought Galileo time by holding his critics at bay. But Clavius went further, about as far as he possibly could have ventured. As a loyal churchman, speaking out in favor of Copernican heliocentric theory would have been unthinkable— heretical, in fact. But Clavius understood that the Ptolemaic system he had spent a lifetime defending was destined for the dustbin. Primitive though his and Galileo's telescopes might have been, they had revealed enough to wreck classic Ptolemaic theory. Maybe there was some theory short of the unthinkable sun-centered theory to explain the universe, but knee-jerk Ptolemaism was no longer tenable. Noting Galileo's observations, Clavius continued: "Since things are thus, astronomers ought to consider how the celestial orbs may be arranged in order to save these phenomena."[16] In other words, the facts were what they were; scientists needed to accept the facts and set about finding a credible theory to explain them.

Clavius died soon after he published these statements. Galileo continued at his peril to propound controversial views. Twenty-odd years later he was on his knees before Vatican inquisitors, abjuring belief in a heliocentric universe and swearing that the Earth didn't move in order to ward off excommunication and perhaps even premature (and unnatural) death.

Clavius endorsed all of Galileo's findings and calculations. Clavius understood that the Ptolemaic system he had spent a lifetime defending was destined for the dustbin.

What role would Clavius have played in Galileo's drama had he lived? Indisputably the leading astronomer-priest of his era, Clavius certainly would have become embroiled in the controversy. It's difficult to imagine a church official defending Galileo, given the church's own unflinchingly militant stance. And yet,

Clavius's own text is elegant, simple testimony to his intellectual integrity and seemingly unwavering commitment to the truth. How he would have reconciled his dilemma remains a curious but unanswerable question.

How Clavius helped fix our day planners

Though Clavius's astronomical views were being eclipsed even before his death, another of his achievements has admirably stood the test of time. Indeed, though few have heard of Clavius, everyone who has ever consulted a calendar or opened a day planner has unknowingly paid him tribute. During Clavius's lifetime, the Julian calendar guided the rhythm of European life, as it had for centuries since its institution by Julius Caesar. But it was malfunctioning. The Scriptures recorded Jesus Christ's crucifixion and resurrection as taking place during the Jewish Passover, which occurs in the first month of spring. The Catholic Church accordingly fixed Easter Sunday to occur on the first Sunday after the first full moon following the vernal (spring) equinox. But for reasons that were not well understood, the spring equinox was slipping backward with each passing century (and therefore, so was Easter Sunday). By the sixteenth century, Easter Sunday was slowly but inexorably migrating toward Christmas.

Pope Gregory XIII asked Clavius to head a commission investigating the increasingly embarrassing problem. What was going wrong with the calendar? As it turned out, the actual solar year was shorter—674 seconds shorter, to be exact—than the Julian calendar year. What's 674 seconds? Not much in a year, but problematic once compounded over centuries. Three days were added every four hundred years, and Easter Sunday continued its march toward Christmas Day.

Clavius's commission largely adopted the analytical approach of the Italian Aloysius Lilius and his elegantly simple solution. Lilius, who died not long before the commission was formed, had proposed that century years only be leap years when evenly divisible by four hundred. In other words, the year 1900 would not be a leap year, but the year 2000 would. This subtle recalibration of the leap-year mechanism remains intact, and Christians regularly celebrate Easter in spring, blissfully unaware of their debt to Lilius and Clavius. Clavius was modest and politically astute—and most likely never given a choice in the matter—when the time came to promulgate what would later become known as the Gregorian calendar in honor of Pope Gregory XIII.

Not everyone immediately rallied around the new calendar. The late 1500s was a decidedly less ecumenical age than our own. Protestants and Catholics engaged in regular, bitter, and often bloody skirmishes all over Christian Europe. Who was to say that the new calendar was not some deviously clever Jesuitical or papist plot? Even if the new calendar *was* superior in its accuracy, Protestant leaders had little interest in backing a calendar revised by the Roman pope and a *Jesuit* mathematician. Catholic Italy immediately adopted the new calendar; militantly Protestant Britain did not. Catholic regions in the German states signed on; neighboring Protestant regions in Germany did not. For years it was one date in one part of Germany and a different date in another.

Loyal Catholics weren't necessarily pleased with the new calendar either. In order to undo more than a millennium of compounded damage from the Julian calendar, Clavius's commission had Pope Gregory XIII proclaim that in the year of 1582—and *only* in 1582, thankfully—the day after October 4 would be October 15. Even loyal Catholics had cause to grumble: their lives had been shortened by nearly two weeks. As confusion over the new calendar dragged on, Clavius prepared what should have been the final word on the subject. With Pope Gregory and all the other commission members long dead, the aging Clavius published his definitive, eight-hundred-page mathematical analysis and proof supporting the new calendar.

Still, old prejudices die hard. Nearly two hundred years passed before Great Britain adopted the Gregorian calendar in 1752. Russia adopted it in 1918, a decade after calendar confusion had caused the country's athletes to arrive twelve days late for the 1908 Olympics. Meeting planners and calendar makers were eventually relieved of the nightmarish scheduling headache brought on by inconsistent calendars, though hardcore partygoers unfortunately were deprived of what would have been a wonderful opportunity to celebrate the second millennium twice.

Old prejudices certainly do die hard. Only in 1822 did the Catholic Church formally allow heliocentricity to be taught in Catholic countries. And only in 1992 did Pope John Paul II definitively close a long-open chapter by issuing the Catholic Church's posthumous apology to Galileo.

A DIFFERENT WAY TO THINK ABOUT LEADERSHIP

Goes, Ricci, and Clavius: three unlikely leadership role models. After all, don't leaders lead other people? And don't the greatest leaders lead *lots* of people? None of these three ever managed more than a handful of others; for most of their respective working lives, each led only himself.

Which is precisely the point: they led *themselves*. They didn't shrink from this task, the first and most crucial leadership challenge that every leader must face.

Leadership lessons from unlikely sources

What do leaders do? A quick study of Goes, Ricci, and Clavius reveals the leadership qualities present in all of them. Leaders

- are always teaching and learning: Matteo Ricci achieved fluency in Chinese and absorbed the wisdom of the Confucian Four Books, introduced Confucian thought to Europe by translating the work into Italian, and all the while taught his mandarin teachers everything from Euclidean geometry to astronomy to the Christian message.

- mold "brilliant and eminent" men and women: Christopher Clavius challenged students in his Collegio Romano master classes year after year for more than forty years.

- persevere: Benedetto de Goes pressed on with his journey through three-mile-high mountain passes despite bitter cold and fear of not finding the mysterious Cathay.

- energize themselves by the sheer ambition of their heroic goals: Goes journeyed through thousands of miles of unmapped Asian hinterland in search for his route to China; Ricci set his sights on the imperial audience that eluded three centuries of Europeans; Clavius envisioned a corps of unparalleled talent unleashed on the world.

- innovate by approaching their challenges in ways their predecessors never imagined: Ricci developed an improbable strategy to win attention for his Christian message— by translating geometry texts and reconfiguring world maps.

- devote themselves to excellence: Clavius painstakingly produced an eight-hundred-page mathematical proof underpinning his calendar reform.

- remain open to new ideas, even in old age: At seventy-three, Clavius carefully duplicated Galileo's observations.

- honor the truth above their egos: Goes
  frankly admitted that he had not found
  an easier way to China, despite all he had
  personally invested in the quest; Clavius
  endorsed Galileo's observations, well
  aware of the threat they posed to theories
  Clavius had spent a lifetime defending.

- influence others by their example, their
  ideas, and their coaching: Clavius
  inspired Ricci and subsequent
  astronomers in China, and all three—
  Clavius, Goes, and Ricci—continue to
  influence Jesuits today.

Leadership is not merely getting the job done; it's *how* the job is done. For all leaders, including Goes and Ricci and Clavius, this means *influencing, visioning, persevering, energizing, innovating, teaching*.

Certain assumptions have over time come to dominate our cultural stereotypes of leaders and leadership:

- A leader is a person "in charge"—the one
  running a company, heading a government, coaching a team, or captaining
  troops.

- Leadership produces direct results, and
  the most effective leadership behavior
  produces *immediate* results.

- Leadership is about "defining moments"—
  the decisive battle, the championship
  game, the new business strategy.

Goes, Ricci, and Clavius make a very different statement about who leaders are and how lives of leadership unfold. Despite the exotic challenges they faced, they nonetheless represent a leadership model relevant to the *real* life that most of us live:

- Most people never face the challenge of
  motivating armies of subordinates; we

face Goes's more prosaic day-by-day challenge to motivate *ourselves* through long and sometimes unpromising journeys.

- Rarely does life unfold with the predictability of the carefully scripted strategic plan; far more leadership is improvised. As with Ricci in unfamiliar China, most life challenges emerge at unexpected times in unanticipated ways. Such circumstances don't come with a leadership handbook and don't fit the well-planned life strategy; instead, we rely on our wits and accumulated wisdom.

- Unlike the general heading into battle or the coach heading into game seven, few of us experience dramatic defining moments. Rather, our defining "moment" is a pattern slowly etched through a lifetime studded with ordinary opportunities to make subtle differences: Clavius's conscientious tutoring of the hundreds and hundreds of Jesuit recruits that passed through his classrooms over a forty-eight-year career.

- And like Goes, Ricci, and Clavius, few of us can discern our leadership impact in the world with the same clarity and certainty of one billiard ball sharply cracking another. Most of us must derive satisfaction not from manifest results but from the mere personal conviction that our actions, decisions, and choices have value.

The stereotypical company counts relatively few leaders, all in positions of substantial authority or influence. The Jesuits built a company in which every employee was a leader. Those at Stereotype, Inc., instinctively look around for one of their few leaders when defining moments arise; those in the Jesuit company

Unlike the general heading into battle or the coach heading into game seven, few of us experience dramatic defining moments. Rather, our defining "moment" is a pattern slowly etched through a lifetime studded with ordinary opportunities to make subtle differences.

looked in the mirror. Moreover, they understood that *every* moment—not just the defining ones—was an opportunity to make an impact, to build a life of leadership.

Everyone leads, and everyone can lead all the time. On rare occasions those leadership moments are dramatic and obvious; more often they are subtle, easily overlooked opportunities that, taken together, can form a lifetime of positive leadership influence. And if everyone is leading all the time, it follows that most inspired, motivated leadership performance must be self-initiated and self-led. Following chapters explore the Jesuits' unique leadership vision and how it helped them maintain a successful track record for close to five hundred years.

CHAPTER 5

"To Order One's Life"

Self-Awareness As the Foundation of Leadership

*T*he person who knows what he or she wants can pursue it ener-getically. No one becomes a great teacher, parent, violinist, or corporate executive by accident.

Only those who know their weaknesses can deal with them or even hope to conquer them. Executives with careers stalled by poor self-confidence can resume an upward trajectory only by identifying and attacking their weaknesses.

Those who have identified what moves them to wholehearted engage-ment have little trouble staying motivated.

There is no news in these statements. Yet as obvious as they are, few people make the personal investment to benefit from them.

Many people invest significant time and money to acquire the professional credentials and skills needed to succeed. Leaders invest equally in their *human* skills, in their capacity to lead. An introspec-tive journey—whether done all at once or over an extended period—builds the foundation for success. This journey involves

- appreciating oneself as talented

- identifying personal, derailing baggage that prevents the realization of full poten-tial, especially weaknesses that manifest themselves as habitual tendencies

- articulating personally motivating goals and ambitions—not being content to merely drift along but instead living according to one's personal sense of *magis*

- determining what one stands for, what impact one wants to make

- developing a worldview that guides inter-action with others

- acquiring the habit of updating oneself regularly, indeed *daily*, on all the above

Those who acquire this portfolio of personal skills become vastly more capable of committed, energetic action. Imagine the consolidated power of a team of thousands who possess these personal skills. No wonder that Vladimir Lenin, no friend of the Jesuits—or of any religious believers, for that matter—envied Loyola's team, reportedly once sighing that with only a dozen cadres as talented and dedicated as the Jesuits, his Communist movement would sweep the world.

The good news is that everyone has the capacity to cultivate these leadership skills by committing to the personal introspective investment that will develop them. No one lacking the requisite technical skills would naively waltz into a company and expect to succeed: who imagines that he or she will be a successful account-ant without ever learning accounting, or a successful lawyer without learning the law? Yet we remain naive enough to believe that those who don't know themselves—their strengths, weaknesses, values, and worldview—can achieve long-term success. As the world becomes even more complex and changes even faster than Loyola's topsy-turvy sixteenth-century environment, it becomes increasingly clear that only those with a deeply ingrained capacity for continu-ous learning and self-reflection stand a chance of surfing the waves of change successfully. Harvard Business School professor Joseph Badaracco has written eloquently of the vital importance of this habit of self-reflection. After interviewing corporate leaders to understand how they successfully navigated crises or decision points for their respective companies, Badaracco concluded:

> They are able to take time out from the chain of managerial tasks that consumes their time and undertake a process of probing self-inquiry—a process that is more often carried out on the run than in quiet seclusion. They are able to dig below the busy surface of their daily lives and refocus on their core values and principles. Once uncovered, those values and principles renew their sense of purpose at work and act as a springboard for shrewd, pragmatic, politically astute action. By repeating this process again and again throughout their work lives, these executives are able to craft an authentic and strong identity based on their own, rather than someone else's, understanding of what is right. And in this way, they begin to make the transition from being a manager to becoming a leader.[1]

If self-awareness is critical to leadership success, as Loyola, Peter Drucker, Daniel Goleman, Badaracco, and others have argued, our ideas about leadership and about how we help leaders develop must be revisited. First, no one can make another person self-aware, so leaders must largely mold themselves. Only I can muster the will, courage, and honesty to search myself. Others—coaches, managers, friends, parents, and mentors—help, of course, but primarily by playing a role similar to that of the "director" in Loyola's key self-awareness tool, the Spiritual Exercises. The director's job is "to point, as with the finger, to the vein in the mine, and let each one dig for himself."[2]

> Only those with a deeply ingrained capacity for continuous learning and self-reflection stand a chance of surfing the waves of change successfully.

Leaders "finger the vein" for others: their children, employees, coworkers, and friends. But first they make their own lifelong

commitment to pursue self-awareness. All leadership begins with
self-leadership, and self-leadership begins with knowing oneself.
First comes the foundation: goals and values, an understanding of
personal strengths and obstacles, an outlook on the world. Then
comes the invigorating daily habit of refreshing and deepening
self-knowledge while immersing oneself in a constantly evolving
world.

A Ten-Man/No Plan Company: The Early Surge of Jesuit Growth

The Jesuits strained to keep pace with their runaway success. The
"ten-man/no plan" operation launched in 1540 grew a hundred-
fold within fifteen years. Loyola found himself running a thousand-
strong company with dozens of outposts on four continents.

Enterprising Jesuits sniffed out opportunities in places known to
few Europeans and visited by a relative handful—what are now
Japan, Brazil, Ethiopia, Madagascar, Sri Lanka, Malaysia, and elsewhere. King John III of Portugal sometimes learned more about his
colonial empire from overseas Jesuits than from his own courtiers,
explorers, or diplomatic corps. While his emissaries hunkered down
in the relative safety of coastal trading posts, Jesuits burrowed into
local communities and mounted embassies to royal courts.

The company was no less adventurous and even more successful
on its home turf of Europe. More than thirty Jesuit colleges were
up and running by the year Loyola died—not bad progress for a
company that a dozen years earlier had never opened or run a
school. European operations weren't limited to establishing institutions of higher education. Church bureaucrats enlisted well-
trained, resourceful Jesuits for Counter-Reformation efforts to
shore up wavering congregations or recapture communities already
lost to Protestantism across central and northern Europe.

As Jesuit triumphs attracted new clients and new demands for their services, opportunities soon outstripped resources. One Jesuit described his brutal counseling workload: "At present, I can't get away until midnight. On some mornings I find that they have scaled the walls and are actually settled inside my house waiting."[3] The cofounders were no doubt thrilled with notoriety and success that surpassed their greatest hopes. But with success came an unshakable, chronic staffing headache. As waves of Jesuits fanned out and established beachheads around the world, they inevitably looked back to headquarters for reinforcements. Back in Rome, Loyola puzzled over a staffing equation that simply didn't work.

Tempers began to fray. Jerome Domenech probably expected a speedy, positive response when he wrote Loyola complaining about understaffing. After all, he was running a Jesuit showcase operation in Sicily: the Jesuits' first school opened primarily for lay students. The response from Rome was speedy, all right. But instead of reading that help was on the way, Domenech learned from Loyola's secretary that his complaints had almost cost him his job. "Indeed, if our father [i.e., Loyola] were not restrained by certain considerations, he would show in a much more effective way his dislike of your reverence's complaints, which reflect discredit on him . . . because you also condemn [his appointments] as bad in the presence of others." Not that Domenech had asked, but Loyola's secretary went on to enumerate the staffing woes vexing Loyola in Italy alone:

> You fail to see (something still more surprising) that our father is obliged to keep the universal good in mind. Thus, besides providing you with sufficient manpower to carry on the works you have undertaken, he must remember others in which our Lord wishes to make use of the Society and its members. The college at Venice has only one priest, who has no knowledge of philosophy or theology; that of Padua has two who are weak in

literature . . . that of Medina has two who are only average in Latin and still mere youths.[4]

Domenech was not the only short-staffed Jesuit, nor was he the only one to stick his arm into a hornets' nest by requesting help. The Dutch Peter Canisius manned the northern European frontlines of the Counter-Reformation, high-profile work that was as critical to the Vatican as it was to the Jesuits. Yet even Canisius had to go begging for reinforcements. And like his colleague in Sicily, all he got was a snappish rebuke: "You ought not to be so persistent in asking us for a new man every hour of the day. We are not rich in experienced teachers."[5]

A COMMON PREDICAMENT, THEN AND TODAY

The Jesuit predicament is a familiar one. Highly successful, rapidly growing companies inevitably face painful staffing constraints. The economic landscape of the late 1990s regularly featured more work opportunities than talented staff to fill them. Fast-growing— if, in retrospect, ill-conceived—"new economy" Internet start-ups battled one another and "old economy" businesses for the limited number of skilled workers. The business press coined a new phrase for the crisis: the "war for talent." And while innumerable carcasses of once-vaunted dot-coms now litter the economic landscape, their demise has not brought armistice in the so-called talent war.

For it's no longer just fast-growing start-ups like the early Jesuit company or the dot-coms that struggle to find talent. The recent economic malaise may make the "war for talent" seem a quaint, outdated notion as employers today seem to have their pick of well-qualified candidates. But the United States's meager birth rate presages a long-term shortage of quality staff that will afflict companies in all kinds of industries. The baby-boom-fed U.S. work force, for example, grew 2.3 percent annually from 1975 to 1990; from 1990 to 2005, the work force will grow only 1.2 percent annually, its slowest growth since the 1930s. The peak-productivity population, workers aged thirty-five to forty-four, will actually *decline* by approximately 15 percent from 2000 to 2015. Worrisome though the statistics sound for the U.S. economy, the numbers are even worse elsewhere. Over the first twenty years of the new millennium, the total work force will *shrink* in four of the world's ten largest economies: Japan, Germany, the United Kingdom, and France.

Employers can't do much to shore up the supply side of this equation: the population of thirty-five- to forty-four-year-old workers for the year 2015 has already been born. It's too late to manufacture more. Even more liberal immigration policies would address only a small portion of the looming gap.

> Over the first twenty years of the new millennium, the total work force will *shrink* in four of the world's ten largest economies: Japan, Germany, the United Kingdom, and France.

Management consultants have become more than accustomed to coaching fast-growing start-ups through staffing shortages, and they would have had ready advice for Loyola and his overstretched colleagues: cast a wider net, recruit as aggressively as possible, and rush new hires through boot camp and into the field. Consultants would have reassured the Jesuits that their staffing woes were ultimately a good sign, the natural byproduct of business momentum arising from their first-mover advantage. They were dominating the emerging education market because competitors had not yet organized themselves to attack the opportunity. Above all else, the Jesuits needed to defend and grow their already dominant market share to lock out potential entrants.

THE IMPORTANCE OF
PERSONAL QUALITY

If the Jesuits' predicament is not unique in corporate history, their response may be. A few of Loyola's lieutenants demonstrated the right stuff that might have landed them lucrative consulting posts had they lived only a few centuries later. They labored over the staffing shortage, brainstormed eighteen distinct recruiting tactics, and included them in a draft of the Jesuit *Constitutions* for Loyola's review. The draft boomeranged back with Loyola's brusque comment scrawled beside the recruiting proposals: "Take them all out, or, leaving a few, still make it very difficult [to gain entry to the Jesuit order]."[6]

Perhaps the general was just having a bad day? Hardly. His rebuff of the recruiting program was no aberration. Indeed, while presiding over a company growing so rapidly that it had more promising opportunities than staff to handle them, Loyola was most concerned about admitting people into the Society too freely. He was far from worried about ratcheting up the recruiting intake; a colleague recalled Loyola confiding that "if there was anything that would make him desire to live on . . . it was that he might be more stringent in admitting into the Society."[7]

So the screening process became even more selective. Surely entry-level training was curtailed to rush recruits into resource-starved worldwide operations? Not a chance. Recruits underwent a longer, more rigorous orientation than that of any other religious order or commercial enterprise—by a striking margin. Recruits of other sixteenth-century religious orders typically became full-fledged members after a year of novitiate training, an intensive introduction to the rules, practices, and lifestyle of their religious order under the tutelage of an experienced superior; Jesuit recruits marched through a spiritual boot camp that lasted twice as long. And after Jesuits had been out working in the field for years, they were reeled in for yet another year of professional development and for some midcareer self-reflection. The company officially called it a *tercer probación*, "third testing," but early Jesuits also called it their *escuela del afecto*, loosely, their "school of the heart."

> After Jesuits had been out working in the field for years, they were reeled in for yet another year of professional development and for some midcareer self-reflection.

As any consultant would have warned, Jesuit recruiting selectivity and extensive training inevitably bottlenecked efforts to reinforce operations. It took its toll. A dozen years after Loyola's death, the Jesuits' third general, Francis Borgia, was shuttering schools selectively, fearing that the talent base was being spread too thin. And the fifth general, Claudio Acquaviva, refused more than 150 new requests to open schools. We don't know what advice these Jesuit generals might have received from the seventeenth-century version of a management consultant. Today they would be warned that they were forfeiting their "first-mover advantage." But Jesuit leadership seemed unfazed. Far from panicking as a few opportunities slipped through their fingers, they reinforced their commitment to personal development: local Jesuit managers were instructed that under no circumstances were the Spiritual Exercises to be sacrificed in order to rush recruits into the field.

At first glance, their instincts seem counterintuitive. They were *already* short-staffed. Surely Loyola and his successors should have focused on surfacing more recruits, not on tightening entrance requirements. By turning down new opportunities and protracting new recruit training, Loyola's successors would only imperil corporate momentum.

But what transpired was far from a loss of momentum. Membership had swelled from ten in 1540 to approximately a thousand at Loyola's death in 1556—and mushroomed to more than five thousand by 1580. The company's first college had opened in 1548; more than thirty were up and running by Loyola's passing, and more than two hundred were established before century's end. In fact, the Jesuits' strategic instincts were anything but counterintuitive. While *first-mover advantage* features prominently in today's management consultancy lexicon, so does *sustainable growth*. An organization can grow only as fast as available capital, talent, and management capacity to oversee the growth. Many an enterprise has imploded from unsustainable growth. Twenty-first-century online customers thrilled by the promise of being able to mouse-click their way through holiday shopping became less enchanted with "e-tailers" who hadn't figured out the tiny detail of delivering the goods by Christmas morning. Most such overly ambitious online companies didn't survive to see a second Christmas.

Jesuit leaders recognized their company's flourishing reputation as the direct result of unique, high-quality services. Municipalities across Europe flooded them with requests to open schools, requests that would likely continue so long as the company's reputation remained unimpeachably solid. The same dynamic explained the Jesuits' recruiting success: their reputation for selectivity, high standards, and outstanding results was precisely what attracted the most-talented recruits. The Jesuits certainly would have culled more recruits in the short term by cutting standards. But the tactic would have severely damaged their long-term ability to attract the recruits they really wanted, what they called *aptissimi*—Latin for the "very best" talent in Europe and beyond. By reining in overly aggressive growth and rejecting "bottom-fishing" recruiting practices, they sustained both their reputation and their steep growth trajectory. Or, paradoxically, the Jesuits kept growing rapidly by not growing *too* rapidly!

The Jesuit case study, now approaching five hundred years, might have proved instructive to innumerable fast-growing start-ups that crashed and burned spectacularly after meteoric bursts of overly aggressive growth. But what does any of this have to do with self-awareness, the first Jesuit leadership principle and this chapter's theme?

Everything.

THE LINK BETWEEN SELF-KNOWLEDGE AND SUCCESS

Neither Loyola nor his successors ever sat around discussing first-mover advantage or sustainable growth. They certainly worried about preserving their company's future and seizing the many urgent opportunities they saw around them. But by all indications, they focused predominantly not on grandiose, company-wide strategies but on the simpler strategy of forming quality Jesuits one by one—or what we might today call *molding leaders*.

Loyola's final project was translating the Jesuit vision into a set of rules and procedures robust enough to govern the fledgling company. The result was the 250-page Jesuit *Constitutions*. Fully *two-thirds* is monopolized by guidelines for selecting and training recruits; every other aspect of Jesuit life is relegated to a measly eighty pages: rules for work, methods of governance, criteria for selecting managers, guidelines for entering new businesses, and so on. Presuming that Loyola didn't simply run out of steam after completing the section on trainees, the implied message in the lopsided *Constitutions* is obvious: ongoing success depends on turning recruits into leaders. Solve that problem, and the leaders you've molded will solve every other problem.

Jesuit-style leadership formation had little to do with technical skills or vocational training. Jesuits were believers in on-the-job training who regularly tossed recruits into the deep end of the pool. Managers shipped junior Jesuits off on two-year ocean journeys to Asia, confident that each would successfully acquire the needed work skills: fluency in the language, assimilation into an alien culture—even, if necessary, the ability to operate an astrolabe, create a map, or build a cannon! The travelers didn't bring with them tactical handbooks addressing every foreseeable contingency. Instead, they brought the most important skill they needed to thrive in unfamiliar and challenging environments: self-awareness.

More than four hundred years later, the Jesuits' uncompromising emphasis on self-awareness is finding plenty of validation. True, one would still be hard-pressed to find corporate annual reports extolling staff self-awareness with the same pride reserved for a lofty P/E ratio. But academics have begun to pinpoint the strong link between mature self-knowledge and success.

Peter Drucker has been a pioneer in management and leadership studies for more than three decades. He has written persuasively on the ramifications of our changing economy, particularly the technology-driven shift toward a "knowledge economy." It wasn't so many years ago that work for most people entailed following orders and performing assigned jobs. Bosses parceled out tasks, and those tasks fit into an orderly and fairly predictable corporate routine. Not so today. Work roles have largely become *self*-managing, and the big picture is anything but predictable. There are far fewer supervisors to give direction. Companies have continuously and sometimes ruthlessly "delayered," eliminating middle management in pursuit of efficiency. Surviving middle managers are responsible for increasingly broad spans of control: they're too stretched to baby-sit subordinates. Most office workers are on their own most of the time, independently prioritizing and plowing through responsibilities. Moreover, in a more competitive and rapidly changing marketplace, companies must respond with ever increasing speed and urgency; this has further decentralized decision making. In the current business environment, "he who hesitates is lost." Employees who once might have been reprimanded for not clearing decisions with managers before making them will today more likely be penalized for not showing enough initiative.

Drucker has focused on the *human* implications of this shift. How do workers succeed in such an environment? Skills once critical only for top management have become essential for *everyone*. No longer can one succeed—or even *survive*—simply by following orders. Each employee is more and more a self-manager, making decisions on his or her own. Moreover, with the accelerated pace of change, roles and tasks evolve constantly, requiring continuous judgment and the ability to learn on the fly.

Who thrives in such environments? Those who can learn, innovate, exercise good judgment, take responsibility for their actions, and take risks. These traits aren't like the technical skills required of a good lawyer, accountant, or salesperson. They come from self-understanding, not vocational training. As Drucker argued in the *Harvard Business Review*, in this new environment, "successful careers are not planned. They develop when people are prepared for opportunities because they know their strengths, their method of work, and their values."[8] Of course, success in any job is impossible without the requisite technical or vocational skills. But whereas those skills alone once might have constituted a success formula, employees today must *also* be able to assess their strengths, weaknesses, and how well their working style equips them for a fast-paced, constantly changing work environment. In other words, they need to become self-aware. Drucker singles out two practitioners of this best practice and offers his own, perhaps generous assessment of how powerfully their self-knowledge served their respective companies:

> John Calvin and Ignatius Loyola . . . incorporated [ongoing self-assessment] into the practice of [their] followers. In fact, the steadfast focus on performance and results that this habit produces explains why the institutions these two men founded, the Calvinist church and the Jesuit order, came to dominate Europe within 30 years.[9]

While more than a few historians would argue Drucker's claim that the Jesuits and the Calvinist Church came to dominate Europe within thirty years, less open to debate is his core thesis. The pace of societal and corporate change *is* accelerating, and whether in their personal or professional lives, individuals are forced to make more decisions and make them faster—with less guidance, incomplete information, and few relevant precedents. Successfully navigating such changed and changing landscapes tests one's self-confidence, good judgment, ability to learn, and comfort in making decisions.

Daniel Goleman's extensive research in the broad field of managerial self-awareness has resulted in two best-selling works, *Emotional Intelligence* and *Working with Emotional Intelligence*. Goleman has generally focused on why and how some senior executives succeed while others fail.

We know what we want these leaders to do: establish direction and vision, motivate teams to pursue goals, smash through obstacles, and produce change for the better. Most corporations have a process for identifying smart, talented, and ambitious employees with the potential to assume leadership roles. But these selection processes don't always work very well. Many rising stars self-destruct, never achieving their early potential. No one really understands why some talented individuals become successful leaders while others crash and burn, why the first in the class is rarely the first in life, or why the hotshot junior executive seldom makes it to CEO. Goleman has focused his research on this puzzle, and his insights have implications for more than just the world of senior executives. The more senior one's role within an organization, the *less* critical to success are intellect and technical skills compared with the bundle of skills Goleman calls emotional intelligence. "When I compared star performers with average ones in senior leadership positions, nearly 90% of the difference in their profiles was attributable to emotional intelligence factors rather than cognitive abilities."[10] Just what is "emotional intelligence"? In Goleman's terms, it comprises five core competencies:

Self-Awareness: the ability to recognize and understand your moods, emotions, and drives. . . .

Self-Regulation: the ability to control or redirect disruptive impulses and moods; the propensity to suspend judgment—to think before acting.

Motivation: a passion to work for reasons that go beyond money or status. . . .

Empathy: the ability to understand the emotional makeup of other people. . . .

Social Skill: proficiency in managing relationships and building networks; an ability to find common ground and build rapport.[11]

Reread the list. How many companies interview candidates with the above criteria in mind? How many companies attempt to develop these traits in employees? And when companies identify "future leaders," how many do so on the basis of these human skills?

The answers to these questions, at least until quite recently, were pretty much none, none, and none. We can draw an obvious conclusion from Goleman's work: it's no wonder that companies suffer erratic results when selecting and forming leaders—most are looking for the wrong skills. Corporate rising stars frequently distinguish themselves by keen intellect, but that's not what equips them to *lead*. And looking for leaders while focusing on the wrong skills is a hit-or-miss proposition—like picking future opera stars by examining their golf swing.

At least one company *did* look for emotional-intelligence potential in candidates—and more important, crafted a program to engender it in recruits. In fact, this company was doing it more than 450 years ago. What we're calling Jesuit self-awareness lines up strikingly well with Goleman's notion of emotional intelligence. It's no surprise. Both the Jesuits and Goleman wanted to identify the personal traits essential to successful leadership.

Goleman's five-pronged summary largely describes the "what," the core behaviors and personal traits characteristic of those possessing emotional intelligence. The Jesuit approach takes it one step further, identifying not only the "what" but also the "how"— a program for imparting those skills. Central to and irreplaceable in the process were the Spiritual Exercises. Each Jesuit recruit emerged from his thirty-day immersion in the program with invaluable personal strengths, including:

- the ability to reflect systematically on personal weaknesses, especially those manifested as habitual tendencies

- an integrated worldview, a vision, and a value system

- profound respect for other people and for all of creation

- appreciation of oneself as loved and important

- the ability to tune out everyday distractions in order to reflect, and the habit of doing so daily

- a method for considering choices and making decisions

Most managers would love to hire candidates with demonstrable evidence of these six credentials. The trouble is, they don't show up on resumés, and we don't know how to interview for them. Nor do we consider it a company's role to inculcate them. Pointing out that a rash manager's lack of self-awareness is jeopardizing his or her career progress is fine and appropriate for the annual performance review. But showing the same manager a path to greater self-awareness? That's what self-help groups do, not companies!

The result of this helpless, hands-off, and haphazard approach to self-awareness is obvious. Most major companies have notoriously poor track records when it comes to identifying future leaders. Rising stars are anointed only to have their careers derail or stagnate, and rarely because they lack smarts or technical savvy—that's usually what made them rising stars in the first place. Instead, their careers derail because they never understand and therefore can never really address their weaknesses, weaknesses that typically revolve around risk taking, managing and interacting with others, and making judgments—in other words, the abilities and managerial courage that come with mature self-awareness. Or they never acquire the skill of learning on the fly, of constantly processing new information and adjusting course.

> Most major companies have notoriously poor track records when it comes to identifying future leaders.

Such talent wastage was unacceptable to Loyola. It was hard enough to find *aptissimi* in the first place. Instead of simply *hoping* that talented junior stars had the human skills integral to long-term success, he had enough confidence in human nature to believe that those skills could be acquired. And he had a revolutionary process to make it happen.

CHAPTER 6

The Spiritual Exercises
A Lifelong Development Tool

The ancient Greek philosopher Socrates is on record for making the most extreme claim for the value of self-knowledge: "The unexamined life is not worth living." Though few thinkers today would echo so thorough a condemnation of an unreflective approach to life, there is no doubt that the value of self-knowledge has been rediscovered as almost never before. Self-awareness, always cherished by philosophers, poets, psychologists, writers, and other "reflective types," is increasingly promoted as an indispensable success tool even in the hard-knuckled arena of the corporate boardroom. Executives employ a broad suite of tools in the quest for greater awareness of their strengths, weaknesses, values, and personality traits—from executive coaching sessions and 360-degree feedback solicited from subordinates to the Myers-Briggs type indicator and the Enneagram personality type test. Even astrology and personal-growth gurus find an audience among self-knowledge–hungry executives.

No company values self-awareness so profoundly as the Jesuits. It is the foundation of their leadership model. Rather than cycle through self-awareness approaches haphazardly, the company developed and promoted one universal tool for all Jesuits: the Spiritual Exercises.

The Exercises were developed by Ignatius Loyola, based on his own journey toward personal and spiritual awareness. He took note not only of what he learned but also of the reflective practices that led him to those insights. He distilled the most effective of these practices into what might be called a self-awareness "handbook."

It is not a book to be read; one achieves self-awareness not by reading how someone else achieved it but through focused reflection on *one's own* experience. It's impossible to overestimate the Spiritual Exercises' importance in Jesuit culture. They encapsulate the company's vision and serve as each Jesuit's preeminent personal development experience. Engaging in the Exercises is the uniquely unifying experience of Jesuit life, shared by recruits from Rome to India, from the founding generation through this year's entering class. Jesuits sometimes refer to themselves as "men of the Exercises," implicitly celebrating the camaraderie born of their common spiritual boot camp but more crucially signaling their allegiance to shared vision and values. The Exercises were designed to help individuals choose or confirm a life direction. Yet they prove an equally potent corporate tool: the merest shorthand reference to "the Exercises" allows Jesuit managers to tap a wellspring of energy and goodwill, as well as remind recruits of their unifying value system.

Loyola called them Spiritual Exercises for a reason—they were actions to be done, not rules to be read or studied: "For just as taking a walk, traveling on foot, and running are physical exercises, so is the name of spiritual exercises given to any means of preparing and disposing our soul to rid itself of all its disordered affections."[1] The person undertaking them was *la persona que se ejercita,* "the person exercising him- or herself"—not someone passively reading about Loyola's experiences and insights but a spiritual athlete building his or her own interior resources.

An experienced, impartial "director" guides each participant, not by teaching but by helping each recruit interpret his own experiences. The director doesn't interject his own opinions but is a sounding board who "ought not to incline in either direction but rather, . . . [stand] by like the pointer of a scale in equilibrium."[2] Why the hands-off approach? An early Jesuit handbook for directors pointed out that "it is a lesson of experience that all men are more delighted and more moved by what they find out for themselves. Hence it will suffice just to point, as with the finger, to the vein in the mine, and let each one dig for himself."[3] Loyola intuitively grasped what every competent therapist understands about self-discovery and what every quality manager understands about motivation: the switches are on the inside.

The Exercises demand total intellectual, emotional, and spiritual engagement. Accordingly, they monopolize focus and energy for their thirty-day duration. This means no contact with family, friends, or coworkers; no involvement with work; no reading matter other than spiritual texts; no engaging in casual conversation (even meals are taken in silence). Why strip away so much of life's customary daily activity? Simply because daily habits and occupations easily become *preoccupations*, a distracting scrim of thoughts, worries, images, and ideas that block genuine introspection. Such was Loyola's conviction in the sixteenth century, *before* the proliferation of telephones, cell phones, e-mail, radio, television, magazines, newspapers, fax machines, billboards, wristwatches, cars, trains, planes, and buses. It's too easy to bob along superficially, distracted by an endless stream of background noise. Loyola purged distractions in order to free time and psychic space.

> The Exercises demand total intellectual, emotional, and spiritual engagement. Accordingly, they monopolize focus and energy for their thirty-day duration.

And so each recruit is left alone with himself. For a month, every day is arranged around four or five one-hour meditations. The rest of each day is cleared for interior percolation of reflections, memories, thoughts, impulses, and convictions that might have been long forgotten, never allowed to surface, not sufficiently ruminated, or simply buried in the muck of everyday preoccupations.

Still, while the Exercises' daily rhythm leaves ample scope for freeform introspection, their progression is anything but random. Rather, the meditations on scriptural events or imaginary scenarios drive relentlessly toward the goal of enabling high-quality, totally engaged human commitment. Of course, Loyola's *personal* commitment was to Christian service, and the Exercises' thrust and subject matter are emphatically Christian. But they work as a leadership tool not because they are grounded in a religious worldview but because they build the personal resources required for freely chosen, powerful, and successful human commitments of *all* sorts: to religious goals, but equally to work, life aspirations, and personal relationships. Over the course of a month, trainees deconstruct themselves in order to erect solid personal foundations of self-awareness, ingenuity, heroism, and love.

THE FOUNDATION OF SELF-AWARENESS: "TO OVERCOME ONESELF AND TO ORDER ONE'S LIFE"[4]

The Exercises immediately plunge trainees into an ice-water bath of painfully frank self-assessment, "that I may perceive the disorder in my actions, in order to . . . amend myself, and put myself in order."[5] Recruits fasten their seat belts for a hellfire-and-brimstone journey through the sights, sounds, and very whiff of hell, "to see with the eyes of the imagination the huge fires and, so to speak, the souls within the bodies full of fire. . . . In my imagination I will hear the wailing, the shrieking, the cries, and the blasphemies. . . . By my sense of smell I will perceive the smoke, the sulphur, the filth, and the rotting things."[6]

This meditative episode comes along more or less on day *two*; surely more than a few trainees regret signing up for thirty days of this stuff. Still, Loyola's imagery reflects the religious mentality of a very different era. While many in the late twentieth century retired Satan to all but metaphorical status, he was a real, formidable enemy to sixteenth-century Europeans. The Exercises of Loyola's day painted a world where the unvigilant, lazy, or unreflective could fall into this enemy's cunning snares.

If anything is surprising, it is less Loyola's graphic portrayal of hell than his empowering message that trainees will not be left cowering, miserable, and helpless against the satanic onslaught. Instead, recruits are exhorted to pick up their cudgels and wade into personal battle with what Loyola calls "the enemy of our human nature." The enemy is no match for anyone who has "ordered" himself. How does one order oneself? First, by taking stock of one's weaknesses ("disordered affections"). This self-discovery alone sends the wily but cowardly enemy of human nature on the run, for the enemy is like "a false lover" who most fears having his sinister doings brought to light.

We sophisticated moderns might be inclined to dismiss all this as an archaic relic of a romantic and superstitious age. But the imagery conveys rich insight. Contemporary culture has by and large replaced "Satan" with all manner of personal, psychological, and societal demons as the cause of our missteps. These demons include addictions, weaknesses, the media, an unloving childhood environment, bad luck, peer pressure, greed, fear of success, narcissism, loose social mores, stupid bosses, and on, and on, and on. But whether personalized (as Satan), psychologized, or explained otherwise, the "enemy of our human nature" *does* exist. The bottom-line human reality is that everyone falls short of peak potential, and usually for identifiable reasons. As Loyola observes, the enemy of human nature does fear discovery. While our weaknesses remain unacknowledged or closeted away, we are powerless over them. The sometimes painful process of dragging our weaknesses into full light of day by understanding them is the first empowering stride toward conquering them. This self-searching assessment of what Loyola calls disordered affections is an assessment of what a Freudian might call "attachments which impede effective ego functioning." Veterans of Alcoholics Anonymous might call the process a "fearless moral inventory," while others more simply recognize it as "taking stock of who I am, where I want to go, and what's holding me back."

THE FOUNDATION OF INGENUITY: "TO MAKE OURSELVES INDIFFERENT"[7]

A colleague once asked Loyola how long he would need to recover if the pope was ever to disband the Jesuits. Loyola's response surely shocked his questioner, and it quickly found its way into Jesuit lore: "If I recollected myself in prayer for a quarter of an hour, I would be happy, and even happier than before."[8]

Perhaps there was a smidgen of posturing in his answer. Loyola had built what was rapidly becoming the world's most influential and successful religious organization. Could he see it dismantled and then stroll away whistling after a mere fifteen minutes in prayer?

Posturing or not, Loyola was sending an unambiguous message grounded in the lessons of the Exercises. Jesuits achieved what we today would call ingenuity—a mix of adaptability, daring, speed, and good judgment—only by first cultivating the attitude he called "indifference."

Trainees approach indifference by imagining three different men who have each legitimately acquired the fabulous sum of ten thousand ducats, then considering their varying reactions to their newly obtained wealth. All three feel more than niggling discomfort with their growing attachment to the fortune. *There's more to life than money, . . . but it feels so nice to have it.* Suddenly it seems impossible to imagine doing without it. The first two types do little or nothing to rid themselves of the wealth that is leading to such inordinate attachment. What does the third type do about the ten thousand ducats? Here is the punch line of the meditation, the person we are to emulate, so the answer seems obvious: he generously distributes the money to the poor and piously rejoices, right?

Wrong. The role model for Jesuit indifference rids himself of the *attachment* to the money, "but in such a way that there remains no inclination either to keep the acquired money or to dispose of it."[9] In other words, the money is not the issue. The problem is slavish attachment to money or to anything else. Inordinate attachments fog one's vision. I might have first pursued a lucrative job so that I could provide for my family, but somewhere along the line the money itself became my goal, and my family became a neglected second. The end became confused with the means. Only by becoming indifferent—free of prejudices and attachments and therefore free to *choose any course of action*—do recruits become strategically flexible. The indifferent Jesuit liberates himself to choose strategies driven by one motive only: achieving his long-term goal of serving God by helping souls.

> Only by becoming indifferent—free of prejudices and attachments and therefore free to choose any course of action—do recruits become strategically flexible.

The meditation isn't about the money; it's about the attachment. And understanding personal attachments means overturning personal rocks to see what crawls out. Attachment to money is usually salve for some other debilitating ego-itch: I'm terrified of failing; I need to feel important and be the center of attention; I'm insecure about my real talent and worth.

This is what Loyola was *really* after: the internal fears, drives, and attachments that can control decisions and actions. Imagine the chief executive who undertakes an ill-advised merger because his ego inflates along with his company's balance sheet—or who backs away from a brilliant merger because he and his counterpart cannot carve out roles commensurate with their enormous egos. Imagine the sixteenth-century Jesuit reluctant to go to China, clinging to the security blanket of working on home turf surrounded by friends—or the twenty-first-century professional forgoing a wonderful career opportunity for similar reasons. Consider the controlling micromanager unable to relinquish authority to subordinates—or the person mired in a destructive relationship out of fear of being alone. All are driven by their attachments just as addicts are driven by alcohol, sex, or drugs.

These people aren't indifferent. They are not freely making choices; their inordinate attachments are in control. As a result, they don't in the end choose what will best serve them, their companies, their coworkers, or their families.

Indifference is the right stuff of ingenuity. And once early Jesuits attained it, Loyola usually set them loose to lead themselves. "In all, I much desire a complete indifference; then with this obedience and abnegation supposed on the part of the subjects [i.e., individual Jesuits], I am very glad to follow their inclinations."[10]

THE FOUNDATION OF HEROISM: *MAGIS*

Loyola described indifferent Jesuits as "poised like a scale at equilibrium," balanced to consider all strategic alternatives.

They don't remain poised for long.

In another meditation, recruits imagine a king preparing for battle. His ambitions are not modest: "My will is to conquer the whole land of the infidels." He issues a call for followers: "Whoever wishes to come with me has to be content with the same food I eat. . . . So too each one must labor with me during the day, and keep watch in the night . . . so that later each may have a part with me in the victory, just as each has shared in the toil."[11]

The meditation continues with "Christ the Eternal King" replacing the earthly king and waging a similarly ambitious *spiritual* battle. His cause is described as so worthwhile, so motivating, and so inspiring that "all those who have judgment and reason will offer themselves wholeheartedly for this labor."[12] Well, actually, they'll do more than just offer themselves wholeheartedly. The meditation continues: "Those who desire . . . to distinguish themselves in total service [will] go further still."[13]

Go further than wholehearted service? How is that possible?

Strictly speaking, of course, it *isn't* possible. No one can give more than wholehearted service. But just as great athletes learn to play "beyond themselves" at peak moments, Jesuits learn through the meditation on the two kings and others like it that it is possible to give more. A heroic Jesuit is as much "coiled" as "poised" at equilibrium. And only heroically ambitious goals will inspire him to spring. Total victory is always the goal. And total victory demands more than total commitment: it requires going further than wholehearted service.

Early Jesuits captured this aggressive drive, this relentless energy, in a one-word motto plucked from elsewhere in the *Exercises: magis*, Latin for "more." Jesuits are exhorted to always "choose and desire" the strategic option that is *more* conducive to their goals. But the simple motto captures a broader spirit, a restless drive to imagine whether there isn't some even greater project to be accomplished or some better way of attacking the current problem.

Motivation is personal. And the meditative exercises transformed Jesuit company goals into personal ones. The meditation on the two kings presents an invitation, not an order. Accepting that invitation is a personal decision. Moreover, the metaphorical meditation lacks specific shape. It doesn't explain what one does to achieve the heroic goal. *That* detail comes as each recruit mentally shapes the mission and the *magis* to his circumstances, not only during the Exercises but throughout his life.

What would so motivate you that you would go further than wholehearted service to achieve it?

Few can answer that question. Most have never even asked it of themselves. But asking oneself, and coming up with an answer, all but guarantees motivated, imaginative engagement.

THE FOUNDATION OF LOVE: "STIRRED TO PROFOUND GRATITUDE, I MAY BECOME ABLE TO LOVE"[14]

What kind of world does the energized recruit reenter after completing the Spiritual Exercises?

The previously mentioned Exercises might suggest a perilous place. Recruits have inventoried their weaknesses to arm themselves against the "enemy of human nature." They've been summoned to enlist in a high-stakes battle to conquer "the whole land of the infidels."

A final integrative meditation, the Contemplation to Attain Love, delivers the recruit back into the world. One commentator has called it "the masterpiece of the *Spiritual Exercises*."[15] Early meditations turn each recruit inward. But the crowning exercise turns his gaze outward to contemplate the world in which he will realize his potential:

> First. Love ought to manifest itself more by deeds than by words.
> Second. Love consists in a mutual communication between the two persons. That is, the one who loves gives and communicates to the beloved what he or she has. . . .

I will consider how God dwells in creatures; in the elements, giving them existence; in the plants, giving them life; in the animals, giving them sensation; in human beings, giving them intelligence; and finally, how in this way he dwells also in myself, giving me existence, life, sensation, and intelligence. . . .

I will consider how God labors and works for me in all the creatures on the face of the earth; that is, he acts in the manner of one who is laboring. For example, he is working in the heavens, elements, plants, fruits, cattle, and all the rest—giving them their existence, conserving them, concurring with their vegetative and sensitive activities, and so forth. Then I will reflect on myself.[16]

The recruit is catapulted back into a world that is charged with love. This love drives *action:* "Love ought to manifest itself more by deeds than by words." And the same energy that courses through each recruit, "giving [him] existence, life, sensation, and intelligence," is also "working in the heavens, elements, plants, fruits, cattle, and all the rest."

The meditation rests on a theological vision of divine love poured out into the world. But nothing about it suggests dry theological argument. Rarely has an abstract notion like love—much less *divine love*—been reduced to more concrete, everyday physical images. And Loyola intended a concrete, everyday impact on recruits: they were made of the same stuff as the people and things around them; they were all equal, all endowed with the same worth, all shot through with the same energy and potential. Recruits shared bonds not only to family and friends but equally to all those who worked with, for, and around them—even the lazy, stupid, competitive ones who didn't bathe regularly. It was a world-view, a lens intended to color a recruit's mindset and every action.

"Love ought to manifest itself more by deeds than by words." This simple principle becomes a mantra of sorts for those who absorb the meaning of the Contemplation to Attain Love. The point of the meditation is not merely for the recruit to bask in the warm and cozy knowledge that he—along with all creation— reflects an outpouring of divine love (although there's nothing wrong with that invigorating feeling). Rather, the point lies in the action unleashed by this realization. Appreciating himself as a loved person of unique dignity and potential inevitably affects the way the recruit lives his life, instilling in him the desire to make the most of his gifts and to avoid squandering them through laziness, self-abuse, poor self-confidence, or an aimless life path. The principle equally influences his relationships with others: the meditation leaves him convinced that *they too* have dignity and potential. They rate profound respect as individuals, because shared humanity means something. And for teachers, parents, managers, coaches, mentors, and friends, expressing love through deeds, not words means helping others bring their potential to fruition.

> For teachers, parents, managers, coaches, mentors, and friends, expressing love through deeds, not words means helping others bring their potential to fruition.

THE *EXAMEN*: "UPON ARISING," "AFTER THE NOON MEAL," AND "AFTER SUPPER"

Recruits who successfully absorb the Exercises are injected back into the world as self-aware, ingenious, loving, heroic leaders. But no monthlong introspective journey, no matter how intense or sophisticated, is enough to fortify someone for a lifetime. Immersed in the world with all hell breaking loose around them, Jesuits—like anyone else—risk slipping away from their goals and values when faced with the pressures, distractions, and competing demands of everyday life.

Loyola anticipated this and made sure that the Exercises could also be used as a daily follow-up tool to maintain focus on newly embraced values. The Exercises were specifically designed for those immersed in a busy lifestyle in an ever-changing world. Every day "upon arising," Jesuits are to remind themselves of key personal goals. And twice each day they make a short mental pit stop, what they call an *examen*. Each *examen* begins by recalling the positive, loving worldview that was the Exercises' culminating meditation: "The First Point is to give thanks to God our Lord for the benefits I have received."[17] Then comes a mental replay of the day thus far, "exacting an account of self with regard to the particular matter decided upon for correction and improvement. He should run through the time, hour by hour or period by period, from the moment of rising until the present examination."[18]

In other words, the recruit recalls in his mind all the events of the day, the opportunities and challenges presented, and how he reacted to them—whether his subsequent attitudes and choices brought him closer to his long-term goals or moved him further away.

This self-reflective habit is as powerful as it is simple. Ambitious goals become manageable when broken down into smaller goals. Not smoking for the rest of one's life is a daunting proposition, but not smoking for the next few hours is a manageable goal. Wanting to become more assertive in order to boost one's career trajectory is a sprawling, ill-defined aspiration, but assessing whether one asserted oneself in the meeting that ended an hour ago is a way of focusing this aspiration with laserlike precision.

Moreover, the *examens* create an ongoing feedback loop. Relevant new information is incorporated and assessed in real time; I remind myelf of key goals each morning, not every six months, and I extract lessons learned from my successes and failures *twice a day*, not once a year. Finally and most important, the

> Few people are willing to set aside even one day a year for self-reflection, but *anyone* can carve out five minutes three times each day.

examens work for busy people. Few people are willing to set aside even one day a year for self-reflection, but *anyone* can carve out five minutes three times each day.

Self-awareness, the first of the four Jesuit leadership pillars, is the foundation of the others. *Ingenuity*—confident, optimistic innovation—hinges on indifference, the freedom to read and respond to a changing world. *Love*, engaging others positively and supportively, flows from the worldview established through the Contemplation to Attain Love. And *heroism* evolves out of the spirit of *magis*, a reflexive response that keeps one motivated through ambitious personal goals.

The self-awareness accomplished during the Exercises is a prelude to action. Cut off from the world for a metaphorical desert experience, each recruit reemerges all the more committed and engaged. So too, our focus now moves from the introspective Exercises to what those Exercises enabled the early Jesuits to achieve—and what they teach us about leadership today.

CHAPTER 7

"The Whole World Becomes Our House"

How Ingenuity Sparks Innovation, Creativity, and a Global Mindset

G ood enough. I'm ready . . ."
If Francis Xavier had more to say about what he'd just been asked to do, it hasn't been recorded. Just *pues sus, heme aqui.*[1]

Xavier was about to become the embodiment of ingenuity. In all likelihood, the term *Jesuit ingenuity* would have meant little to Xavier and his sixteenth-century colleagues. *Ingenuity* appears nowhere in Jesuit regulations or correspondence. But every early Jesuit would have instantaneously recognized ingenuity's telltale attitudes and behaviors as core to their *modo de proceder,* their way of doing things. Ingenuity is the readiness to cross the world at a moment's notice in full-hearted pursuit of a good opportunity, as Xavier was about to do. It is the willingness to work without a script and to dream up imaginative new approaches to problems that have stymied others, as Matteo Ricci demonstrated in China. And it is the creative embrace of new ideas and foreign cultures, as Roberto de Nobili exemplifies later in this chapter.

What distinguishes Jesuit ingenuity is not so much its characteristic behaviors. After all, leadership pundits have long championed the virtues described thus far: imagination, adaptability, creativity, flexibility, and the ability to respond rapidly. Rather, the defining mark of Jesuit ingenuity is what makes these behaviors possible in the first place. Loyola didn't merely exhort recruits to be adaptable and creative; he ensured through the Exercises that recruits would adopt the demeanor, attitudes, and worldview that make adaptability and creativity possible.

There are two vital ingredients for Jesuit ingenuity. Indifference frees Jesuits from the prejudices, attachments, fears, and narrow-mindedness that can block the enthusiastic pursuit of new ideas and opportunities. And the Exercises' final meditation—the Contemplation to Attain Love—endows recruits with an optimistic vision of a world thoroughly shot through with divine love. Ingenuity blossoms when the personal freedom to pursue opportunities is linked to a profound trust and optimism that the world presents plenty of them. Imagination, creativity, adaptability, and rapid response become the keys for finding and unlocking those opportunities. The Exercises equipped early Jesuits such as Xavier with the gift of ingenuity; Loyola then unleashed them on the world and let them lead.

> Ingenuity blossoms when the personal freedom to pursue opportunities is linked to a profound trust and optimism that the world presents plenty of them.

A SMALL COMPANY WITH BIG PLANS: THE JESUIT WHO TOOK ON ASIA

It is fitting that the Jesuits' first great overseas opportunity came from a country taking its own rare turn as star on the world stage. Tiny

Portugal had long languished at Europe's literal and littoral periphery. But if its remote location removed the country from the commercial mainstream, it proved an ideal launching point for Atlantic Ocean voyages of exploration. Portuguese and Spanish expeditions didn't waste the opportunity. The Portuguese explorer Bartolomeu Dias had reached the southern tip of Africa by 1488; four years later Columbus planted the Spanish flag in the Americas.

As the two nations undertook an aggressive campaign of conquest in Asia and the Americas, Europe's balance of power was fundamentally realigned. Tiny Portugal was tiny no more. And in a rare if fleeting moment of sanity, Portugal and Spain decided that the world just might be big enough for both of them. Rather than rushing headlong toward potentially ruinous confrontation, they cut a deal—an elegantly simple, charmingly naive, and incredibly arrogant deal. Their ambassadors agreed to divide the world between them from a point 370 leagues west of the Cape Verde Islands. (Neither country, incidentally, even remotely understood just where this point lay.)

From their imaginary and poorly defined starting point, Portugal and Spain sketched a line girdling the globe through the North and South Poles, dividing the world in two. Half the world went to Spain, half to Portugal—what could be simpler? Portugal waltzed away with exclusive rights to colonize newly discovered or undiscovered lands east of the demarcation line if not already occupied by Christian princes. Not a bad outcome for a country half as large as the state of Idaho and about as populous then as Idaho is today.

All these "undiscovered" lands had already been occupied for millennia, of course, but their governing "non-Christian princes" had somehow been overlooked when invitations to the negotiating party were engraved. They weren't the only ones slighted: no other European power had been invited either. Not surprisingly, no other nation ever recognized the treaty's validity. But rather than giving in to messy, protracted multilateral negotiations,

Spain and Portugal enticed a higher authority to bless the arrangement. In return for each country's pledge to propagate Christianity throughout its conquered lands, the Vatican gave approval for their Treaty of Tordesillas.

Nearly fifty years after the treaty's ratification, King John III of Portugal received reports of "certain learned clerics of exemplary life" from a courtier in Rome who knew Loyola's team from Paris.[2] They were exactly the kind of men the king wanted for his "spices and souls" expeditions to the Indies, and he instructed his delegate in Rome to retain them. The king's ambassador asked Loyola for six Jesuits. Loyola, putting a suave spin on his sorry staffing situation, replied, "And what will your Lordship leave for the rest of the world?"[3]

If Portugal was a dark-horse candidate for world dominion, the Jesuit company was entirely out of the running. In fact, the Jesuits weren't even really a "company," still scrambling after formal papal approval for their charter. Loyola wasn't being flip in his response to the Portuguese ambassador. His whole "company," such as it was, numbered *ten* full-fledged Jesuits, and only six of them were in Rome at the time. So sending six would truly have left none "for the rest of the world." Still, it was an opportunity no ambitious fledgling company could pass up. Twenty percent of the company (two Jesuits) was designated for India. One fell ill on the verge of departing. Informed that he was needed to replace his sick colleague, Xavier instantly replied, "Good enough. I'm ready" or "Splendid. I'm your man," as later Jesuit generations often rendered it.

> Within forty-eight hours Xavier had patched up his extra pair of pants, visited the pope for a blessing, packed up his life, and departed.

Within forty-eight hours he had patched up his extra pair of pants, visited the pope for a blessing, packed up his life, and departed.

The Jesuits' first hero

Francis Xavier is here depicted drafting his farewell letter to Loyola, presumably on the island off the Chinese coast where Xavier died. The print was based on a sketch by Jesuit-educated Peter Paul Rubens.

MAKING IT UP AS HE WENT

It was just as well that Xavier didn't plot a strategy before leaving, for any plans would have soon become laughably outmoded. Xavier's companion didn't even make it past their Lisbon transit stop. The same King John who later gushed that he would sacrifice his empire to bring the Jesuits to Portugal started by insisting that Simão Rodrigues remain there instead of traveling on to India. Xavier was left to travel onward without his Jesuit companion.

Rodrigues missed the fun of ocean cruising, sixteenth-century style. A journey anticipated to take six months lasted more than a year. More than four hundred passengers and crew stewed in unsanitary conditions while the ship sat in doldrums off the coast of Guinea. Passengers afflicted with scurvy nursed bleeding gums and teetered on swollen legs, praying for relief from the sweltering equatorial sun—that is, until rain actually fell. Xavier's biographer stitched together correspondence from Xavier and others to describe what happened next:

The tropical showers brought no relief. The rainwater was luke-
warm and toxic. If it was left standing for an hour before drinking, it swarmed with worms; if rain fell upon the hanging meat,
it also began to crawl with life; if it fell upon clothes, they too
became wormy and musty and began to rot if they were not
immediately washed in sea water. . . .

Food also became spoiled. Drinking water turned yellow and
stank. It was so nauseating that one who drank it had to hold his
nose and close his eyes or hold a cloth in front of his mouth, and
yet it was still drunk in order to stifle the dreadful thirst that tor-
mented all.[4]

Well, at least Xavier survived. That's about the best one can say
about the journey, no small feat in an era when barely half the ships
bound for Goa, India, safely completed the trip there and back.

Xavier was so long in transit that he lost his chance to become
the first Jesuit ever to work outside continental Europe. Well after
he departed, two other Jesuits set out on an overseas mission, and
they ended it, tails between their legs, while Xavier's ship was still
a good three months shy of India. Granted, the two had a shorter
trip: over to Ireland to rally resistance against Henry VIII's impo-
sition of Protestantism. One had the foresight to buy a kilt in
Scotland before crossing the Irish Sea. Apparently it took more
than native clothing to impress the Irish clan chieftains, and the
underwhelmed feelings proved mutual: "We actually met some of
the chiefs, such as MacQuillan and O'Cahen, and some others.
But our eyes were opened to the fact that the disease of internal
strife in this country is a hopeless thing . . . because of a savage
and barbarous way of life, worse than bestial and hardly to be
believed unless actually seen."[5] The two accomplished nothing,
but merely making it back alive was achievement enough to
impress the hard-boiled Scots who welcomed them back from
unruly Ireland as returning heroes, because "they had not believed
they would ever see us again until the day of the resurrection."[6]

Neither Xavier nor any other European knew just what he would be dealing with once he arrived in Goa. No one briefed him about Asia before his departure. Who could have? Xavier's own letters were the first correspondence from the Far East ever published in Europe. The map of Asia was still in flux, changing constantly as explorers and traders logged new discoveries. Xavier ended up devoting his most substantial efforts to Japan, a country that was yet undiscovered by Europeans the day his ship weighed anchor in Portugal.

The prudent course for Xavier would have been to stay put in Goa, the administrative capital of Portugal's emerging Asian empire. The enormous Indian subcontinent would have offered an ambitious enough start to Jesuit multinational operations. After all, the full Jesuit company at the time could have squeezed around an oversized dining table. But Xavier operated according to a more ambitious logic. Far from holing up in colonial Goa, he was almost constantly on the move. He worked his way south to India's Fishery Coast and then traveled east along the spice trade routes to Malacca (Melaka), Java, Amboina (Ambon), and Morotai.

NEW BUSINESSES IN A NEW WORLD

These weren't mere reconnoitering trips. By the time Xavier was finished, the tiny Jesuit company had somehow found itself committed to a string of outposts in what are today India, Malaysia, Indonesia, Japan, and the Persian Gulf port of Hormuz. It wasn't only *where* he went; it was *what* he did. While Jesuits back in Europe were wondering whether they should enter the education business, a letter from Xavier arrived enthusiastically describing a school he had founded to educate both native children and those of Portuguese colonists. It was the first Jesuit-operated school of its kind anywhere in the world and perhaps the first school of its kind ever. Xavier launched it without even bothering to consult Jesuit headquarters in Rome, and he suggested that his poky colleagues in Europe might want to try the field of education themselves.

He moved no less aggressively in other directions. Although Jesuits purchased their first company printing press for their showcase Collegio Romano, they only barely beat Xavier. He had a Jesuit printing press operating in Goa by the end of that same year of 1556, well ahead of Jesuits working in Paris, Venice, or other more cosmopolitan settings.

By the time Xavier was finished, the tiny Jesuit company had somehow found itself committed to a string of outposts in what are today India, Malaysia, Indonesia, Japan, and the Persian Gulf port of Hormuz.

By force of his own imagination and energy, Francis Xavier had elevated Asia—and, by extension, *all* overseas activity—to a company priority. Consider, for example, that all ten cofounders had studied in Paris, and four were French nationals. Yet within a few years of Xavier's arrival in Goa, thirty Jesuits—both European expatriates and Indian nationals—were working there, while a mere thirteen were posted to familiar Paris. What modern American or European multinational has ever been able to make a similar claim? When he landed in Goa, Xavier *was* the Jesuit presence in Asia. He created a genuine, "if I build it they will come" success story: by the time of his death, more than seventy European and Indian Jesuits labored across Asia, with long lines of volunteers ready to join them.

Xavier's peripatetic, adventurous lifestyle lends context to the subsequent journeys of men such as Goes and Ricci. These later generations blazed new trails, but in equal measure they simply embraced Xavier's legacy. And the Jesuit style of trailblazing pioneered by Xavier was far more imaginative than merely hitting the highway. Long before Ricci set his sights on Beijing's imperial court, the instinct to aim high inspired Xavier's winter-long journey through rural Japan to the Japanese emperor's court at Miyako (Kyoto). Xavier intended not only to present his credentials but also to pitch history's first East-West academic exchange: to bring professors from the University of Paris and other European universities to the imperial University of Hiei-zan in Japan and to send Japanese professors to Europe. No European before Xavier had even set foot in Kyoto. What madness, or chutzpah—or combination of both—convinced him that he would even reach the capital alive, much less win an imperial audience and approval for his academic exchange?

Xavier returned from Kyoto empty-handed, his petition for an imperial sit-down summarily rebuffed. No problem. He bounced back soon enough, his restless radar now trained on a new opportunity.

> The people of China I have so far seen are of penetrating intelligence and lofty mind, more so than the Japanese, and they are people much given to study. The country is blessed with all manner of goods, most populous, full of large cities with houses of finely worked stone and, as everyone proclaims, very rich in all manner of silks. . . .
>
> I think that in this year of 1552 I shall leave for the place where the King of China dwells.[7]

Xavier left reinforcements behind in Japan working out of an abandoned Buddhist temple. The Japan team soon realized that Xavier had miscalculated the power of the emperor and his court anyway; the real power lay with the shogun. And two generations after Xavier, a Portuguese Jesuit linguist named João Rodrigues found a key to attracting the shogun's interest and favor. It was nothing so high-minded as academic exchanges or astronomy debates. Instead, it was Rodrigues's service as a commercial liaison: when Portuguese ships sailed into the port of Nagasaki to trade cargoes of Chinese silk, they found themselves dealing with an intermediary savvy enough in European ways to negotiate a fair

deal for the Japanese—the Jesuit João Rodrigues, business attaché
for shogun Tokugawa Ieyasu.

Xavier never made it to China. He died on the island of
Sancian (Shangchuan) some thirty miles short of the mainland.
Years passed before letters announcing his death reached Jesuit
headquarters in Rome, after retracing the same thousands-of-
miles-long journey that had begun with "Good enough. I'm ready."
Months after Xavier's death—and still months before word
reached Rome—Loyola drafted a letter to his friend and
cofounder, recalling him to Europe—a poignantly ironic end to
Xavier's story. It's clear from Loyola's letter that Xavier hadn't
been the only visionary Jesuit at work. The ten-person Jesuit company had sprawled over four continents in less than a decade.

> You also know that much depends for the good of India on the
> kind of men that are sent there. . . . You could see who are suit-
> able and who are not, who for one place and who for another. . . .
>
> Over and above these reasons, all of which look to the good of
> India, I feel that you would stir the [Portuguese] king's interest in
> Ethiopia. For so many years now he has been on the point of doing
> something, but nothing is ever done. From Portugal you would also
> be of no little help in the affairs of the Congo and of Brazil.[8]

Although it may seem irreverent to suggest, it certainly redounded
to the Jesuits' benefit that Xavier died as he did, when he did.
Whatever he might have accomplished in China, the mythology sur-
rounding him was vastly more valuable to succeeding Jesuit generations. And his death within sight of the Chinese coastline was the
perfect bookend to his "Good enough. I'm ready." His letters,
copied and circulated among Jesuit houses, created an electric
impact. One Jesuit manager in Coimbra, Portugal, reported that his
team was so charged up after reading the letters that he would
"have little difficulty in transferring the whole college to India."[9]

Before Xavier, the Jesuit vision had existed largely on paper. Now the Jesuits had a genuine hero who brought it to life. Sent to India, but single-handedly taking on all of Asia instead, Xavier exhibited the holy ambition so valued by Jesuit managers; heading to Asia on a day's notice, he displayed the indifference Jesuits were encouraged to cultivate; and molding his company's direction as he saw fit, he revealed that prized entrepreneurial instinct.

Ingenuity was manifest when a nimble Xavier decamped Japan to pursue a more promising opportunity in China, and it was manifest centuries later when manufacturers and financiers made the same strategic shift, fleeing Japan's post-bubble economy in the early 1990s to focus on business opportunities unfolding in China and emerging Southeast Asia. Ingenuity was Xavier's inspired adaptation to unexpected circumstances, just as it was the 3M researcher's insight that the botched batch of glue that didn't hold permanently might be good for something—and the Post-It was born.

DEPARTURES FROM CLASSIC RELIGIOUS TRADITIONS

The early Jesuits had exhibit A to prove that their model worked. No religious company had ever tried anything quite like it. Jesuit strategic values—speed, mobility, responsiveness, and flexibility—were the opposite of everything religious companies had always embodied. To live those Jesuit values, Loyola jettisoned whatever traditional religious practices stood in the way, like *praying*, or, more accurately, praying according to the monastic tradition. To appreciate the innovative leaps the Jesuits took with their company model, we must dip into some history of how earlier religious organizations operated and show how the Company of Jesus departed radically from the norm.

Embracing the world rather than
retreating from it

It's little wonder that the disciplines of mainstream religious life in sixteenth-century Christendom didn't serve Jesuit priorities. The Jesuits embraced the world and immersed themselves in its everyday life, living in its cities and cultural centers and traveling and working with its people. The traditions of religious life at that time were rooted in the *opposite* impulse. Instead of running to embrace the world, the pioneers of religious life had mostly headed fast in the other direction. The third-century St. Anthony of Egypt abandoned his village at age twenty, wandering off to live alone in the desert until his death at 105. Others followed his example all over Christendom, some pressing their desire for solitude to creative extremes. The Syrian monk Theodoret wrote of a hermit who lived for ten years perched above the ground in a tub suspended between two poles. Food was raised in a bucket secured with a rope; presumably other matter came down the same way—one hopes in a different bucket. St. Simeon Stylites played a variation on the theme. Plagued by crowds seeking spiritual counsel at his wilderness hermitage, Simeon erected a series of pillars, the last one sixty feet tall, so that he could live out his final thirty-five years in solitude. As one might have predicted, the stratagem backfired. Simeon and similarly inspired "stylites" became spiritual tourist attractions, even drawing the occasional Byzantine emperor out into the wilderness for a peek.

> The Jesuits embraced the world and immersed themselves in its everyday life, living in its cities and cultural centers and traveling and working with its people.

Colorful though these hermits may have been, early religious more typically submitted to a far more prosaic, communal lifestyle. Hundreds of monasteries peppered the fifth-century landscape from Europe to North Africa and Egypt. Each sheltered like-minded souls who left behind worldly pursuits for monastic study, prayer, and manual labor. But aside from gravity, many monastic communities were bound by little else than their own local traditions and the guidance of a (one would hope) wise abbot.

The sixth-century Italian St. Benedict lived the full sweep of these traditional monastic lifestyles before pioneering a new approach. Repelled by the vice-ridden mores of his native Rome, Benedict retreated to a hermitage. Like Simeon Stylites, his reputation soon attracted wisdom seekers. But unlike Stylites, Benedict was eventually coaxed from his hermitage to reform a monastery grown lax under a succession of degenerate abbots. When his strict leadership proved more than the monks could stomach, they did what any enterprising, disgruntled, wayward monks would do: tried to poison his food.

Praying on the run rather than in a controlled environment

The durable Benedict survived, his appetite for monastic reform now truly whetted. He gathered more resolute companions to establish a new monastery at Italy's Monte Cassino, where he authored a fifty-page "rule" that ultimately became the dominant guiding protocol for western monasticism. Benedict's monks gathered for communal prayer at seven set times each day, starting with Matins at 2:00 A.M. and continuing at regular intervals before retiring each night after Compline at 7:00 P.M. The schedule varied only to accommodate the seasonal changes of daylight hours. The summer sun rose early, so the appointed time for morning prayer (Lauds) was accordingly shifted to follow the 2:00 A.M. office, "after a very short interval, during which the brethren may go out for the necessities of nature."[10] Hand it to Benedict: his rule ran only fifty pages, but it covered life's most pressing daily contingencies.

What does it matter how a few monks organized their daily routine? Perhaps not much today, but it mattered far more to a Europe slipping into the darkest of its Dark Ages. As barbarian hordes overwhelmed a dissipated Roman Empire, its cities plunged into decay. Public education, libraries, and even literacy itself were becoming distant memories of a more civilized time. The light of learning was dimming, and monastic scholars and copyists were among the very few torchbearers preserving the light from flickering out entirely. Hence, monastic practices mattered enough that two centuries after Benedict, the Holy Roman Emperor, Louis I— a.k.a. Louis the Pious or Louis the Debonair—saw it fit to summon church bigwigs to debate monastic discipline and afterward ordered all monasteries in his empire to take up Benedict's Rule.

Was the decree implemented thoroughly? Who knows? News traveled slowly in the ninth century. Some remote monasteries undoubtedly knew little of Louis the Pious *or* St. Benedict, much less that the former was their emperor and that the latter had composed what was now a binding monastic rule. But whether universally recognized or not, Benedict's vision of religious life fundamentally influenced monastic practices for centuries—right up to Loyola's time.

Benedict's personal impulse to flee Rome—and indeed the world—profoundly colored that vision. Benedictine communities were self-supporting, self-contained islands. They produced their own food, clothing, and other necessities. They elected their own leaders, each monastery operating autonomously. No one superior was responsible for all the Benedictine houses in any given country, much less throughout the world. Nor did the rule foster an expansionist or missionary impulse to establish new branches. Quite the contrary. Benedict was scandalized by Europe's "gyrovagues," those wayward monks "tramping from province to province, staying as guests in different monasteries. . . . They indulge their own wills and succumb to the allurements of gluttony."[11] As a remedy, each Benedictine monk vowed "stability," to live out his remaining years in the monastic house he joined. Benedictine stability clearly complemented the monastic regimen of daily communal prayer at fixed hours. Centuries later, Loyola and the Jesuits would find little value in stability, or in communal prayer at set times. Instead, Jesuit prayer was individual, on-the-go, and self-regulating—like the *examen*.

But Benedict's model was exceedingly well suited to the agrarian Dark Ages in which it was introduced. After all, it wasn't as if the monks could have bought groceries in the nearest large city. Nor were they missing out on a hip, urban scene by retreating to a monastery. Trade had collapsed. There were few cities to speak of.

Still, European cities did once again stir to life. The growth of the continent's new economy was nothing so thrilling as the recent dot-com craze (R.I.P.). But towns slowly came back to life, thanks in part to twelfth- and thirteenth-century cloth merchants, the weavers they employed, and the carpenters, builders, bankers, shippers, food sellers, and others who catered to their worldly needs. These reemerging urban communities had religious, social, and spiritual needs as well. Benedictine monks were ill positioned to deal with the needs of these populations, cloistered as they were and often far removed from emerging town centers. A new model was needed for a new era. And two great monastic reformers happened along to provide it. As Europe moved into the thirteenth century, St. Francis of Assisi and St. Dominic punched a small hole in the monastery walls to experiment with new approaches to religious life.

Francis of Assisi renounced substantial familial wealth to heed the mandate proclaimed in Matthew's Gospel: "Take no gold, or silver, or copper in your belts, no bag for your journey, or two tunics, or sandals, or a staff; for laborers deserve their food" (Matthew 10:9–10). Francis took the gospel passage literally. His earliest followers lived hand-to-mouth and day-to-day as itinerant preachers relying on freely given food offerings. Saving money for a rainy day was not an option: his friars were prohibited from even *touching* coin. Though he never ambitioned a large religious order, his charismatic appeal attracted thousands to live a poor, simple life while finding God present in all natural things.

Striving for global growth rather than maintaining monastic traditions

If history best remembers Francis for his simple piety and uncom-promising embrace of religious poverty, he might also be remem-bered as the founder most desperately wanting for a good chief operating officer. Francis envisioned a loosely bound, small band of brothers, and he structured his company accordingly. *Every* Franciscan enjoyed the authority to accept new members into the ranks. By what criteria? No one seemed too worried about such details. Once new members joined, there was no organized novi-tiate system to train them. The approach worked fine while Francis ran the equivalent of a corner deli, but the same seat-of-the-pants style didn't lend itself to oversight of a company the scale of McDonald's.

The early Franciscans convened their full membership for annual "general chapters" to resolve strategy. This worked well for a small band of brothers, but in 1221 as many as five thousand fri-ars descended on Assisi for what surely became more circus than strategy session. They straggled in from all over Europe, some after months of travel, each recognizing no clear chain of command other than Francis's ultimate leadership, each informally trained by whatever monk or monks had admitted him—it's little wonder that the general chapters were unproductive.

To their great credit, Francis and the similarly inspired founder of the Dominican order (St. Dominic) refocused religious life. At the core of each man's vision was engagement with the pressing problems of an urbanizing Christendom. Their members sallied forth each day to preach or teach. But they remained tethered to the monastery, retaining Benedict's tightly scheduled communal prayer at appointed hours. An impulse to be actively involved in the world inspired their corporate efforts, but each order struggled to shoehorn that impulse into the withdrawn-from-the-world monastic model they inherited. It wasn't a natural fit.

Both reformers also groped toward "global management," in contrast to the fully autonomous Benedictine monasteries. The Dominicans elected a worldwide master general, but his authority was checked within an exquisitely balanced system that would have wowed the framers of the U.S. Constitution. Each Dominican community elected its own leaders, and each region largely managed its own affairs. As a result, the master general didn't enjoy the broad authority of a modern CEO. In contrast, the Franciscan minister general enjoyed more substantial authority but lacked the organizational infrastructure to wield it effectively.

Widely distributed authority and democratically elected leadership checked the Dominicans' full corporate potential, and severe "undermanagement" weakened the Franciscans. Neither order managed or even tried to invent a leadership or management model specifically geared to a proactive, mobile, large-scale modern company, as Loyola later would do. And in fairness, neither *intended* to build a large-scale modern company. Dominic, Francis, and their followers undoubtedly remained quite pleased with what they had created: a balanced life of active service complemented by contemplative prayer. The elegantly simple Dominican motto eloquently conveys the essence of this approach to life, work, and prayer: "to contemplate and to give others the fruits of contemplation."

Well, Ignatius Loyola *did* intend to build a proactive, mobile, large-scale modern company—although he probably wouldn't have put it in quite those terms. And while Dominic and Francis stretched the garment of traditional religious life to cover their more activist ambitions, Ignatius Loyola decided that a completely new garment was needed. A thousand years after Benedict and three hundred after Francis and Dominic, Loyola started drafting the Jesuit *Constitutions*. The finished product incorporated ideas from all three monastic traditions, but they were draped on a model so radically different from what had preceded it that they were almost unrecognizable.

First to go was the very organizing principle of monastic life: daily communal prayer at fixed hours. The Jesuits' priority was fully engaged fieldwork, which is fundamentally incompatible with a shackling obligation to hurry home periodically each day for communal prayer. The monastic communities prayed in common at multiple fixed times each day; Loyola's Jesuits would pray individually, sandwiching prayer between their work obligations. It was a radical departure from the way things had been done in the past, an ingenious leap that created scope to seize unplanned and unanticipated opportunities to "help souls."

Basing ministry on opportunity rather than on strict definitions

Prior to the Jesuits, religious orders frequently confined their missions to particular areas of service or types of work. While Dominic had articulated a clearly focused mission of "preaching and teaching," Loyola refused to pin his Jesuits down. Opportunities would evolve over time, and even in 1540 Protestant Germany's needs differed utterly from those of non-Christian Japan. So Loyola articulated a wide-open mission: "The aim and end of this Society is, *by traveling through the various regions of the world* at the order of the [pope] or of the superior of the Society itself, to preach, hear confessions, and *use all the other means it can . . . to help souls*" (emphasis added).[12] What might "helping souls" include? Apparently, whatever made sense to a self-aware Jesuit and his superiors, from expeditionary treks to mapmaking to astronomical research. Instead of specifying businesses his Jesuits should pursue, Loyola only warned them to avoid occupations that could tie them down or limit strategic flexibility: "Likewise, because the members of this Society ought to be ready at any hour to go to some or other parts or the world, . . . still less ought they to take charge of religious women . . . or similar burdens which are not compatible with the liberty that is necessary for our manner of proceeding."[13]

Well, political correctness was not exactly a hallmark of the sixteenth century.

The cofounders ensured rapid responsiveness by vowing to mobilize immediately at the pope's request, "without any excuse . . . to any place whatsoever where [the pope] judges it expedient to send them, . . . whether among the faithful or the infidels."[14] By explicitly putting themselves at the pope's disposal, they made it impossible to turn back and therefore enforced flexibility. Like it or not, when the pope came knocking they were committed to go.

Of course, companies don't become strategically flexible and change-ready merely by repeating these goals throughout the company handbook. If it were that simple, corporate America would be awash in nimble, resourceful leadership. It's easy to talk about embracing change; it's far more difficult to live it by risking one's career on untested tactics or by leaving home and friends for distant assignments. The indifference meditations of the Spiritual Exercises mentally prepared early Jesuit recruits for these and other challenges by surfacing attachments that might hinder them. Jesuits not only talked about change-readiness but developed recruits to live it.

In case he didn't fully absorb the message, each trainee was given a sole-testing. Each was dispatched on a monthlong "Christian man against the elements" pilgrimage. Trainees set out empty-handed, begging for food and lodging along the way, the challenge symbolic and unmistakable: be resourceful, mobile, creative, free of attachments, and able to operate independently. No wonder so many Jesuits ended up with a taste for exploration. When Jacques Marquette joined with Louis Jolliet to explore the Mississippi River, it was hardly Marquette's first journey. His novitiate had included a monthlong, two-hundred-mile roundtrip pilgrimage between Nancy and Trier. Granted, trekking through northeast France was considerably tamer than canoeing past buffalo herds en route to a rendezvous with Illini tribal leaders. But the one-two punch of the Exercises and the monthlong pilgrimage made a far profounder impact on trainees than would a corporate handbook encouraging flexibility and resourcefulness.

Finding God in the world rather than behind walls

Loyola had spun the very structure of religious life onto its head. While Benedict's monks pronounced a vow of *stability*, remaining in one monastery for life, Jesuits were instead committed to *mobility*. Loyola's lieutenant Jerónimo Nadal barnstormed Europe framing the distinctive Jesuit mindset and lifestyle: "[Jesuits] realize that they cannot build or acquire enough houses to be able from nearby to run out to the combat. Since that is the case, they consider that they are in their most peaceful and pleasant house when they are constantly on the move, when they travel throughout the earth, when they have no place to call their own."[15] The world-friendly sentiment is unmistakable. Far from squeamishly recoiling from change or fleeing the world, the ideal Jesuit embraces life on the move as his "most peaceful and pleasant house." Or, as Nadal told another team, "It must be noted that in the Society there are different kinds of houses or dwellings. These are: the house of probation, the college, the professed house, and *the journey—and by this last the whole world becomes [our] house*" (emphasis added).[16]

Speed, mobility, imagination, and flexibility were the goals. Obstacles were uprooted, including the very practices most often associated with priestly life. Nadal described a particularly unpleasant dressing down by Loyola: "On the next day [Loyola] sharply denounced me in the presence of others; and, thereafter, he did not make great use of my services."[17] What was the extraordinary offense? Nadal had yielded to Spanish Jesuits' request to pray for as long as an hour and a half each day, and Nadal's saintly, mystic Jesuit boss was apoplectic to hear that Nadal had allowed the Spaniards to do so much praying! Loyola insisted instead that "a truly mortified man needs only a quarter of an hour to be united with God in prayer."[18]

> Obstacles were uprooted, including the very practices most often associated with priestly life.

His point? Not that Jesuits shouldn't be prayerful, but that success in their activist mission hinged on finding ways to remain prayerfully re-collected without withdrawing from action. Or, as Nadal put it when proposing Loyola as the role model, Jesuits should be *simul in actione contemplativus"* ("contemplative even in action"). Another colleague put it more plainly: "It is unbelievable with what ease our Father [i.e., Loyola] recollected himself in the midst of a tide of business."[19]

What was the key to Loyola's ability to shift gears? Like so much else, the skill traced back to the Exercises. Loyola had abandoned fixed communal prayer but had substituted strategies for maintaining focus and composure in a busy lifestyle. The short mental pit stops of the daily *examen* enabled refocusing on the fly.

But refocusing is useless without a focal point. Equally vital was the up-front investment each recruit had made to understand his weaknesses, establish his worldview, and cultivate indifference. So he instinctively knew what to look for when he stopped to refocus. He measured his performance over the past few hours against key goals, the weaknesses that habitually tripped him up, and the attachments that blocked indifference. After the spiritual and mental fine-tuning, he got back into the race.

No less important to re-collection amid the tide of business was the Contemplation to Attain Love, which first attuned recruits to the divine presence all around them. Jesuits didn't consider it necessary to gather in chapel every few hours to remind themselves of the sort of world in which they worked. Instead, their worldview—their lens, their outlook toward others—had been set through the Exercises, allowing them to move through the day with their radar fixed to "find God in all things." What did that mean? Exactly what it said. Loyola told Jesuits to find God "in all things, for example, in conversing with someone, in walking, looking, tasting, hearing, thinking, and in everything that they do."[20]

Previous pages depicted the slow-motion evolution of religious life, the ten-century journey from Benedict's monks to Francis's friars to Ignatius Loyola's world-engaged Jesuits. If religious life evolved slowly, so did the medieval world it mirrored: Loyola's Jesuits would have had no place in Benedict's feudal, agrarian era, or in Francis's thirteenth century, for that matter.

Today's world changes at a more frantic pace; modern managers pride themselves not only on coping with change but on *driving* change to seize the competitive advantage in constantly shifting markets. But we may not be as good at change management as we would like to think. In 1982 Thomas Peters and Robert Waterman released *In Search of Excellence: Lessons from America's Best-Run Companies*; the landmark work was a fixture on bestseller lists for more than three years. The authors' prescriptions for achieving corporate excellence stand up surprisingly well twenty years later. Unfortunately, the same can't be said for many of the companies they lauded as "America's best-run companies." Peters and Waterman sifted corporate America through rigorous sieves and proclaimed that thirty-six companies cleared "all the hurdles for excellent performance" over their twenty-year study period. Some of those thirty-six still shine. But others struggle for their corporate lives, no longer paragons of excellence but fodder for case studies analyzing good companies gone bad (Eastman Kodak, Kmart). Still others are dimly remembered ghosts, casualties of corporate takeovers (Amdahl, Chesebrough-Pond's, Raychem).

Peters and Waterman didn't make injudicious choices. They chose excellent companies—for 1982. But excellence—like the leadership that engenders it—is no timeless plateau that once attained is never forfeited. The thousands who lost jobs as these one-time corporate role models disintegrated need no reminder that the modern world is tumultuous and always shifting;

succeeding in this world requires individuals to cultivate the personal skills needed to thrive in an environment of near permanent change. And thriving amid change is not merely a workplace concern; the same social, technological, and cultural changes that convulse the workplace present an endless stream of threats and opportunities in every facet of life. The abilities to adapt, create, and respond quickly are core *personal* leadership skills for the twenty-first century.

Loyola and his colleagues understood the urgency of molding a change-adaptive, creative Jesuit team in the sixteenth century; surely those same skills are all the more critical in the tumultuous twenty-first century. Yet the snuffed-out corporate stars of the *In Search of Excellence* class of 1982 suggest that many today are far less resilient than the sixteenth-century Xavier who crisscrossed Asia. Why? Perhaps we don't focus as energetically as Loyola's Jesuits did on assembling the internal, personal building blocks of ingenuity.

About sixty years after Xavier left India, another Jesuit arrived there. Roberto de Nobili would push Jesuit ingenuity to limits that would draw the attention of a wary Vatican—neither the first nor the last time that this would happen in Jesuit history.

THE JESUIT WHO WORE RED: THE INNOVATIONS OF DE NOBILI

Not much was overlooked in Loyola's obsession with inventiveness and flexibility—not even clothes. Other religious orders proudly sported distinctive habits as their "team colors." Loyola instead opted for plain priestly attire, "conformed to the usage of the region where one is living."[21] He was referring to nuances in Catholic priestly custom and dress across Europe. In Loyola's mind, the dress code must have been little more than a minor grace note in his broader concern that Jesuits blend into local

Groundbreaking multiculturalist
This sketch of Roberto de Nobili, the Italian noble turned sannyasi, was done by his Jesuit colleague Balthasar da Costa. Though da Costa's crude sketch hardly rivals the Jesuit portraiture executed by masters like Rubens and del Conte, it nonetheless captures de Nobili's thorough attempts to adapt to his host culture.

cultures, not set themselves apart. But even Loyola might have been surprised at how aggressively his adventurous Jesuits interpreted "conformed to the usage of the region where one is living" once they found themselves working amid non-Christian priestly classes dressed in anything but priestly black.

Jesuits likely arrived in Asia primed for cultural experimentation, given the themes rattling around their heads. Their company mission demanded they use *all the means they could* to help souls. Each trainee had meditated on the ten thousand ducats to rid himself of controlling personal attachments and to cultivate indifference. Managers like Nadal had reinforced the change-ready message that they were *in their most peaceful and pleasant house when they were constantly on the move*. No wonder many were quick to shake off the cultural trappings of sixteenth-century Europe in order to *conform to the usage of the region where one is living*. Few tested cultural frontiers as thoroughly as the twenty-eight-year-old Italian Jesuit and former noble who reached the southern Indian city of Madurai in 1606.

Roberto de Nobili's pedigree would have been extraordinary almost anywhere other than a Jesuit company that already boasted more than its share of well-connected Europeans. The grandnephew of a pope and son of a papal army general, de Nobili renounced his own title as count of Civitella to remain a Jesuit. Who knows what else he passed up to enter Jesuit life: a sizable inheritance, for sure; probably a palazzo on the family's Tuscan estates; and likely a cardinal's hat had he pursued a conventional clerical career.

Instead of sitting in cardinal's robes in a Tuscan palazzo, by 1610 de Nobili was sitting in a grass hut a few degrees north of the equator. Dressed in a red-ocher robe, his head completely shaved but for a small tuft of hair and his forehead marked with sandalwood paste, de Nobili took his one daily vegetarian meal of rice seasoned with herbs—and didn't complement it with wine from the de Nobilis' Montepulciano vineyards. Noble-born in his native Italy, de Nobili had at first presented himself as a member of the rajah caste, according to his adopted country's practices, a calculated strategy to avoid the label of "untouchable" that Indians invariably accorded his missionary colleagues, forever after hobbling their efforts. But as de Nobili immersed himself in his host country's culture, he adjusted his strategy. He began draping a distinctive triple strand of white cotton from his shoulder down to his waist, marking himself as a member of the Brahmin (priestly) caste. Moreover, he adopted the austere diet and disciplined regimen of a sannyasi, a religious man "who abandons all."

The sannyasi de Nobili convinced the Brahmin scholar Sivadarma to tutor him in the Hindu scriptures, the Vedas—a double first of sorts. Not only was de Nobili the first European to consult the sacred Vedas with any thoroughness, but he also became the first European to master Sanskrit, the classical language of Hindu India and the language of the Vedas. It was a triple first, actually; de Nobili was there not only to learn but also to

> Not only was de Nobili the first European to consult the sacred Vedas with any thoroughness, but he also became the first European to master Sanskrit, the classical language of Hindu India and the language of the Vedas.

participate actively in religious discourse. So after absorbing the Sanskrit Vedas, the sannyasi shifted to colloquial Tamil to draft his *Nitya Jivana Callapam* (*Dialogue on Eternal Life*). In what was almost certainly the first theological treatise written by a European in an Indian language, de Nobili offered Hindus his interpretation of the way to attain knowledge of the true Veda.

Alarm bells went off in Rome when word arrived that the one-time count of Civitella had become a Hindu and was worshiping idols. For not every Jesuit—in Rome or even in Madurai, for that matter—was of one mind on just how to interpret "use all the means you can" in a tricky, unfamiliar world. Some in Rome were dithering over far more pedestrian squabbles. Not long after word of de Nobili's activities reached Rome, Jesuit bureaucrats were fussily debating whether nonordained Jesuits should be entitled to wear the distinctive black beret that was becoming de rigueur Jesuit haberdashery; what in the world did they think upon learning that de Nobili had shaved his head and was suiting up in red ocher?

These early reports to Rome weren't positive; nor were they framed in sympathetic terms. It wasn't de Nobili himself sharing the news but his colleague Gonçalo Fernandes. Working alone in Madurai for eleven years before de Nobili's arrival, Fernandes had managed to attract exactly *no one* to Christianity. With a flock of none, he presumably had plenty of time to write Rome accusing de Nobili of engaging in superstitious practices. The bureaucrats in Rome were surely scandalized by the reports from India, especially as it became clear that Fernandes wasn't the only unhappy one. The bishop of de Nobili's diocese in India was also complaining about the wayward Jesuit.

CULTURAL PRACTICES VERSUS
RELIGIOUS EXPRESSION

Most large, multinational companies deal regularly with analogous crises: low-level employee in remote, relatively unimportant market exceeds authority and strays so far out on a limb that the company's reputation is threatened. And most large, multinational companies have a well-honed, sensitive policy for handling such situations: saw off the limb, and fast. What support in Rome could the upstart de Nobili count on as he sat half-naked halfway around the world? Lucky for de Nobili, the Jesuit general at the time, Claudio Acquaviva, left the saw in the toolshed and instead solicited de Nobili's input on his missionary methods and Indian culture.

Like de Nobili, Acquaviva was of Italian nobility, the duke of Atri's son. And just as the thirty-year-old de Nobili challenged the tactics of much older, more experienced, and inevitably irritated Jesuit colleagues in India, Acquaviva was something of a prodigy himself. Joining the Jesuits after a meteoric ascent through Vatican ranks, Acquaviva was eventually elected the Jesuits' youngest general ever at age thirty-seven. When Jesuit delegates informed Pope Gregory XIII of their choice, the stunned, seventy-nine-year-old pontiff blurted out a less than hearty endorsement: "Good heavens. You have chosen as your ruler a young man who isn't even forty years old!"[22]

But Acquaviva's stake in the India controversy might have been still more poignant and personal than superficial similarities between his background and de Nobili's. When Acquaviva first became a Jesuit it was largely assumed in nepotistic church circles that his nephew Rodolfo would simply slide into Acquaviva's vacated slot in the Vatican bureaucracy. But Rodolfo had different ideas. Over family objections he announced his own intention to join the Jesuits. It was not an attempt to seek his well-placed uncle's patronage and secure a cushy assignment; Rodolfo instead signed up for the miserable yearlong ocean voyage to India, a place where the noble Acquaviva name didn't count for much.

If he hoped to set aside the trappings of nobility for a life of humbler service, he experienced an ironic twist of fate. While Claudio was steadily rising through Jesuit ranks in Italy, word arrived that Rodolfo had been invited to live and work at the royal court of the Mughal emperor Akbar. He remained there for nearly four years, founding the Jesuit embassy that Benedetto de Goes would take up some twenty years later.

Not long after Claudio became Jesuit general, the Acquavivas experienced another ironic twist, this one bitter. As Jesuit general it would have fallen to Claudio to write the formal sympathy letter to his brother: Rodolfo Acquaviva had been murdered in India along with three Jesuit colleagues. Sketchy, delayed reports suggested that the murderers were venting long-nursed outrage over the indiscriminate leveling of Hindu shrines that had punctuated Portuguese subjugation of Goa. Rodolfo and his companions had done nothing particularly wrong; they were merely symbols of a broader—and just—grievance.

Perhaps because his nephew's death left the Jesuit general Acquaviva feeling a personal stake in India, he took the impolitic course, trying to understand de Nobili's approach rather than summarily sanctioning him. If this was the time for de Nobili to eat humble pie and temper his radicalism to save his career, no one told him so. He might have devoted the previous years to studying Sanskrit classics and drafting treatises in Tamil, but de Nobili still remembered how to whip up convincing arguments in church Latin. Neither Acquaviva nor his theological advisers—nor anyone else in Europe, for that matter—had ever seen anything like de Nobili's 175-page "*Informatio de Quibusdam Moribus Nationis Indicae*" ("Report on Certain Customs of the Indian Nation"). His readers must have wondered if he had somehow sneaked back to the Collegio Romano library to marshal arguments rich in ammunition from sources spanning everything from Roman mythology to Jesus Christ to St. Augustine and St. Thomas Aquinas to the Hindu Laws of Manu. De Nobili's obscure references likely sent leading theologians scurrying to their concordances in befuddlement: "Take for instance the testimony of Bardeseres the Babylonian, a writer highly commended by Eusebuis in the 6th Book on his Propagation of the Gospel."[23]

If his references were at times obscure, his central argument was straightforward. Unlike many of his detractors, de Nobili had troubled himself not only to understand Indian culture but to grasp thorny distinctions between religious faith and its cultural trappings. He systematically dissected and adopted the cultural practices of Brahminism: the *kutumi* (a tuft of hair on an otherwise shaven head), the *tilakam* (sandalwood paste), and so on. He pored over Hindu classics and consulted Brahmin experts to unlock the origins and received meaning of these practices. While many Europeans ignorantly assumed unfamiliar practices to be superstitious and associated with idol worship, de Nobili demonstrated that many such practices were traditional ways of identifying civil status or adorning oneself and conveyed no religious significance. De Nobili argued that he had instructed his converts to forgo overtly superstitious and traditional Hindu religious practices, but he himself had adopted and had allowed his Brahmin converts to retain purely civil-status signs and nonreligious cultural practices.

He then turned full-bore on his detractors who systematically forced prospective converts to adopt European names, don European dress, and otherwise abandon all signs of status within Indian society. De Nobili accused these detractors of cruelly and needlessly condemning converts to surrender respectability in their society. Non-Christian Indians saw the converts "as degenerates, in reality cut off from their former grade and . . . deprived of every civil advantage. . . . [Non-Christians] could not understand

why we made it a strict condition for following the law of Christ
that one should lower one's civil status and deny oneself all human
dignity and every human benefit."[24]

After all, de Nobili pointed out, "as for cosmetics and perfumes
[like the sandal-paste mark reserved for high-caste Indians], . . .
Christ himself, the master of preachers, allowed himself the use of
such things."[25] De Nobili closed his tour de force with a testimo-
nial from "108 Brahmins with the Degree of Doctor in their
Several Branches of Learning" that there was indeed no overtly
religious symbolism in the practices de Nobili had allowed his converts to retain. He pointed out that these doctors were "neither
Christians nor Catechumens, . . . nor a single one of them has
received either money or any other gift."[26] And he assured his
Jesuit superiors that he had saved each doctor's signature, "written
on Indian palm leaves," should it ever become necessary to verify
their testimony.

Not even de Nobili's most erudite critics could counter with a
commensurately well-informed response. Not only was the
breadth and depth of his western theological knowledge extraordinary, but the 108 Brahmins he consulted equaled just about 108
more expert sources than most of his critics had ever consulted.
None of his critics were fluent in Sanskrit; the Hindu classics he
quoted were closed books to them.

Still, the issues de Nobili agonized over were and *are* profoundly
complicated. Cultural practice and religious expression can't be
untangled into two neatly distinct strands, as de Nobili tried to
prove. And embedded in his missionary approach were other controversial strategic considerations. He had noted, for example,
that his beef-eating, leather-wearing, ritually unclean (by Indian
standards) missionary predecessors had rendered themselves
"untouchable" to high-caste Hindus. De Nobili's adoption of
Brahmin status and its complicated cultural regimen was part of a
carefully plotted top-down strategy to appeal first to high-caste

Indians, betting that the lower castes would follow their lead. But the strategy enmeshed de Nobili in practices he would have rather not appeared to endorse: for example, preventing low-caste Hindus from even touching his person or preparing his food. Finally, no matter how remarkable de Nobili's cultural sensitivity was in its seventeenth-century context, his work spotlights a question that vexes even twenty-first-century missionary experts: where does one draw the line between interfaith dialogue and aggressive proselytization?[27]

It's safe to say that de Nobili's seventeenth-century critics were not preoccupied with such complicated issues. Instead, they attacked him and other Jesuits across Asia with arguments that seem in retrospect only to confirm the advanced sensibilities of the Jesuits. For example, one non-Jesuit missionary in China dashed off a scandalized report to Rome because Jesus *wore shoes* in a Jesuit-commissioned painting of the Last Supper. The charge was taken seriously enough that the Jesuits actually had to waste time responding. Their defense was simple. The Chinese considered it unsanitary to go barefoot. How could prospective Chinese converts be expected to respect the so-called Son of God if he lacked elementary manners?

Other missionaries in China attacked the Jesuits for straying from the church's formal baptismal rites: "The Fathers [i.e., the Jesuits] in baptizing women fail to apply saliva to their ears, salt to their mouths, and oil to their breast and head."[28] Guilty as charged. The Jesuit superior in China explained: "Among the Chinese it is highly irregular and indecent to expose a woman's breast, to touch her hands and her mouth. If it is necessary everywhere for ministers of the Gospel to observe circumspection in their conduct with women, it is certainly far more necessary in China."[29] The Jesuits had departed from what they considered nonessential traditional aspects of the European baptismal rite in deference to what they deemed important cultural mores in China.

Acquaviva died years before the matter of de Nobili's methods was resolved. Although the general had tentatively ruled in support of de Nobili's fundamental approach, his hands had been tied from offering blanket approval. For de Nobili's doings in a hut near the equator had eventually attracted the attention of a higher authority than a mere Jesuit general. The Vatican itself had become involved, ultimately impaneling a theological commission to conduct a thorough investigation. It would have been little solace to de Nobili that his colleagues in China were also being pilloried for their inculturation strategies. What mattered to the Italian sannyasi was that he was prohibited from accepting converts while investigation of his methods lurched along at a bureaucratic pace. Daunting though the investigation must have seemed to de Nobili, there could have been worse alternatives. The Portuguese archbishop de Sa e Lisboa of Goa, primate of all the Indies, his knickers well and truly twisted over the Italian Jesuit troublemaker in his jurisdiction, had invited the grand inquisitor of Portugal to have a go at de Nobili. But the Inquisition authorities ruled they had no right to intervene in a matter actively under Vatican review. Lucky for de Nobili.

But not completely lucky. The president of the theological troika investigating de Nobili was the seventy-year-old archbishop Peter Lombard. The Irishman had participated in a previous papal investigation of another controversial Italian, and that process hadn't turned out very well for its subject, a Mr. Galileo. At least Galileo had been offered the chance to participate in his own inquiry. De Nobili, far away in India, wasn't interviewed by the commission, asked for his input, or made privy to the report.

Too bad he never had the chance to read it. If he had, he would have been pleasantly surprised to read Archbishop Lombard's citation from St. Augustine's *City of God*: "It is a matter of no moment in the city of God whether he who adopts the faith that brings men to God, adopts it in one dress and manner of life or another, so long as he lives in conformity with the commandments of God."[30] While the commission's report was confidential, Pope Gregory XV's ruling was announced to the world in the 1623 bull *Romanae Sedis Antistes,* although it took a while for the bull to reach Goa on the slow boat from Lisbon: "We grant by the present letters, in virtue of the Apostolic authority, to the Brahmins and other gentiles who have been and will be converted to the Faith permission to take and wear the thread and [grow] the kudumi as distinctive signs of their social status, nobility and of other offices."[31]

A vindicated de Nobili went back to work. Years later, at age sixty-eight and nearly blind, it was well past time to retire. For most people, that is. For de Nobili it was time to start another career. He shipped across the Palk Strait to the Jaffna peninsula in Ceylon (Sri Lanka). After having dazzled the Brahmin with his Tamil treatises and wowed the papal theologians with his Latin polemics, de Nobili put his literary talents to use for a no less discerning but more readily responsive audience, writing stories for children.

The former count of Civitella died in the Indian city of Madras at age seventy-nine not long after the fiftieth anniversary of his arrival in India.

THE ADVANTAGE OF OBEDIENCE

The creative, freewheeling likes of de Nobili suggest that Jesuits were ever poised to pounce innovatively on unfolding opportunities. But there was a flip side to this innovation and daring. The Jesuits vowed *obedience* to God, as represented by their Jesuit bosses and the pope as well. The ideal obedient Jesuit, according to the *Constitutions,* behaved "as if he were a lifeless body which allows itself to be carried to any place and to be treated in any manner desired, or as if he were an old man's staff which serves in any place and in any manner whatsoever in which the holder wishes to use it."[32]

"Lifeless body" and "old man's staff"? What invigorating imagery! It doesn't exactly seem the stuff of ingenuity and creativity. How does one reconcile even the *idea* of obedience with ingenuity and creativity? After all, a "lifeless body" or an "old man's staff" isn't very flexible, strategically or literally. Whatever attributes one associates with obedience, ingenuity surely falls pretty far down on the list.

But in Loyola's mind, obedience was *entirely* consistent with ingenuity. Most of the innovators profiled thus far—Goes, Ricci, Clavius, Xavier, and de Nobili—performed their most creative heroics as order *takers*, on the short end of that old man's staff, so to speak.

Strict obedience and ingenuity: opposites perhaps, but not to those schooled in the Jesuit *modo de proceder*. With his simple "Good enough. I'm ready," Xavier packed up his life on short notice and headed to Asia as the ultimate "old man's staff" and exemplar of Jesuit obedience. Yet once there he was an "independent entrepreneur," resourceful and confident enough to set strategy for a continent without guidance from headquarters: *Oh, did I tell you that I've committed us to a new country I found called Japan? Or that I've committed us to a new line of business—running schools?*

Recall the punch line of the meditation concerning the three men and the ten thousand ducats: the ideal response was not to rid oneself of the money but to rid oneself of the attachment, "in such a way that there remains no inclination either to keep the acquired money or to dispose of it." In other words, be free to do whatever the situation calls for—in the case of the Jesuit innovators, to be flexible enough to give an order, take an order, or plot one's own course. The spirit of indifference cast obedience in an entirely new light. It was not about who got to give orders and who had to take them; in one way or another, most early Jesuits—and most *everyone*—usually did both, even in the course of a day. The focus was on cultivating the freedom—the indifference—to do either and to do either *well* in order to deliver results. Jesuits didn't manage to exempt themselves

totally from the human condition; few things make the head
swell like giving orders, and
plenty of Jesuits liked the feeling when it came their way. But
at their best they avoided crippling, ego-drenched tugs of
war in order to focus instead on
a common goal: making and
implementing well-informed decisions that would "help souls."

> The spirit of indifference cast obedience in an entirely new light. It was not about who got to give orders and who had to take them; the focus was on cultivating the freedom to do either in order to deliver results.

Obedience conferred *speed* on the Jesuit enterprise, allowing managers to recognize and respond to opportunities aggressively. And rapid response was clearly on Loyola's mind when he drafted this choice nugget from the *Constitutions:* obedient Jesuits "should be ready to leave unfinished any letter or anything else of ours which has been begun and to apply our whole mind and all the energy we have [to the task requested by a superior]."[33] Lest there be doubt about his meaning, he didn't instruct Jesuits to leave unfinished the three-page letter *(la carta)* home to Mom; he exhorted them to leave unfinished the letter *(la letra)* M in the let-ter home to Mom. Granted, no modern corporation is going to elicit a vow of obedience from staff members, no matter how attractive the pay package and perks. But anyone in today's fast-moving, competitive business environment will immediately rec-ognize the power of having team members who can take orders, give them, plot their own course . . . and do all these quickly.

THE COURAGE TO DELEGATE AGGRESSIVELY

This indifferent approach to exercising authority started at the top. Those who had founded religious orders before Loyola had bequeathed him a menu of centralized and decentralized business models. Benedict's Rule had counseled that "whenever any important business has to be done," the abbot should "call together the whole community" and solicit input. Dominicans and Franciscans summoned delegates to Rome for triennial global leadership congregations. All three orders—the Benedictines, Dominicans, and Franciscans—nurtured grass-roots democracy, empowering local communities to elect their own superiors.

Loyola had no time for any of it—literally. Rome was a one-month trip from Madrid in the sixteenth century, and a roundtrip drained two valuable months—not to mention the disruption caused by postponed decisions and interrupted work. The critical meeting that elected Loyola general was a pretty good indication of things to come: only six of the ten founders even made it, the others off on far-flung missions that were deemed more important. While Dominican and Franciscan delegates gathered for general congregations every three years, the Jesuits convened only eight such congregations in their first hundred years.

Nor would Loyola countenance local election of superiors. The Jesuit general appointed all senior managers. This practice alone profoundly colored the whole company's mindset. Instead of loosely agglomerated "federal Jesuit republics" focused on regional priorities, the Jesuits were decidedly global, with authority radiating from a strong hub to many spokes. As Jesuit generals considered candidates to head Jesuit teams, nationality was rarely an overriding concern: instead of a community of Spaniards being led by one of their own, Jesuit communities might find themselves headed by expatriate troubleshooters or rising stars being groomed for yet bigger assignments to come.

What did Jesuit generals do with the vast authority Loyola's *Constitutions* harvested for them? If they were true to his style and to the company's *modo de proceder*, they lavishly delegated it to whoever could make the best informed, fastest decisions in the field. Jesuit Pedro Ribadeneira described the kind of manager anyone would want to work for, in the sixteenth century or the twenty-first, recalling

> The confidence [Loyola] showed to those to whom he was entrusting some important affair, by giving them complete freedom, and credit, and allowing them authority to act according to the capacity and talent of each one. And to the instructions which he was giving them he added: "You who are on the ground will see better what should be done."[34]

Those comfortable assuming authority were not reined in but given more. Francis Borgia had been duke of Gandia before joining the Jesuits. Given his administrative experience, it's no surprise that Loyola endorsed one of Borgia's decisions before even knowing it: "Whatever means you shall judge to be better in our Lord, I fully approve. . . . In this matter we have but one will, but you are in closer touch with affairs where you are."[35] This wasn't special treatment for a favored lieutenant. A similarly worded letter to Simão Rodrigues betrays Loyola's habitual instinct to delegate aggressively: "I leave everything to your judgment and I will consider best whatever you shall decide."[36]

More telling was his treatment of those who hung back from flexing authority. When a vacillating Olivier Mannaerts looked to Loyola to decide a local management issue, the ball was quickly batted right back to Mannaerts: "Olivier, cut your suit according to your cloth; only let us know how you have acted."[37] As luck would have it, when Mannaerts screwed up the nerve to "go with his gut," he screwed up the decision as well. Confessing the bungle to Loyola elicited not a reprimand but immediate encouragement to get back in the saddle: "I wish for the future you do, without scruple, as your judgment tells you to do according to the circumstances; rules and ordinations notwithstanding."[38] Nurturing Mannaerts through early fragility paid off handsomely. Years after Loyola's death, Mannaerts was given charge of Jesuit operations in the Netherlands and Belgium, transforming a region in ruins into an operation of seven hundred Jesuits running nearly thirty colleges.

Loyola resolved the complicated management challenge of building responsive, innovative, globally focused teams. It takes not just "lots of delegated authority," as conventional wisdom would suggest. To be sure, innovation and creativity happen when individuals enjoy a wide berth and the managerial support to take risks and experiment. But speed and a global mindset often require the opposite: a centralized authority to weigh opportunities and mobilize resources quickly against emerging opportunities. In other words, speed, innovation, and global focus happen only when lots of delegated authority sits alongside lots of centralized authority.

That's certainly the way Loyola and his cofounders saw it. Holy obedience, the very extreme of tightly centralized authority ("as if he were an old man's staff"), lay beside wide-open self-initiative ("cut your suit according to your cloth; only let us know how you have acted"). Indifference made it work. Self-aware Jesuits stayed focused on their goal (helping souls). They didn't get tripped up confusing the *means* with the goal itself. Take an order today, chart a course tomorrow—just as long as we're heading where we need to go.

Ingenuity blossomed when Jesuits layered the "whole world is our house" spirit on top of an indifferent attitude. Ingenuity inspired the confident optimism that solutions were out there, and with imaginative, out-of-the-box thinking, men like de Nobili and Ricci uncovered those solutions time after time.

THE CHALLENGE REMAINS: INGENUITY IN A WORLD OF CHANGE

"The urgent question of our time is whether we can make change our friend and not our enemy."

Ignatius Loyola could have said something like this while launching his Jesuits into a Europe that had changed more in fifty years than during the previous thousand. But in fact, former United States president Bill Clinton said this in his first inaugural, nearly 450 years after Loyola's death. It's unlikely that the Jesuit-educated Clinton was consciously echoing the change-ready message Loyola hammered into his team. But the former president's observation suggests that we haven't gotten much better at coping with change from the sixteenth century to today.

What was Jesuit ingenuity? In Clinton's terms, making change a friend instead of an enemy. Jesuit ingenuity is the ability to innovate, to absorb new perspectives, to respond quickly to opportunities or threats, and to let go of strategies that no longer work in order to embrace new ones. As Loyola put it, ingenuity is being comfortable traveling through the various regions of the world and using all the means you can to reach your goals.

Jesuits have negotiated change since well before the industrial revolution and continuing through the "e-economy," from a monarchical Europe through a democratic Europe that's seen the birth and death of Communism, from a predominantly Catholic world to a predominantly Christian world to a multicreed world to a largely secularized world.

> Corporate ingenuity is cultivated and won one person at a time. The Jesuit company embraced change because individual Jesuits embraced change.

So what wisdom do they have to teach?

First, that corporate ingenuity is cultivated and won one person at a time. The Jesuit company embraced change because individual Jesuits embraced change. Xavier embraced change by picking up and going where needed at short notice and being confident enough to make major decisions once he arrived. De Nobili embraced change by being imaginative and fearless enough to look at the world from other perspectives and courageous enough to take on the hierarchy in defense of his ideas. Loyola embraced change by trumpeting the goal of flexibility but also walking the walk by delegating power and providing generous personal encouragement to subordinates who assumed that delegated authority.

Jesuit managers focused their energy on freeing recruits from personal obstacles to ingenuity. The now predictable refrain? Self-awareness is the cornerstone of ingenuity. Three aspects of self-awareness are essential for pursuing personal ingenuity:

- indifference-inspired freedom from unhealthy attachments

- knowledge of personal nonnegotiables: the values, goals, and ways of working that are not up for discussion

- confidence to embrace new approaches and explore new ideas or perspectives, born of a "whole world becomes our house" attitude

Indifference enabled the count of Civitella to trade in an Italian noble's lifestyle for a sannyasi's single daily serving of rice. But Jesuit-style indifference is not ultimately about the *material* dimension of trading a European lifestyle for an unfamiliar new-world lifestyle. It's about those internal drives, fears, and prejudices that prevent flexibility and openness. Indifference is seen in the ego health of a Xavier, willing to accept orders and just as ready to turn around and plot his own course. Loyola himself provides the mirror image. The ex–military man, well used to commanding troops, designed a company that focused authority at its center. Yet the same Loyola freed himself from the controlling impulses that inhibit delegation. De Nobili provides the most relevant modern example. His greatest detachment was not from the trappings of a noble lifestyle but from the personal fears that so often cripple initiative: fear of failing, fear of falling out of favor with managers, fear of taking risks—not to mention the considerable fear of looking like a complete idiot in front of peers. Taking risks inevitably exposes us to some or all of these natural fears, and few people detach themselves from them as effectively as de Nobili did.

A second dimension of self-awareness is no less critical to personal ingenuity. Men such as de Nobili, Ricci, and their successors in India and China tested the boundaries of Christian practice and expression in ways that baffled and at times outraged many of their sixteenth- and seventeenth-century contemporaries. Their confidence to do so depended not only on their indifference but also on their ability to identify their nonnegotiables. Some people shrink from change, paralyzed by plain old fear of whatever is different. Others drift aimlessly from one set of values and strategies to another. Both responses—paralysis and incoherent lurching—indicate the same underlying problem: lack of core values and principles. The time to hash these out is not when one is confronted with complicated choices, when one is under stress, or when one is grappling with an urgent problem or opportunity. Those who come to the table with a strong understanding of their nonnegotiables can pounce instinctively on opportunities that suit their broader objectives. Sitting in a Madurai hut with his *kutumi* and *tilakam* would not have been a good moment for de Nobili to begin wondering about core Christian values. He had had that discussion with himself years earlier, most intensively when he and his fellow Jesuit recruits had undertaken their monthlong Spiritual Exercises.

Attaining indifference and knowing nonnegotiables are only preludes to what really brings ingenuity to life. When Nadal told trainees that for men on a journey, the whole world would become their house, he was encouraging far more than mobility alone. He was pronouncing a fundamentally hopeful, optimistic, adventurous, and even playful outlook. Leaders with a "whole world is our house" attitude eagerly look forward to what lies around life's next bend. Ingenuity rests on the conviction that most problems have solutions, and that imagination, perseverance, and openness to new ideas will uncover them.

If ingenuity helped early Jesuits identify counterintuitive, risky strategies that took them far beyond European mainstream culture, their third leadership pillar—love—brought the courage and passion to execute those strategies. Men such as Xavier and de Nobili took enormous personal risks while doing difficult, often lonely work. These Jesuits and others like them energetically took on challenges because they worked in environments charged with trust and mutual support. The next chapter explores this third pillar of Jesuit leadership—the energy, courage, and loyalty Jesuits discovered in a company bound "by greater love than fear."

CHAPTER 8

"Refuse No Talent,
Nor Any Man of Quality"
How Love Uncovers Talent
and Unites Teams

Ignatius Loyola exhorted Jesuit managers to govern "with greater love than fear." Francis Xavier explained that "'Society of Jesus' means to say 'a Society of love and conformity of minds,' and not 'of severity and servile fear.'" Loyola's successor as general, Diego Laínez, wrote to Jesuits in India: "It does not seem necessary to write a special letter to you since I often communicate with your superiors about essential matters. . . . However, I wanted the satisfaction of writing and speaking to you at this time as a mark of my affection for you, whom I carry in my heart, inscribed and impressed upon my soul."[1]

Jesuit correspondence and the *Constitutions* brim with such expressions. The cofounders were determined to enshrine love as a cornerstone of their fledgling company.

Why? Their sentiments were not merely pious echoes of the great Judeo-Christian mandate to "love thy neighbor as thyself." Instead, by relentlessly urging their teams to a generous, wide-ranging vision of love, Loyola and his cofounders tapped an invigorating leadership principle. Love was the glue that unified the

> Love was the lens through which individual Jesuits beheld the world around them. It changed not only the way Jesuits looked at others but *what they saw.* Their vision became more acute, their eyes open to talent and potential.

Jesuit company, a motivating force that energized their efforts. More profoundly, love was the lens through which individual Jesuits beheld the world around them. Loving their superiors, their peers, their subordinates, their enemies, and those they served changed not only the way Jesuits looked at others but *what they saw.* Their vision became more acute, their eyes open to talent and potential.

In short, love-driven leadership is

- the *vision* to see each person's talent, potential, and dignity

- the *courage, passion, and commitment* to unlock that potential

- the resulting *loyalty and mutual support* that energize and unite teams

REFUSING NO TALENT: THE OUTSIDER TURNED LEADER

It must have been quite a conversation stopper.

Jewish people had been *expelled* from Spain, Loyola's homeland, and Rome was on the verge of herding them into ghettos. Most Europeans wouldn't be seen in the company of a Jew, yet here was the Jesuit founder telling dinner companions that Jewish lineage would be a special grace: "Why imagine! That a man could be a kinsman by blood . . . of Christ our Lord."[2]

Loyola was raised in the most militantly anti-Semitic nation in Europe. Most Americans instinctively associate Spanish sovereigns

Ferdinand and Isabella with Columbus's pioneering voyage to the New World in 1492. But their highnesses took other noteworthy royal initiatives that year. They had finally succeeded in vanquishing the Moors in order to unite Spain under their leadership—their *Christian* leadership. The monarchs lost little time underscoring the point with a 1492 decree expelling Jews from their realm. Faced with the ultimatum of convert or flee, as many as fifty thousand Spanish Jews became at least nominally Catholic, and three times as many fled to North Africa, Italy, or elsewhere.

Loyola had been studying in Paris for five years when Diego Laínez, the son of wealthy Castilian merchants, arrived. The two met on Laínez's first day in Paris. It no doubt relieved the new arrival to find a fellow Spaniard who was comfortable navigating the alleyways of the university quarter. But Laínez didn't need help for long. Whether navigating Paris streets or scholastic treatises, Laínez soon outpaced Loyola and was later hailed by one of the cofounders as "endowed with a singular, almost divine, intellect."

But there was something far more noteworthy about Laínez in the particular circumstances of the sixteenth century: he was descended from Jews. His great-grandfather had converted to Christianity, and in the code of the era that made Laínez a *nuevo cristiano* (New Christian). It was not intended as a compliment. Still, *nuevo cristiano* was less offensive than most other labels hung on descendants of Jewish converts to Christianity. Far more popular was a less technical term: *marrano* (swine).

Loyola's Paris circle numbered fewer than half a dozen when Laínez the *marrano* joined them. Xavier was already part of the group; so was the Portuguese Simão Rodrigues, who was chosen to accompany Xavier to India but never made it past Lisbon. A few years later, Loyola, Laínez, Xavier, Rodrigues, and a few others founded the *Compañía de Jesus*, setting Laínez on a most unlikely path. He would not even have been allowed through the door at any other major religious order; they excluded New Christians from theirs ranks. Yet somehow Laínez—together with Loyola and the others—was founding and running a religious order. Moreover, before long Laínez distinguished himself even among the leadership group; according to Loyola, "To no one, not even to Francis Xavier, does the Society owe more than to Master Laínez."[3] So none were surprised when Loyola charged Laínez with oversight of Jesuit Italy. Not only the nerve center of church power, it was far and away the early Jesuits' largest, most important center of operations.

Which isn't to say the job was fun. Xavier in faraway Asia enjoyed free rein to craft Jesuit strategy for an entire hemisphere. Poor Laínez had to run a countrywide operation with his boss, Loyola, sitting across the hall. Two strong leaders sharing one city with overlapping responsibilities isn't typically an ideal formula for smooth collegial relations. Loyola "forgot" to consult Laínez, the country head, before summoning a talented Jesuit from Venice to Rome; Laínez promised Venice an equally talented replacement from Loyola's staff without consulting Loyola.

Laínez began to complain to colleagues that Loyola's meddling was becoming more than a minor irritation. (It's a relief to know that even enlightened, saintly Jesuits fell prey to the same dysfunctions that enliven modern corporate life.) Then one day a stern letter arrived for Laínez from Loyola's secretary. Loyola *was* the general, after all, and publicly badmouthing the boss was no wiser a career move in the sixteenth century than it is in the twenty-first. The letter "clarified" the working relationship between the Jesuit boss and his Italy country manager:

> Our father [i.e., Loyola] is not a little displeased with your reverence, and the more so, that the faults of those who are loved are always more serious to those who love them. . . .
>
> What is more, he has told me to write to you and tell you to attend to your own office, which if you do well, you will be doing more than a little. You are not to trouble yourself in giving your view of his affairs, as he does not want anything of the kind from you unless he asks for it; and much less now than

before you took office, since your administration of your own
province [Italy] has not done much to increase your credit in his
eyes. Examine these mistakes in the presence of God our Lord,
and for three days take some time for prayer to this end. Then
write, if you admit that they are mistakes and faults. Choose
also the penance you think you deserve; write it out and send it
to him. But do no penance in this matter before you receive the
answer of our father.[4]

Laínez didn't have to employ his singular, almost divine intellect to realize that it was time for a helping of humble pie. In his
response, he plunged headlong into overzealous proposals for the
penance he thought he deserved.

I now choose . . . that for the love of our Lord you relieve me of
the care of others, take away my preaching and my study, leaving only my Breviary [i.e., prayer book], and bid me come to
Rome, begging my way, and there put me to work in the kitchen,
or serving table, or in the garden, or at anything else. And when
I am no longer good for any of this, put me in the lowest class of
grammar and that until death, without any more care for me (in
external things), as I have said, than you have for an old broom.
This penance is my first choice.[5]

Loyola was not about to take up an overscrupulous Laínez's
request to beg his way to Rome "to work in the kitchen, or serving
table, or in the garden." Laínez was not going to be underutilized
in a company committed to "refuse no talent, nor any man of
quality." Loyola's anger had probably passed well before Laínez's
penitential letter arrived. If Loyola imposed any punishment at all,
it was nothing so drastic as the over-the-top ideas Laínez had
dreamed up.

Laínez's talent was as clear to his colleagues as it was to Loyola.
When Loyola died, Laínez was elected his successor.

A COMMITMENT TO EXCELLENCE

Laínez, the papal adviser and Italy country manager, was only the most prominent of a long line of New Christian Jesuits. He embodied a principle for Loyola, that a person's qualities were more important than his or her lineage. While other religious companies shunned New Christians, Loyola snapped them up as the Jesuits' gain: uncontested talent for a growing company. Henrique Henriques had been booted out of the Franciscan order upon revelation of his Jewish heritage because Franciscan rules did not allow descendants of Jews or Moors to be members. Loyola scooped him up, eagerly hurdling the additional obstacle of obtaining the Vatican approval that was required before one could admit someone dismissed from another religious company.

Henriques more than vindicated Loyola's trouble. He's an oft-forgotten Jesuit, sandwiched between the company's two more prominent heroes in India—Xavier and de Nobili. But his contributions were no less vital. True, Xavier opened up India for the Jesuits, but it was Henriques who authored the first Tamil grammar ever published in Europe, enabling generations of Jesuits to extend Xavier's legacy productively. De Nobili tested the boundaries of Christian expression by incorporating imagery and language from Hindu classics, but it was Henriques's original Tamil catechism that jump-started de Nobili's work. Granted, Henriques's Tamil wasn't perfect. When he innocently (but naively) chose the word *misei* for "Mass," he left his Tamil audience, already befuddled at the Europeans' physical appearance and strange habits, wondering why the western preachers were continually rattling on about the holy sacrifice of the "mustache" (the meaning of *misei* in Tamil).

The New Christian Jesuit Alexandre de Rhodes made an equally valiant effort to master Vietnamese. Like predecessor colleagues in Japan, China, and India, Rhodes entered Cochin China (southern Vietnam) primed for acculturation. Yet Rhodes made a fundamental contribution to his host culture that surpassed even

Ricci's accomplishments. He helped fashion a romanized script for the Vietnamese language to replace the adopted Chinese characters that had been used up to that point, and centuries later the script was formalized as the *quoc ngu* (national script) of Vietnamese. For his efforts, he won a posthumous tribute accorded very few westerners—a statue commemorating Rhodes was erected in downtown Saigon (now Ho Chi Minh City).

Not only in faraway India and Vietnam but also all across Europe, New Christian Jesuits became prominent drivers of the fast-growing young company's operating style and vision.

The policy of admitting converts didn't go without notice. The manager of the Jesuit college at Córdoba wrote headquarters explaining why students weren't joining the Jesuits upon gradua-tion: "Those possessing the [priestly] vocation enter the Dominican monastery of San Pablo which, they say, is a commu-nity of *caballeros*, whereas in our school only Jews turn Jesuit. Prejudice on this point is so strong that whenever anyone is bold enough to join us, he is looked upon as one who has received the *san-benito* [i.e., the yellow tunic that Inquisition officials draped on false converts from Judaism]."[6]

Despite the pressure, Loyola remained committed to recruiting *aptissimi*, whatever their origin. When the country manager for Spain complained that the liberal attitude toward Jewish candi-dates was jeopardizing the company's reputation at the royal court, he received a tart reply from Loyola's secretary: "If in consequence of the attitude of the Court and King you deem it impossible to admit converts in Spain, send them here as long as they be of good character: In Rome we do not trouble ourselves as to the origins of a man, only his qualities."[7] The underlying message was clear, and Spain continued to admit qualified converts.

The tension in Spain was real and intense, not simply the inven-tion of a weak-willed, anti-Semitic country manager. Loyola got his own earful on the subject from the count of Eboli, one of the coun-try's leading courtiers. But Loyola did not yield: "I am told that

Your Lordship is displeased that we admit so many 'New Christians' to our company. The company may and must not exclude anyone. . . . It may refuse no talent, nor any man of quality, whether he be 'New Christian' or noble knight or another, if his religious comportment is useful and conforms to the universal good."[8]

The watchwords that paced Loyola's team to success are no less relevant to any company today in any industry. Find as many as possible of the very best, the *aptissimi*. And welcome all talent, whether they are "noble knight or another." What separated Loyola's team from the rest was not merely that they were willing to "hire" the talent that other religious orders shunned, but that they *saw* human talent and potential where others didn't even look for it. Love was the guiding vision that enabled them to do so.

THE ESSENCE OF
LOVE-DRIVEN LEADERSHIP

How is it that while most of Christendom looked at Henrique Henriques—or Diego Laínez, for that matter—and saw unworthy converts, Ignatius Loyola saw potential recruits and colleagues? Or that Loyola could so brazenly challenge European power brokers and the mindset of his era by declaring that his Jesuits would "refuse no talent, nor any man of quality, whether he be 'New Christian' or noble knight"?

That's love-driven leadership: the vision to see each person's talent, potential, and dignity; the courage, passion, and commitment to unlock that potential; and the resulting loyalty and mutual support that energize and unite teams.

That vision had first taken hold during the Exercises, when the culminating meditation reminded each Jesuit of his own potential and dignity, of the divine energy giving him "existence, life, sensation, and intelligence; and even further, making [him God's] temple." The meditation then urged each recruit to consider how the very same energy quickened all the earth's creatures, "giving them their existence, conserving them, . . . and so forth."

In other words, Loyola was saying: first look at self; then regard others. No one perceives others accurately without first achieving healthy self-regard. Appreciate your potential, unique talent, and fundamental human dignity. Then see others, their birthright nothing less than the very same human dignity.

Still, love is not merely seeing, but doing something about what one sees. The Contemplation to Attain Love not only endowed Jesuits with a worldview but committed them to make that worldview a living, day-to-day reality for those they encountered: "Love ought to manifest itself more by deeds than by words."[9]

Love as vision and commitment? What about simpler lessons learned in Sunday school, when love entailed less complicated duties, such as being nice to your neighbor? The commitment—indeed, the *passion*—to develop human potential goes further than simply being nice. Love leads to confrontation when human potential is disrespected, wasted, or frustrated. Love emboldened Loyola to challenge the count of Eboli, and love compelled Jesuits to take on colonial settlers in Latin America, as following pages will show. Love, in today's business world, drives the manager who takes the time he or she doesn't have to help the passable employee do better, to help a promising junior employee chart a career path through the company, to initiate the awkward conversation that forces the high-performing boor to confront his or her grating behavior.

> Love, in today's business world, drives the manager who takes the time he or she doesn't have to help the passable employee do better or to initiate the awkward conversation that forces the high-performing boor to confront his or her grating behavior.

Love sometimes even causes confrontation within a family or team. Despite Loyola's generous assessment that to no one else "does the Society owe more than to Master Laínez," it surely didn't always feel that way to Laínez. His run-in with Loyola over staffing was far from the only confrontation he ever had with his mentor. Indeed, an exasperated Laínez once complained to a colleague, "Lord, what have I done against the Society that the saint [Loyola] treats me so?"[10]

What *had* he done? Perhaps nothing more than fall short of the vast potential Loyola saw in him. The Jesuit Pedro Ribadeneira once described Loyola's management approach: "To those who were still children in virtue Ignatius gave milk; but to those who were more advanced, bread with the crust; while he treated the perfect more rigorously still, in order to make them run at full speed towards perfection."[11] This description, if a bit sappy, captures the unmistakable passion for excellence that animates loving leaders. For Loyola, leading was about helping others "run at full speed towards perfection." Or, in other words, it was about the commitment to see others realize their full human potential.

Of course, most tyrannical managers could cook up similar self-justifications. Maybe those maniacs driving the rest of us insane are just helping us run at full speed toward perfection. Yet no one is calling what *they* do love-driven leadership. What makes Loyola different? Perhaps this: his motivation was *developing* others to achieve a common Jesuit agenda, not *using* others to achieve a self-interested agenda. In another part of Laínez's penitential letter to Loyola was its most telling phrase: "I really accept in love what is said in love." And Laínez, like *anyone*, paid attention to what was said in love, that is, by managers who inspired the trust that they were supporting rather than manipulating their subordinates. More important than what a manager says to extract improved performance from team members is the attitude that motivates him, as Loyola's secretary counseled one Jesuit manager: "For

[criticism or feedback] to be successful it will help much if the cor-
rector has some authority, or *acts with great affection, an affection
that can be recognized.* If either of these qualities is absent, the correction will fail" (emphasis added).[12]

What distinguishes love-driven leaders from tyrants? "Great
affection" coupled with the passion to see others "run at full speed
towards perfection." Love-driven leadership is not urging others
forward without concern for their aspirations, well-being, or personal needs. Nor is it being the nice-guy manager who overlooks
underperformance that could damage a subordinate's long-term
prospects. Instead, love-driven leaders hunger to see latent potential blossom and to help it happen. In more prosaic terms, when do
children, students, athletes, or employees achieve their full potential? When they're parented, taught, coached, or managed by
those who engender trust, provide support and encouragement,
uncover potential, and set high standards.

When love-driven leadership takes root on a widespread basis,
it energizes performances and creates unique bonds of team unity.
Early Jesuits were globally dispersed, not conveniently corralled
within monastery walls, as were Benedictine monks. Jesuits were
well-educated, talented, ambitious, and opinionated men. Their
top-down tactics brought regular interaction with influential academic, cultural, and political leaders who competed for their allegiance. In sum, the early Jesuits faced the same obstacles to unity
that any large global company does. How was corporate unity
forged among far-flung, talented Jesuit teams regularly exposed to
competing viewpoints? Was it inspired by a splashy orientation
program outlining the nifty corporate mission? By golden-handcuff
pay packages that tied key Jesuits to the company? By deferred
compensation plans with cliff-vesting provisions? By a monthly
corporate newsletter? These all create ties of a sort, perhaps, but
they fall short of what Loyola wanted—strong bonds of mutual
affection that he called "unity of hearts." And unity of hearts
began with leaders:

Among other qualities, [the general's] good reputation and prestige among his subjects will be very especially helpful; and so will his having and manifesting love and concern for them. . . .

Further help will be found in his having his method of commanding well thought out and organized, through his endeavoring to maintain obedience in the subjects in such a manner that the superior on his part uses all the love and modesty and charity possible in our Lord, so that the subjects can dispose themselves to have always toward their superiors greater love than fear, even though both are useful at times.[13]

The Jesuit team strove for an environment of greater love than fear. Loyola was—and is—challenging the prevailing wisdom that those foolish enough to operate with all the love and modesty and charity possible will only get eaten alive. Niccolò Machiavelli eloquently summarized *that* viewpoint, advising leaders, "If you have to make a choice, to be feared is much safer than to be loved." While Loyola's team focused on human talent, potential, and dignity, Machiavelli saw humanity through a different lens: "For it is a good general rule about men, that they are ungrateful, fickle, liars and deceivers, fearful of danger and greedy for gain. . . . People are less concerned with offending a man who makes himself loved than one who makes himself feared: the reason is that love is a link of obligation which men, because they are rotten, will break any time they think doing so serves their advantage; but fear involves dread of punishment, from which they can never escape."[14]

> The Jesuit team strove for an environment of greater love than fear. Loyola challenged the prevailing wisdom that those foolish enough to operate with all the love and modesty and charity possible will only get eaten alive.

The Jesuits disagreed and took the road of love, to their great success and the benefit of those they served.

WHAT RESEARCHERS SAY
ABOUT MOTIVATION

Four hundred years after Loyola and Machiavelli, social psychologist Douglas McGregor outlined a variation of the ideological conflict between the two. McGregor theorized that managerial behavior toward subordinates often reflects underlying attitudes toward humanity in general. "Theory X" managers assume, often at a barely conscious level, that humans are fundamentally "lazy and must therefore be motivated and controlled."[15] "Theory Y" managers assume that humans "are basically self-motivated and therefore need to be challenged and channeled."[16] For Machiavellian Theory X managers, the challenge is *making them work*. For Loyolan Theory Y leaders, the challenge is making them *want* to work.

It's not some abstract theoretical distinction. MIT economist Paul Osterman's research convinced him that Theory X is playing itself out all the time in the American workplace. "Companies are finding that they can achieve their goals by maintaining a certain level of fear in the work force [i.e., of layoffs] and that leads people to work hard."[17]

Loyola, Machiavelli, and McGregor all agree on this much: our basic worldview—our vision of humanity—will inevitably affect our day-to-day dealings. Our worldviews are rarely as clearly framed as those of Loyola or Machiavelli, but even when ill formed and barely conscious they steer behavior. If humans are "ungrateful, fickle, liars and deceivers, fearful of danger and greedy for gain," you'll treat them accordingly, ever wary of what damage they might wreak if not controlled, prodded, herded, or micromanaged by their bosses. But if a divine energy is giving them "existence, life, sensation, and intelligence; and even further, making [them God's] temple," you're going to support them, encourage them, even—dare one say it—love them.

Both visions of humanity were on display when a small Jesuit team arrived in South America's Río de la Plata region.

A TRIUMPH OF HUMANITY: THE REDUCTIONS IN SOUTH AMERICA

Diego de Torres Bollo was simply obeying the law. But obeying *this* law meant choosing sides. And the side he chose headed the Jesuits down a road with no turning back. By journey's end, thousands would be dead and Torres's Jesuit company would be expelled from a continent.

In 1608, Torres arrived in the Río de la Plata region as the newly appointed manager of a backwater. The Jesuit Paraguay province sprawled across an area almost half the size of continental Europe: all of modern-day Chile, Argentina, Paraguay, and Uruguay and slices of Brazil and Bolivia. The Americas' southern cone had disappointed virtually every gold-hungry colonial to set foot there. Early explorers had named its gateway Río de la Plata (river of silver). Fat chance. Not only wasn't there much *plata,* but there wasn't much of anything else that mattered to Europeans. Where Lima dangled Inca gold, Asunción (the first permanent settlement in the Río de la Plata area) offered little more than mud and mosquitoes.

At the time of Torres's arrival, the *encomienda* system, established to promote colonization of Spain's overseas possessions, was entrenched in the culture. It hadn't been easy for Spain to entice its citizens to settle in South America. A dangerous ocean voyage left settlers with uncertain economic prospects and far removed from friends and family. The *encomienda* system had been one of very few carrots the Spanish crown could wave. *Encomenderos* in South America not only received substantial land grants but also were "entrusted"—the meaning of the root word *encomendar*—

with native people to work that land for a designated period each year. The system offered something for everyone: for the *encomendero*, land and labor; for the Spanish crown, a means of enticing emigrants to settle recently colonized territories; and for the indigenous people, protection and evangelization.

Protection from what, one might wonder. Well, protection from their enemies. Of course, the indigenous people and their ancestors had been protecting themselves against local enemies for centuries before the Spaniards arrived. The only enemies against whom they lacked protection were the Spanish settlers themselves. It was a convenient if odd exercise in circular logic: *encomienda* boiled down to protection *by* the colonials *from* the colonials. Worse yet, it wasn't long before the designated period of annual service started to become "full-time/all the time." The *encomienda* system degenerated into thinly veneered slavery, and to its credit the Spanish crown soon responded with laws aimed at the eventual eradication of the system.

It was eventual, all right. The system was still flourishing in 1609, when Torres declared that he would obey decades-old Spanish laws by ending *encomienda* on Jesuit estates and rehiring the indigenous laborers as salaried workers. It was no gesture of idealistic innocence. Torres was challenging a system that buttressed the whole regional economy, and he surely knew it. That it was one of his very first acts as Jesuit provincial in Paraguay only heightened its symbolic impact.

No one applauded. In fact, those whose economic survival depended on *encomienda* were furious. Torres wrote that the local magistrate made himself scarce to avoid certifying the Jesuit's action, "as he was afraid of the citizens' anger."[18] And the citizens made their displeasure known more directly by "the cutoff of donations and food for some days during which cornmeal was the menu of the [Jesuit] refectory."[19] It was to get worse.

If Torres didn't win many friends by his debut performance, it's not clear he much cared. His sights weren't set on the one or two thousand Spaniards and Creoles hunkered down in Asunción, Córdoba, or Buenos Aires, but on a population at least one hundred times larger and scattered all over the Río de la Plata region. The Guaraní, Guaycurú, and other indigenous tribes weren't very likely to come calling at Jesuit houses in Asunción or elsewhere. So Torres dispersed his Jesuits along the Paraguay and Paraná Rivers to find them. After establishing trust with local tribes, each Jesuit team worked with a tribe to construct a small settlement. The Jesuits called these towns *reducciones* (reductions) after their aspiration to "reduce" the seminomadic tribes to permanent settlements. One of the very first settlements was christened "San Ignacio," a name presumably chosen by the Jesuits and not by the Guaraní.

Were the expeditions dangerous? Probably. Torres reported to Rome that one team worked in a region menaced by savages "so cruel that they devour those slain in battle and make flutes of their shinbones and mugs from the skulls."[20] Still, everything is relative. The Jesuits might well have reasoned that whatever dangers the South American jungles harbored were nothing compared to what they had suffered at the hands of their fellow Europeans. In the more than century-long history of the Guaraní missions, twenty-six Jesuits suffered violent deaths; but in only one year, Europeans had massacred exactly twice that many Jesuits. In 1570, a Huguenot corsair had intercepted a ship transporting Jesuits to Brazil. Forty Jesuits were dumped overboard, some beheaded first, others with limbs hacked off. By the end the pirates must have grown bored or simply exhausted by their carnage; they dumped the last few of the forty overboard while they were still alive, leaving them to wade through the blood slick left by their dead and dying colleagues. Maybe it was done for sport, for the amusement of seeing what would happen once the blood in the water attracted nonhuman predators. As it happened, another dozen Jesuits traveling to Brazil over the following year also lost their lives to pirate raiders: fifty-two in all, twice the number that fell working in the reductions.

Of course, the number of Jesuits savaged by European pirates or Amerindians was miniscule compared to the number of indigenous people killed by Europeans. Torres's colleagues knew the people who needed protection were the Guaraní, not the Jesuits themselves. So Torres attempted a strategy that amounted to starting from scratch. He negotiated with the crown to obtain protection for the Guaraní settlements from so-called civilized Europeans. The Jesuits settled with the Guaraní in newly built cities that were subject directly to the Spanish crown and far removed from the control and influence of Spanish settlements— and from the *encomienda* system.

How well did the Jesuits and their Guaraní partners do? To be sure, the Jesuit vision was far from perfect. Whatever liberties the reductions afforded the Guaraní came within a patronizing system that hardly granted them total human respect and freedom. Still, the Jesuits' visionary, courageous experiment shamed the practices and mindset of their seventeenth-century contemporaries. Histories have heaped praise on the Jesuit effort, the titles alone telling the story: *The Lost Paradise* and *A Vanished Arcadia*. Even Voltaire, no great friend of what he called "that stupid power, the [Catholic] church," hailed the reductions as "a triumph of humanity [that] expiates the cruel deeds of the earliest conquerors."

Musicians, astronomers, and authors: Realizing human potential

The Tyrolean Antonio Sepp could attest to this triumph of humanity. Sepp had graduated alongside other musical prodigies from the Viennese court school of Les Petits Chanteurs only to choose an unusual career path—as a Jesuit and as maestro of a reduction conservatory. Years after his schooling in Vienna and on an entirely different continent, Sepp reported that his conservatory at Yapeyú de los Reyes had churned out "the following future music masters: six trumpeters, four organists, eighteen cornetists, ten bassoonists."[21] In *one year*, that is. Sepp had known more than his share of talented musicians in his youth, so presumably he had some basis for comparison when noting, "The characteristic of [the Guaraní's] genius is in general music. There is no instrument whatsoever that they cannot learn to play in a short time. And they do it with the skill and delicacy that one admires in the most gifted masters."[22] Perhaps Sepp lacked objectivity. He was their teacher, after all. But Sepp wasn't the only aficionado of Guaraní talent, nor was his tutelage the source of their musical genius. Years before Sepp ever set foot in South America, the governor of Buenos Aires had reported to Spain on a musical troupe from Yapeyú, "outstanding in their music and dances as though they had been educated at the court of Your Majesty, and all that in so few years."[23]

Buenaventura Suárez also witnessed the triumph of humanity. The great astronomer and mathematician Clavius had envisioned his Jesuit scientific protégés "distributed in various nations and kingdoms like sparkling gems, to the great honour of the Society." It wasn't only his protégés at the astronomical bureau in Beijing who made that vision a reality. A hemisphere away, Suárez, the region's first native-born astronomer, was complementing his Beijing colleagues' work with equally accurate observations of the southern skies. From an observatory planted in the middle of the jungle at the San Cosme reduction, with telescope lenses fashioned from polished crystalline rock, the Jesuit and his Guaraní team recorded and traded calculations with astronomers in Sweden, Russia, and China.

But perhaps those who could testify most eloquently to the triumph of humanity are those Guaraní who for the first time in their long history had their own written language with which to do so. Long before Buenos Aires boasted a printing office, the Austrian Jesuit J. B. Neumann constructed the first printing press in the Río de la Plata region out of wooden frames and tin type. But before Neumann could shape his tin letters, someone had to shape the language. The Creole Jesuit Antonio Ruiz de Montoya reduced

The product of love: Realizing human potential

Shown here are examples of the art and architecture created by Guaraní Indians of the Paraguay reductions. With the Jesuit expulsion from South America, most of these settlements were abandoned and fell into decay. Ruins and artifacts give eloquent if silent testimony to the unparalleled achievements of the Guaraní craftspeople and their Jesuit collaborators.

dozens of disparate dialects into a standard, unified Guaraní language. It became the basis of one of the very few indigenous languages today to be formally recognized as a national language in Latin America. Nicolas Yapuguay's Guaraní sermons and commentaries made him only the most famous of various published Guaraní authors.

Of course, people do not live on music, science, and literature alone. Guaraní craftspeople found time to fashion musical instruments and observatory equipment only after siting, surveying, engineering, and building their reductions. More than thirty reductions housed more than a hundred thousand Guaraní across a broad swath of modern Paraguay, Argentina, and Brazil. Each reduction accommodated up to a thousand families and the two Jesuits who served them. Interaction with the colonials had brought little good to the Guaraní, so Torres had instructed his teams to "with courage, prudence and tact prevent [colonials] entering the reduction."[24] As a result the Guaraní made their towns as completely self-supporting as possible.

Letters home from Sepp, the conservatory maestro, described vibrant, fully functioning, self-contained communities: "After the sick I visit the offices: first the school, where the boys are instructed in reading and writing. . . . I also visit my musicians, singers, trumpets, hautboys, etc. On certain days I instruct some Indians in dancing. . . . After that I go among the workmen, to the brick makers and tile-makers, the bakers, smiths, joiners, carpenters, painters, and above all the butchers who kill fifteen or sixteen oxen a day."[25]

Sepp the priest, counselor, music teacher—and dance teacher? Is there anything the reductions Jesuits *didn't* do? Not really, it seems: a Czech Jesuit's reduction memoirs explained how to cope with jaguar encounters: "Direct [a stream of urine] into the eyes of a tiger threatening you at the foot of a tree and you are safe: the beast will immediately take to flight."[26] Presumably he was relating local folk wisdom rather than personal experience—but who knows.

Unfortunately, the Jesuits discovered no such deterrent for the Guaraní's most virulent predators—the colonists. For whether the Jesuits did indeed create a utopia, it was smack in the middle of what would become a living hell. Voltaire's generous assessment that the reductions somehow expiated "the cruel deeds of the earliest conquerors" was a bit naive. The earliest conquerors were long dead when the first reduction opened, but the cruel deeds were yet to shift into high gear.

It was the Jesuits themselves who unwittingly helped set the table for the worst of those cruel deeds. Across the ill-defined border established by the Treaty of Tordesillas, in Portuguese territory, teams of Jesuits had been serving Brazil's indigenous people with the same visionary commitment as that of their colleagues on the reductions. The year 1570 proved a particularly bittersweet one for these Jesuits in Brazil: the awful massacre of their forty seaborne colleagues by French pirates had come in the same year as a bold legislative coup. Jesuits lobbying against the mistreatment of Indians in Brazil had moved King Sebastian of Portugal to outlaw virtually all enslavement of the colony's indigenous people. He entrusted welfare of the native people to the Jesuits, who had already begun creating landed communities, *aldeias,* to house and employ them; going forward, plantation owners would have to *pay* for indigenous labor by negotiating wages through each *aldeia*'s managers.

It was a stunningly unpopular decree. Sugar cane cultivation had allowed long-suffering Brazilian settlers to finally glimpse some hint of prosperity. The king's edict now threatened the engine of that prosperity, the slave labor that made the business profitable. It had been challenging enough to maintain an adequate slave labor force even *before* the royal decree. Native populations all across the Americas were perishing under the onslaught of imported European diseases. According to one estimate, for example, the Peruvian population dropped from three million to slightly more than one million in only sixty years (1520–80). There were similar, if not so drastic, stories about populations all over the continent. Free labor was already dying (literally), and now King Sebastian was ruling Brazil's indigenous people off limits.

Decades later, however, an unanticipated, far more convenient labor source fell into the plantation owners' laps. What the Brazil Jesuits had snatched away from the slave owners, the Paraguay Jesuits now seemed to dangle in front of them. *Bandeirantes* (slave raiders) from São Paolo had long hunted Guaraní tribes in the Spanish territory east of the Paraná River. It was unrewarding work, hacking deep into unfamiliar terrain in search of nomadic tribespeople to take into slavery. But thanks to the success of the reductions, in the early 1600s the *bandeirantes* stumbled upon thousands of Guaraní in settled communities within a hundred miles of São Paolo. The Jesuit vision of self-sufficient Guaraní communities had overlooked a key ingredient: defense.

An awful irony slowly unfolded. The Brazil Jesuits' success in protecting local indigenous groups from slavery had only fueled the search for slaves farther afield: in Africa and in South America's Spanish colonies. And the Paraguay Jesuits' efforts to liberate and settle the Guaraní had increased the Guaraní's vulnerability to *bandeirante* raids. The good fathers had unwittingly made the Guaraní sitting ducks for slave hunters swooping down from São Paolo. Between 1628 and 1631, more than sixty thousand Guaraní were captured and sold in Brazilian slave markets. Thousands more were killed during slave raids or forced marches, and just as many died during the Jesuits' hurriedly organized forced evacuations from reductions bordering Portuguese territory.

No help came from the Spanish colonial administration in Asunción. What was to be gained by protecting the Guaraní? The Jesuits had released and shielded them from *encomienda*. The Guaraní towns traded little with the colonials, indeed *competed* with them in yerba maté export trade. The only possible support was across an ocean: the Spanish king and the pope. And it wasn't as if the Jesuits could fax Europe requesting a cease and desist order. Years passed before reductions Jesuits reached Europe to plead the Guaraní case. For Jesuit Antonio Ruiz de Montoya, the South American–born compiler of the first Guaraní dictionary and grammar, his European odyssey on behalf of the Guaraní was no boondoggle. He wrote morosely to colleagues back in South America, "Not for me all this bustle, hand-kissing, courtesies, waste of time, and especially having my mind occupied with business, anxieties, and projects, which rarely come to anything. In sum, Father mine, I remain here an exile. Not a day goes by but for my consolation I imagine they are already taking me to the ship [to return to South America]."[27]

Depressed or not, the Jesuit envoys achieved their objective with the assistance of well-connected European colleagues who helped them navigate diplomatic Rome and the Spanish court. The papal bull *Commissum Nobis* recounted the brutal treatment of the Guaraní before commanding the Portuguese procurator general to "severely prohibit anyone from reducing to slavery, selling, buying, exchanging, giving away, separating from wives and children, depriving of their property, taking away to other places, depriving of liberty in any way and keeping in servitude said Indians."[28]

Not that anyone in São Paolo had the slightest intention of abandoning slaving.

Promulgation of the papal bull in São Paolo elicited no remorse or compliance, only demands to oust the meddlesome Jesuits. They had wreaked havoc through King Sebastian's 1570 decree, outlawing enslavement of indigenous people native to Portugal's Brazilian territory, and now the Jesuits had compounded that offense by inducing the pope to declare indigenous groups in Spanish territory off-limits to Portuguese slave traders as well. Jesuit houses in Rio de Janeiro and São Paolo were attacked by outraged colonials. As Brazilian settlers ignored the papal decree, it seemed Jesuit diplomacy had succeeded mostly in angering the colonial slaveholders and in whipping slave fever into an unprecedented frenzy. Less than a year after the bull's publication in São

Paolo, a huge slaving party of five hundred *bandeirantes* and three thousand Tupi Indian warrior allies sailed toward Guaraní territory in a flotilla of hundreds of boats.

When love meant war

In retrospect, the raid of the *bandeirantes* proved Jesuit diplomacy spectacularly effective, albeit not quite in the way that the pope, king, or Jesuit diplomats themselves had envisioned. For this time, it was not the Guaraní but their enemies who were the sitting ducks. Absent the papal incitement, it's unlikely the *bandeirantes* would ever have mounted so massive a raiding party as the one that furiously paddled down the Uruguay River toward Guaraní lands—and into a waiting ambush. The Jesuit emissaries in Europe hadn't been the only Jesuits at work. Back in the reductions, their colleagues hadn't waited for royal permission before arming the Guaraní. The legacy of military men turned Jesuits hadn't ended with Loyola and Goes: Jesuit and ex-soldier Domingo Torres brushed up on long-dormant skills to help redress the one missing element of Guaraní self-sufficiency. His Guaraní militia destroyed the slaving party during the weeklong battle of Mborore.

If the Jesuits and the Guaraní had fashioned a utopia with their reductions, from this battle forward the communities bore the very nonutopian marks of civilization elsewhere. Guaraní militias went into battle at least fifty times over the following decades while struggling to defend their way of life. They regularly beat back incursions by slave raiders and hostile neighboring tribes. But frequently they were called into battle by a Spanish colonial government that at last appreciated the Guaraní—though perhaps cynically—as an effective buffer against Portuguese forays onto Spanish territory.

The Guaraní towns thrived for more than a century after Mborore. Not until February 10, 1756, did they finally meet their match, when joint Spanish and Portuguese forces fell upon them

in one of the two countries' few cooperative ventures since dividing up the world in the Treaty of Tordesillas.

Border instability in the region threatened not just the Guaraní
but the commercial interests of Spain and Portugal. So in 1750,
ambassadors engaged in a round of remedial horse-trading over
Guaraní native land. The Guaraní weren't invited to negotiate
what became the 1750 Boundary Treaty, just as they hadn't been
invited to Tordesillas. The new treaty endorsed Spanish claims to
the Colonia region near Asunción while ceding to Portugal land
housing seven reductions. But no one could claim that the treaty
didn't consider the Guaraní. The negotiators remembered the
tribes, all right, in Article XVI: "The missionaries will leave with all
their movable property, taking with them the Indians to re-settle
in Spanish territories. . . . The villages, with their church, houses,
buildings and property and the ownership of the land shall be
given to the Portuguese."[29] Oddly enough, the two colonial powers
had somehow found it within themselves to resent the Guaraní for
the inevitable outcome of their own sloppy, arrogant deal-making
at Tordesillas.

Neither the Guaraní nor the Jesuits saw much justice in the
treaty. The Guaraní prepared to defend the cities they had built
rather than conveniently disappearing to suit the drafters of
Article XVI. The colonial powers grew outraged with Jesuit and
Guaraní stonewalling of what, after all, was a perfectly legal treaty
concluded by two sovereign states. Eventually Portugal and Spain
did something about it. On February 10, 1756, the colonial powers ended their joint campaign against the Guaraní with a glorious
victory. Three Spaniards and two Portuguese were killed; about fifteen hundred Guaraní died.

That great imaginary Tordesillas treaty line that divided the
globe came back to haunt the Jesuits as well. Tordesillas had
underwritten the legitimacy of Portuguese conquest, and
Portuguese conquest had afforded Xavier and his Jesuit colleagues
their precarious leap into the world beyond Europe. But by the

Guaraní War, the "learned clerics of exemplary life" that had so impressed King John III of Portugal had become a major irritant. The ranks of aggrieved Jesuit enemies were swelling, and the Jesuit general was preoccupied with deeper worries than defending the Guaraní against Spain and Portugal. Seventy Jesuits manning the reductions met to craft formal protests against the two European powers' treatment of the Guaraní. A century earlier the Jesuit diplomatic machine in Europe had gone to work on behalf of the Guaraní; this time the Paraguay Jesuits were muzzled and ordered by their general to stand down.

When the Tordesillas negotiators signed their 1494 treaty, they had no idea what lay across the ocean in South America. Strangely, the Spanish negotiators in 1750 still hadn't managed—or bothered—to understand just what exactly they had blithely signed away to Portugal. Only after the ink had dried did they begin to learn. The Spanish governor of Montevideo first toured the San Miguel reduction only after the new border treaty was a done deal. He was flabbergasted by what he saw: "Surely our people in Madrid are out of their senses to deliver up to the Portuguese this town which is second to none in Paraguay."[30]

The Jesuit/Guaraní utopia suffered a second blow when the Jesuits themselves were entirely expelled from the territory within a decade of the Guaraní War. The reductions slowly decayed. Some of the Guaraní consented to resettlement, many drifted out of the reductions and resumed a seminomadic lifestyle, and others were pressed into slavery. Some of the reductions became ghost towns, others the basis for new cities under Spanish or Portuguese colonial administration.

Still, a century later enough remained for a Swiss visitor to discern a clear fault line in the Trinidad reduction: "The houses from the Jesuit period were in cut stone and roofed with tiles, while the later buildings were of clay and straw."[31] Trinidad streets were paved and arcaded, while dirt streets dominated the capital of Asunción. Yet although the Guaraní might have outbuilt and outcivilized their enemies, they lacked the resources to outfight them.

In 1537, Pope Paul III had unequivocally condemned New World slavery in the bull *Sublimis Deus*. He didn't take much for granted, starting with a pretty basic assertion: "The Indians themselves are true men."[32] Few of his readers saw it that way; the Jesuit pioneers of the reductions did.

The reductions drew Jesuit volunteers from more than thirty countries—some were native-born South Americans, such as Antonio Ruiz de Montoya and Buenaventura Suárez, while others came from Spain, Italy, Portugal, Austria, Ireland, and two dozen other countries. Each came with a vision refined by the Contemplation to Attain Love. Unlike most other colonials in the Río de la Plata region, they were willing to see true men and women *as* true men and women—and to commit themselves with courage and passion to helping them explore their human potential.

HOW DOES LOVE MAKE A COMPANY BETTER?

We don't live in the romantic world of heroic clerics building a utopia in an era long gone. We live a decidedly less utopian struggle to get through a day peopled with those who vindicate Machiavelli more often than Loyola. And let's face it—few are rushing forward to champion love-driven leadership in the real world. Only crackpots or entrepreneurs burnishing edgily eccentric reputations would dare prattle on about love in today's antiseptic corporate environment.

A quick scan of the management bookshelf reveals guidance on nearly every imaginable human emotion and behavior in the workplace: aggression, deception, joy, anger, envy, greed, play, war, and so on. But the *L* word crops up rarely, and then only in fleeting, vaguely embarrassed snippets. *In Search of Excellence* author

Thomas Peters tentatively floated the notion in two subsequent works but left it playfully light and nonthreatening. In *A Passion for Excellence*, Peters stresses *loving what you do*, hailing McDonald's impresario Ray Kroc's "love stories about hamburgers." In *The Circle of Innovation*, he devotes a full chapter to the theme "love all, serve all." But he's quoting the credo of the Hard Rock Cafe, and the "all" we're supposed to love are our customers (just as the Hard Rock Cafe does?). The promisingly titled *Getting Employees to Fall in Love with Your Company* advocates what turns out to be a pretty one-sided love affair. There are five terrific suggestions for getting employees to fall in love—but no rallying cry for management to require it. *The Guru Guide* gleans insights from more than seventy superstars of management consultancy, crediting one with the unconventional belief that "leadership requires love." Aha, we're on to it! Alas, anyone hoping to see the idea developed—or even find out which guru believes it—reads three hundred more pages of that book in vain.

Why is it that military imagery provides comfortable metaphors for what we do all day (take, for instance, *The Art of War for Executives*), while "love talk" remains a third rail of leadership punditry? Here's one reason. We've noted that the very notion of leadership has progressively been hijacked by corporate-speak. Corporate managers and their consultants or academic advisers are those most obsessed with the leadership gap. And the corporate work force is the greatest consumer of leadership literature. So it's no surprise that it's written in terms that appeal to a corporate audience.

And what appeals to corporate America? Let's be honest. All claims about our enlightened, inclusive business sensibilities notwithstanding, U.S. corporate culture remains a towel-snapping, take-no-prisoners macho arena. Is it really that shocking, then, that our leadership role models strut forward flashing macho credentials? Heading the guru list by a wide, wide margin are the sports coaches and superstars: Pat Riley, Phil Jackson, Coach K,

Joe Torre, and so on. Trailing not far behind are the military leaders: Sun Tzu, Attila, Patton, Ulysses S. Grant, Robert E. Lee, and on and on. The work you're reading is no less guilty of hailing a he-mannish leader as a role model. Loyola's own machismo was established many chapters before I started talking about this love stuff. Remember, he hasn't gone soft on us. He's the same guy who was tough enough to take a cannonball at Pamplona and complete a solo trek from Spain to Jerusalem.

Anyone bold enough to proclaim even softly the very unmacho love idea might want an unimpeachable spokesperson. Who better than legendary football coach and universally acclaimed "man's man" Vince Lombardi? At least three separate works have quoted the same excerpt from a speech Lombardi once gave to the American Management Association. And now at least four. Enumerating the qualities of winning leaders, Lombardi concluded, "And one other, love. The love I'm speaking of is loyalty, which is the greatest of loves. Teamwork, the love that one man has for another and that he respects the dignity of another. The love that I am speaking of is charity. . . . Heartpower is the strength of your company."[33]

Rhetoric reserved for Lombardi's off-season musings on the rubber chicken circuit? No, Lombardi pitched this vision not only to finely groomed business executives but also to the sweaty behemoths who anchored the Green Bay Packers' offensive line. In fact, with his own team, cliché fell away, revealing Lombardi's version of "love ought to manifest itself more by deeds than by words."

One retired Packer remembered how Lombardi demanded every player treat each teammate: "You've got to love him, and maybe that love would enable you to help him."

One retired Packer remembered how Lombardi demanded every player treat each teammate: "You've got to love him, and maybe that love would enable you to help him."[34] Where did Lombardi develop his vision of love-driven leaders? Most likely it was wisdom won through years of coaching and motivating teams. But it may not be entirely coincidental that Lombardi received a Jesuit education.

Well, corporate Pooh-Bahs and pundits may be shy to promote the leadership strategy of engaging others with a positive, supportive (read: loving) attitude, but plenty of others haven't been so reticent. In fact, the bottom-line benefits of love-driven leadership seem obvious wherever humans interact intensively, *except* in the workplace. The one "team" in which virtually everyone has participated is a family. Few would suggest that loveless families function as efficiently as loving families do, or that they are as supportive, motivating, or satisfying. Nor would anyone argue that threatening or brutally competitive schools are our most successful ones. Students learn best and produce most in environments that provide genuine support, care, and encouragement; why have we somehow convinced ourselves that our adult needs are so different? The Jesuit principle of love-driven leadership proposes nothing more radical than absorbing the obvious wisdom of these other human environments.

How did love make the Jesuit company better? And how does love make any company better?

A company that implements love-driven leadership

- refuses no talent, nor anyone of quality:
  Love-driven companies recognize, honor,
  and hire the talent that others shun or
  overlook—in Loyola's time, a Laínez, a
  Henriques, a Rhodes. Or today, those
  with the "wrong" pedigree, skin color,
  accent, background, or education.

- runs with all speed toward perfection:
  Love-driven managers are dedicated to
  developing untapped potential rather

than presiding over a Darwinian sink-or-
swim workplace.

- operates with greater love than fear:
  Love-driven environments make people
  want to work instead of merely making
  them work.

The real payoff is the energy and loyalty catalyzed by environments of greater love than fear. Terms such as *teamwork* and *team
spirit* fail to capture the attitude among Xavier's Asia team: "I thus
am coming to a close without being able to stop writing about the
great love which I have for all of you as individuals and in general.
If the hearts of those who love each other . . . could be seen in this
present life, believe me, my dearest brothers, that you would see
yourselves clearly in mine."[35]

Teams cemented by such mutual regard effortlessly outdo most
organizations, which settle for the basic teamwork behaviors:
respecting colleagues, listening to their views, sharing information
proactively, giving others the benefit of the doubt, mentoring the
newcomers. Anyone who's worked in a close-knit, loyal, trusting
team—be it a family, sports team, or circle of friends—knows that
such minimal teamwork standards pale when compared with the
behaviors of unified, love-driven teams. Unlike energy-sapping
workplaces riddled with backstabbing and second-guessing, environments of greater love than fear *generate* energy. Team members
in such environments are supported by colleagues who want them
to succeed and help them succeed. Individuals perform best when
they are respected, valued, and trusted by those who genuinely
care for their well-being. Loyola was wise enough to perceive this
bundle of winning attitudes as the essence of "love," secure enough
to call it such, and eager to tap its energizing, unifying power for
the Jesuit team.

Just as love united the Jesuit team, it also profoundly colored
their appreciation of those whom they served. The Paraguay
reductions were a Jesuit labor of love not in any sentimental sense

but precisely because love enhanced those Jesuits' ability to perceive the dignity and human potential of the Guaraní—and that
these were assaulted and squandered under the colonial
encomienda system. Love gave Jesuits the vision to see that wasted
potential; heroism spurred them to do something about it.

Not long before Xavier departed for China in late 1552, he
received a letter from Loyola. He dashed off a response:

> Lord knows how my soul was consoled at receiving news of your
> health and life, which are so dear to me; and among many other
> holy words and consolations of your letter, I read those last
> which said, "Completely yours, without my ever being able to
> forget you at any time, Ignatio." Just as I read those words with
> tears, so I am writing these with tears, thinking of the time past
> and of the great love which you always showed and are still
> showing towards me. . . .
>
> Your holy charity writes to me of the great desires which you
> have to see me before you leave this life. God our Lord knows
> the impression which these words of such great love made upon
> my soul and how many tears they cost me every time that I
> remember them.[36]

No wonder Loyola considered his other organizational innovations insignificant compared to love-driven leadership. The pre-
amble to his Jesuit *Constitutions* says as much, pointing Jesuits to a
guiding principle far more important than any rule they will find
in its nearly three hundred pages: "What helps most on our part
toward [the preservation, direction, and carrying forward of the
Jesuits] must be, more than any exterior constitution, *the interior
law of charity and love*" (emphasis added).[37]

That interior law of charity and love begins with vision. Long
before love is a corporate virtue that improves team performance,
it is a personal leadership stance. The love-driven leader possesses

the vision to see and engage others as they are, not through the cultural filters, prejudices, or narrow-mindedness that diminishes them. Early modern Europe saw Amerindians as "beasts of the forest incapable of understanding the Catholic faith, . . . squalid savages, ferocious and most base, resembling wild animals in everything but human shape."[38] Love-led Jesuits from more than two dozen countries instead found in Amerindians that same divine energy that gave them "existence, life, sensation, and intelligence" and made them God's temple.

If the interior law of charity and love begins with vision, it is completed in action: "Love ought to manifest itself more by deeds than by words." It doesn't take an enterprise the scale of the Guaraní reductions to achieve what Voltaire called "a triumph of humanity." Innumerable triumphs of humanity occur every day when parents, teachers, coaches, and others invest themselves selflessly in developing others.

But triumphs of humanity are also evident in actions we are too hesitant to label as love: in the dedication of managers to their subordinates, in the loyalty and support of teammates. Those who would rather help peers succeed than watch them fail are creating environments of greater love than fear. And so are all who make outsiders feel welcomed and supported. Such people are motivated by more than a desire to "do a good job"; some profounder, more personal motive drives them, and their workplace interactions are only one expression of a more fundamental commitment to respect and support those they encounter. Those who treat others with respect and love are leading the way to environments of greater love than fear, where many more people will enjoy the chance to achieve their full human potential.

And everyone knows such leadership is needed. So too are more triumphs of humanity, including those of the grand scale once attempted by seventeenth-century Jesuits in Paraguay. Whatever the imperfections of their vision, they saw further than did their contemporaries. And that's what love-driven leaders do. They see further. They move themselves beyond what blocks our vision in order to see what a fairer, more welcoming world might look like. They point the way to a future in which true men and women will enjoy greater chances to reach their potential. And leaders guided by the resolve that "love ought to manifest itself more by deeds than by words" help create that better future.

Creating a better future—that's quite a task. How much difference can any one person make?

Ask the heroes.

CHAPTER 9

"An Uninterrupted Life of Heroic Deeds"
How Heroic Leaders Envision the Impossible—and Do It

A t a company that I'll call XYZ Telco, unionized telecommunications operators downed headsets and went on strike, citing job stress as a key grievance. The beef originated with customer service representatives, those frontline warriors charged with placating the thousands who call each day complaining about incorrect billings, lost dial tones, and tardy repairpeople.

As if these beleaguered customer service reps didn't have enough trouble, they had recently been presented with "new operating procedures," no doubt crafted by bureaucrats squirreled away in an ivory tower, well insulated from the realities of dealing with angry customers. Created to inculcate stated company values of integrity, respect, imagination, passion, and service, the new operating procedures instructed customer service representatives to end each call with a scripted question: "Did I provide you with outstanding service today?"

One supposes that the master motivators who devised this question expected to inspire the very same outstanding service it inquired about. Needless to say, it only succeeded in unleashing renewed torrents of complaints on these already put-upon souls in customer service. It didn't help customers, nor did it win employees over to the company's values or vision. The local union president commented, "Employees understand the values statement. But I don't know that they believe the company is following its own words. . . . People sort of just look at the values statement and go, 'yeah, right.' It's just a piece of paper."[1]

One thing was right with the picture; a lot more was wrong. Excellence doesn't occur accidentally, so we can at least credit XYZ management with consciously targeting outstanding service as a goal. So far so good. But things drift downhill from there. First, there was the script. How many of the scriptwriters themselves had ever been inspired to excellent performance by a memo instructing them to perform excellently? None, of course. Why did they imagine the customer service reps would react differently? Outstanding service might have been the *company's* mission, but no process had made it meaningful to individual employees.

> They had been set up to fail—or at least to feel like failures—not positioned to succeed.

Second, even if XYZ's operators had enthusiastically embraced the mission, they weren't empowered to do much about it. Irritated customers were unlikely to feel they had received outstanding service no matter what the operators did, because the operators lacked the means to address root problems. They had been set up to fail—or at least to feel like failures—not positioned to succeed.

Finally, and most damaging of all, managers didn't model the ambitions they preached. Operators didn't see their managers "following the company's words" and thus became cynics, drawing the logical conclusion that the values statement was just a piece of paper.

LEADERSHIP THE JESUIT WAY

The challenge, whether for individuals, teams, or whole companies, is how to move from cynical, going-through-the-motions performance to motivated, even heroic, performance. What separated the early Jesuit team from XYZ Telco? What made one an organization in which so many were fired up and convinced that they were contributing to the "greatest enterprise that there is in the world today" while the other suffered from weak management? Both companies aspired to outstanding performance within their fields. But the similarities end there. The Jesuit team took at least three steps that XYZ Telco didn't to turn their aspiration into a reality:

- First, they invited recruits to turn a corporate aspiration into a personal mission.

- Second, they created a company culture that stressed heroism, modeling the virtue themselves.

- Third, they gave each person an opportunity to enlarge himself by contributing meaningfully to an enterprise greater than his own interests.

Loyola's most powerful practical insight about heroic leadership was that it is *self*-motivated. The Spiritual Exercises enabled each recruit to personalize the company's mission. Invited to "go further still" than wholehearted service, each recruit made the personal choice to respond. Unlike the employees of XYZ Telco, the Jesuit recruit wasn't simply handed his company's vision. Moreover, he had to figure out what going further than wholehearted service—the *magis*—would mean in the concrete circumstances of his life. The dynamic of the Exercises highlights a key difference between heroic and run-of-the-mill organizations: widely dispersed leadership in which each person considers, accepts, shapes, and transforms a general mission into a personal one.

Of course, those who made the personal commitment needed support. Jesuit recruits found that support in constant reinforcement from the top. Jesuit leaders relentlessly reinforced the commitment to excellence and to (holy) ambition. Loyola's exhortation to a team in Portugal was typical: "No commonplace achievement will satisfy the great obligations you have of excelling. If you consider the nature of your vocation, you will see that what would not be slight in others would be slight in you."[2] His colleague Jerónimo Nadal rendered it in more concrete, personal terms for trainees in Spain: "The Society wants men who are as accomplished as possible in every discipline that helps it in its purpose. Can you become a good logician? Then become one! A good theologian? Then become one! . . . and do not be satisfied with doing it half-way!"[3]

Those words energized Jesuit teams *only* because they saw the Loyolas, Nadals, and others modeling the sentiments they preached. Personal commitment evaporates into cynicism when, as in XYZ Telco, individuals see managers talking the talk but not walking the walk. As it happened, the early Jesuit team boasted plenty of heroes walking the walk and made sure every Jesuit heard about those heroes. Esprit de corps soared as letters from the field, copied in Rome, were circulated throughout the Jesuit world. Jesuits in Brazil conveyed the impact of one such letter from Japan, describing how even its late-night arrival couldn't keep them from reading it: "From [midnight] till morning, there was none who could sleep, because the Father Provincial began at once to read the letters." After devouring what they called the "great news from Japan," the Brazil Jesuits wrote to headquarters, urging them to continue forwarding such reports and explaining that the "consolations" they derived from hearing of colleagues' exploits "excel all others."

If making the mission personal and creating a supportive culture were two ingredients of the Jesuit formula for instilling heroism, the third ingredient was giving each individual the
opportunity to contribute meaningfully. Jesuits in Brazil were not
just sitting around reading about what their heroic colleagues
were doing. After all, their own letters to Rome boasted of work
so satisfying that it made them feel that they were "working to
lay the foundations of houses which will last as long as the world
endures." They had committed themselves to "go further still"
than whole-hearted service, and unlike the employees at XYZ
Telco, they were given a meaningful opportunity to do just that.
The Jesuits believed what behavioral psychologist Frederick
Herzberg would later observe: "You cannot motivate anyone to
do a good job unless he has a good job to do."[4]

The Jesuits had many good jobs to do—and heroes emerged to
fill them. First were those who conceived a revolutionary new
company—Loyola, of course, but Xavier and Laínez as well.
Then there were scientific and cultural pioneers—Ricci, Clavius,
de Nobili—as well as explorers like Goes and a long list of
others: Pedro Paez, who first paddled to the source of the Blue
Nile at Lake Tana; Jacques Marquette, who charted the Upper
Mississippi River; and the "wise, visionary" Jakob Baegert, who
already in 1771 foresaw the future of his remote outpost:
"Everything about California is of such little importance that it
is hardly worth the trouble to take a pen and write about it."[5]

They were committed individuals who enjoyed meaningful
opportunities to contribute their own gifts and visions. They
came out of supportive environments where managers demonstrated the same commitment. Few organizations become so rich
in these traits that observers call them heroic or visionary.
Reaching that performance plateau is enormously challenging
in its own right; remaining on that plateau is even harder. A
restless, countercultural instinct to keep challenging the status

> A restless, countercultural instinct to keep challenging the status quo was built into Jesuit heroism.

quo was built into Jesuit heroism. The built-in energy of the *magis* pointed always toward some better approach to the problem at hand or some worthier challenge to tackle. The daily *examen* shed steady light on behavior or results that fell short of aspirations; the Jesuits' self-reflective habits denied them the luxury of "just going with the flow." And when a better path presented itself, their change-ready posture of "living with one foot raised" inclined them to leap into action instead of stewing indecisively.

Good leaders share this restless, eternally questioning posture. It keeps them a little ahead of the curve. It's what keeps them pointed toward the future, toward solutions and opportunities that others might overlook or be too timid to try or lack the energy to pursue. It's the scrappy, indefatigable, persevering spirit of "throw me out the door and I'll find a way to climb in the window." Invigorating though such a leadership lifestyle may be, it can be difficult as well, as Jesuits learned.

Undaunted by the various challenges that frequently derail would-be leaders, one Jesuit team pulled off something so remarkable that Pedro Ribadeneira gushed to King Philip II of Spain that "all the well-being of Christianity and of the whole world" depended on their work.

He was speaking of high school teachers.

While Ribadeneira was convinced that the world's well-being rested on the able shoulders of Jesuit teachers, he suffered no starry-eyed delusions about life in the classroom trenches. It's clear from his observations that the day-to-day challenges of teaching have not changed all that much from the sixteenth century to the twenty-first:

> It is a repulsive, annoying and burdensome thing to guide and
> teach and try to control a crowd of young people, who are natu-
> rally so frivolous, so restless, so talkative, and so unwilling to
> work, that even their parents cannot keep them at home.
> So what happens [is] that our young Jesuits, who are involved
> in teaching them, lead a very strained life, wear down their
> energies, and damage their health.[6]

Heroic leadership is not just teaching high school kids but looking past the flying spitballs to see that the well-being of the whole
world depends on what you're doing. Heroic leadership
is motivating oneself to above-and-beyond performance by focusing on the richest potential of every moment. Jesuits characterized
it more simply with their company motto, *magis:* the restless drive
to look for something *more* in every opportunity and the confidence that one will find it. It's not the job that's heroic;
it's the attitude one brings to it. The Jesuits weren't heroes because
they were high school teachers; they were heroes because they
brought a spirit of *magis* to their work. And *magis* popped up all
over the Jesuit world. So it wasn't only Ribadeneira who saw himself involved in a world-changing endeavor; they *all* did. Witness
the sentiment echoed by a Jesuit in Japan feeling no less energized
about very different work: "Your Paternity should understand that
this is, beyond a doubt, the greatest enterprise that there is in the
world today."[7] Or by a Jesuit in Brazil: "We are working to lay the
foundations of houses which will last as long as the world endures."[8]

Were they all delusional? No, like the rest of us they sometimes
complained about dreary, monotonous work and irritating colleagues. But they could also look beyond these things, envisioning
the richest possible outcomes of what they were doing. The spirit
of *magis* transformed their work and their product. By approaching
their work as the greatest enterprise in the world, it became just

that. Their conviction and intensity of spirit, multiplied across thousands of opportunities, built the world's largest, most successful education system.

HOW THE WORLD'S LARGEST EDUCATIONAL SYSTEM CAME TO BE

It would make the Jesuits sound a bit more traditionally corporate to pretend that a task force emerged from a conference room one afternoon in 1543 with a master plan to dominate the world education market. It didn't exactly occur that way. It just kind of happened. And the truth is, more corporate successes have "just kind of happened" than any strategic planner would ever care to admit.

To begin with, the Jesuits had a problem. The founders had made the naive assumption that the European educational system would churn out an endless stream of candidates fitting their recruiting specs. Bear in mind the candidates they sought: those who were spiritually engaged, totally committed, intellectually superior (in the top 1 percent of Europe's elite), capable of debating theology in Latin with leading Protestant theologians and of explaining the same ideas in the vernacular to peasant children, ready to cross the globe on forty-eight hours' notice, equally comfortable working in university lecture halls as in plague hospitals, ready to take orders or design their own strategies.

What a surprise that such candidates weren't there for the picking. As the Jesuits later put it in their *Constitutions*: "Those who are good and learned are few."

There might have been an easy way out of the predicament—lowering standards just a bit—but that wasn't an option for the Loyola who went to his grave wishing that he could have tightened standards even more. Only certain candidates were up to snuff, what one Jesuit called *aptissimi*, "the very best." It made for a memorable recruiting slogan: *quamplurimi et quam aptissimi*—"as many as possible of the very best." And since Europe's colleges weren't producing enough ready-made *aptissimi*, eventually the Jesuits resorted to molding the raw human material themselves. Already short-staffed, they decided to address the lack of qualified entrants by diverting Jesuits from already stretched field operations into training the new recruits. It wasn't the most appealing business solution.

The scope creep of serving an unmet need

What happened next was a classic case of scope creep, as corporate teams charged with a narrowly defined mandate to educate Jesuit recruits slowly watched their mission mushroom. Their initial plan addressed the problem at hand without excessively taxing Jesuit resources. They opened residential communities for their trainees within the precincts of universities at Paris, Louvain, Cologne, and elsewhere. Jesuit managers supervised trainee spiritual development while Europe's finest faculties provided academic formation. Problem solved. Well, not quite. Even at Europe's best universities, teaching quality seemed uneven to Jesuit managers measuring on a scale of one to *aptissimi*, and it soon seemed entirely sensible—and no great incremental burden—to supplement the university education their recruits were receiving with courses taught by the Jesuits themselves.

And once they began tutoring their own recruits, the duke of Gandía's proposal didn't seem an impossible leap: that they teach their recruits in Gandía, shoehorning some of his non-Jesuit subjects into the classes as well. Why not? What extra trouble would it be to include a few others in classes they were teaching anyway? And the duke's offer to endow the school was welcome news to the cash-strapped company. But it *was* extra work and extended the thrust of Jesuit education in a new direction. There was no university in Gandía at the time. So for the first time, Jesuits were doing all the teaching, not to mention running the school itself. It was little more than a year later that Messina, Sicily, city officials proposed yet another slight twist: that the Jesuits open a school there for the city's youth and shoehorn a few of their own Jesuit trainees into the classes.

So what started as residential, nonteaching communities housing Jesuit recruits somehow morphed into Jesuit-staffed, Jesuit-run colleges serving lay students. Scope creep. The goal hadn't emerged as a brainstorm from their (nonexistent) strategic planning department; it just kind of happened. But we must credit the Jesuits with the savvy to recognize and jump all over a winning idea, however it had emerged.

Recognizing and building on a good idea

Loyola approved nearly forty college openings during the last ten years of his life. No Jesuit had ever run a school. Somehow the company managed to get more than thirty up and running before Loyola died: a dozen in Italy alone, others in Lisbon, Paris, Vienna, Louvain, Cologne, Prague, Ingolstadt, and even beyond Europe in Goa and São Vicente, Brazil. Nearly three-quarters of available Jesuit manpower was suddenly being poured into a business that hadn't been contemplated at the company's founding. By the company's fortieth anniversary, their 150 colleges formed the bedrock of Catholic higher education in Europe. Theirs was the world's largest, most influential higher-education network long before it reached its high-water mark of more than seven hundred high schools, colleges, and universities on five continents. Education historians have estimated that by the mid-eighteenth century, nearly 20 percent of Europeans pursuing a classical higher education were studying under Jesuits.

Pundits would say the Jesuits were the first well-organized entrant into a market that was largely a vacuum, and their leaders were bold enough to bet the company on seizing the opportunity. But the real leadership came from the trenches, as motivated Jesuits in one region after another saw schools as the ideal way to make a unique, long-range impact while cementing local status and reputation. Scrappy managers fought to get schools up and running, shaking sponsorship and funding out of local communities and nobles and squeezing approval and resources out of Jesuit headquarters. Sponsorship was usually the easy part, relatively speaking; as the Jesuit reputation flourished, new school requests poured into Rome. Securing manpower from Rome was usually the tricky part.

The education market presented Jesuits with a perfect opportunity. The existing system was badly fragmented at all levels. Education was a catch-as-catch-can affair. Most European cities and towns had no elementary or secondary education systems whatsoever. There were virtually no broad-based systems of free or subsidized education—those who were educated were those few whose families could pay. As a result, as few as a third of school-aged males and less than a tenth of females learned even rudimentary reading and writing skills. But the averages mask stark socioeconomic disparity: virtually all children of the wealthy received some schooling; virtually none of the less well off did. Because elementary teachers were not organized into craft guilds, there were no established minimum standards for entering the profession. Nor was there oversight or curriculum guidance from local governments. If one could attract paying students, one was a teacher. More than 80 percent of Venetian students in the late 1500s, for example, were served by independent operators running tiny schools out of their homes.[9]

Protestant reformers deplored the obvious inequities and deficiencies of these education nonsystems. Martin Luther urged civil authorities to organize primary education systems, arguing the benefits to the state of a broadly educated citizenry. But the reformers' efforts focused almost exclusively on elementary education. The few networks implemented in response greatly improved elementary education in some regions. But these networks rarely crossed state borders or encompassed higher education, and in any case they were few and far between as the sixteenth century ended.

Unlike those who taught at the primary education level, those wishing to teach at the university level had to at least meet minimal standards for entering the profession. Though professorships did not require the schooling that they do today, the privilege of a university lectureship and designation of "Master" required years of university study and successful examination results. Needless to say, the quality requirements for entering the profession were relevant only to those lucky enough to attend a university, and the most salient feature of formal higher education at that time was its utter scarcity. If only a quarter of those residing in Europe's wealthiest cities attained basic literacy, less than 1 percent pursued formal higher education.

The secondary education marketplace—fragmented, stagnant, underserved and underled, yet facing "ideological competition" from Protestant communities—perfectly suited the Jesuits' competitive strengths. Their global organization and ready responsiveness were two obvious advantages. Whereas staffing a new college was a daunting challenge even for a town with the will and resources to found one, the Jesuits could rapidly staff new schools by reallocating teams from existing schools and other operations, or by bringing in fresh trainees. The founding faculty in Sicily comprised ten Jesuits representing at least five different nationalities.

While the Protestant reformers focused on primary schooling, the Jesuits instead claimed a field almost entirely devoid of organized competition. In a Europe where curricula and practices were haphazardly thrown together even within a single school, not to mention from country to country, the Jesuits engineered a global plan of attack. Best practices were gathered into a *Ratio studiorum* (plan of studies). The Jesuit brand became associated with consistently high standards, a boon to parents lost among the dozens of tiny, independent schools serving any large city. In an environment where neither guilds nor civil authorities dictated minimum standards for entering the teaching profession, each Jesuit's rigorous training left him far more qualified than the average secondary school teacher.

In sum, the Jesuit company's strengths uniquely matched the needs of the times. No other organization boasted a similar array of competencies, and Jesuit leaders exhibited the risk tolerance, creativity, and aggressiveness to capitalize on the opportunity.

THE PERFECT NETWORK

But why *this* business? After all, plenty of occupations fit the Jesuits' broad mission of helping souls, and education was hardly the only field where a well-organized, intellectually superior, nimble company could excel.

They dove into education so aggressively because they realized how neatly it dovetailed with their broader agenda. The Jesuits were eager to influence those who would make the greatest impact on society—that their students would, by virtue of their education, often become the elite of their respective communities was a great advantage. A better-educated Catholic populace would shore up efforts to check the spread of Protestantism, another goal dear to Jesuit hearts. And higher education supported the Jesuit mission in countless other ways. It reinforced the scholarly ranks of Jesuits involved in polemical warfare with Protestant reformers; it kept ingenuity-driven Jesuits at the cutting edge of science and scholarship; it provided an academic outlet for the scientific, geographic, and cultural findings constantly flowing in from Jesuits stationed in Asia, Africa, and the Americas.

Students were concentrated in Europe's emerging urban centers, so Jesuits located new schools in key cities that waxed in prominence as the early modern European economy developed. Jesuit schools became civic nerve centers. And once a school infrastructure was in place, other Jesuit activities made use of the facilities. Thus, Jesuit churches, social service centers, and other operations frequently found themselves fortuitously situated at the heart of major cities, catering to Europe's most influential citizens.[10]

Finally, the schools tempered Jesuit staffing woes in ways they had not foreseen. As envisioned, the colleges enabled them to educate their own recruits to a high standard. But the schools also gathered a vast pool of young, impressionable *potential* recruits. The diversion of experienced Jesuits into teaching paid for itself many times over as new recruits enlisted annually from the schools' graduating ranks. And if Jesuits scrupulously steered clear of overt recruiting tactics, they were far from naive about the potential to augment their numbers with prospective recruits studying right under their noses. The same Jerónimo Nadal who encouraged Jesuit managers to recruit *quamplurimi et quam aptissimi* (as many as possible of the very best) also advised each Jesuit faculty to nominate "a *promotor* who would be especially charged with keeping his eyes open for likely candidates and guiding those who came seeking."[11]

So Jesuit capabilities and strategic interests uniquely and symbiotically coincided with the needs of an era. Most runaway business successes are rooted in the same happy marriage of core capabilities and market needs.

But one other minor detail further supercharged the product appeal: it was free. Not only were Jesuits offering Europe's best secondary education, they were offering it *free of charge*. No wonder cities clamored for them. Aside from a handful of isolated civic experiments, nothing remotely so ambitious was being attempted by any other company—or by any government, for that matter. Only a company enamored with "heroic goals" would be foolish enough to launch such a vast, novel, and labor-intensive experiment while plagued by a lack of manpower and funding—and, characteristic of heroes, pull it off.

> Jesuit capabilities and strategic interests uniquely and symbiotically coincided with the needs of an era.
> Most runaway business successes are rooted in the same happy marriage of core capabilities and market needs.

It was free. That fact alone announced a revolutionary social vision: even the poor should have the chance to learn. As it stood, formal education was available only to those few whose families could afford to pay. The resulting inequity only reinforced Europe's social and economic stratification. It would be a gross exaggeration to claim that Jesuits leveled the playing field for those seeking an education in cities with Jesuit schools. No social revolutions or triumphs of humankind came about because of their school openings. Nor did the Jesuits understand themselves as social revolutionaries. They were merely helping souls, driven by their loving outlook on the world. Even though their network dwarfed other privately organized efforts, it was still just a drop in the ocean of illiteracy and inadequate education. Still, the schools afforded a unique opportunity to many poor children who would otherwise never have been educated. The children of the wealthy enjoyed a unique educational opportunity as well: by sharing their classroom with poor children, they experienced what was often their first peer-level interaction with the less privileged and learned a none-too-subtle lesson about human equality.

The Jesuits' revolutionary vision was eventually threatened by its very success. The network rapidly expanded even beyond the Jesuits' own heroic imaginings. Loyola himself was responsible for spurring the aggressive expansion; how he and his colleagues dealt with the consequences of that unsustainable growth was to have implications that the Jesuits may not have fully understood—and that Loyola might well have handled differently had he seen those unintended consequences unfold.

THE DIFFICULTY OF MAINTAINING A VISION

Working from an extensive survey of CEOs in 1989, Stanford Graduate School of Business professors James Collins and Jerry

Porras identified eighteen premier companies across industries—what they called "visionary companies"—and studied them to uncover common traits leading to consistently superior performance. They published their findings in *Built to Last: Successful Habits of Visionary Companies*.[12] Prominent among the successful habits was committing one's company to—even betting it on—extraordinarily ambitious, barely attainable missions, which the authors call BHAGs—big, hairy, audacious goals. For example, building, within a generation, the world's most extensive, highest caliber higher education system. Pretty audacious for a chronically understaffed company that had never opened a single school.

There was only one problem. It was B, H, and A, all right, but no one had ever proclaimed it a G. The Jesuits hadn't even set out to build a school system, nor—once they started—had any enterprising Jesuit general resolved to build the world's largest. Instead, Jesuits in the field pressed to open schools wherever they would further their corporate ambition to help souls. And when a school opened, motivated Jesuit faculties usually made it the best secondary education alternative in the region.

The network was built from the bottom up, not visioned top down. Insofar as there was an overarching vision, it was a decidedly retail one: *magistri sint insignes*—"the teachers should be outstanding." And so they ended up with the best network of schools in the world—one outstanding teacher at a time, one school at a time. It epitomizes the Jesuit principle of heroic leadership. The result was extraordinary, but it was accomplished person by person, each one internalizing and shaping the company mission. Each one was motivated by a spirit of *magis* to look beyond an ordinary potential outcome and wonder if there wasn't something more, something greater he could accomplish.

Lesson learned about BHAGs from the early Jesuits? Heroism—and the BHAGs that come with it—percolates *bottom up*, from *magis*-driven leaders. Such heroism can't be bought, bartered, manipulated, or forced. It's freely offered and passed along by self-motivated individuals enthused about their work. Successful leaders know that eliciting heroism is not as simple as dreaming up an ambitious enough BHAG. Instead, they spend their time creating environments where individuals will *choose* heroism as a way of working and living.

Heroic leadership gets difficult: Coming up short on human rights

As the company waded deeper into uncharted cultural and ideological waters, they navigated a difficult, lonely, and sometimes contradictory course.

Grant Brazil's slave raiders this much: they were consistent. Whether an African, an indigenous Brazilian, or a resident of a Jesuit-run reduction in Paraguay, a slave was a slave was a slave. It wasn't so simple for the Jesuits. The Portuguese Jesuit Antonio Vieira had traded a cushy royal appointment in Lisbon for a controversial commission investigating abuse of indigenous people when he arrived in Brazil in the 1650s. It didn't take him long to alienate every element of Portuguese colonial society; as he wrote to King John IV in Portugal, "We have against us [here] the people, the [other] religious [orders], the proprietors of the captaincies, and all those in the Kingdom and in this State who are interested in the blood and sweat of the Indians whose inferior condition we alone defend."[13]

Not content to limit his brief to degradations suffered by indigenous people, Vieira spoke out as well against brutal treatment of African slaves arriving in Brazilian ports, "the masters decked out in courtly dress, the slaves ragged and naked; the masters feasting, the slaves dying of hunger; the masters swimming in gold and silver, the slaves weighed down with irons."[14] If his championing of indigenous rights had aligned colonial society against him, the rhetorical flourish that came next in the same sermon utterly isolated him from virtually all seventeenth-century

Europeans: "Are these people the children of Adam and Eve? Were not these souls redeemed by the blood of Christ? Are not these bodies born and do they not die as ours do? Do they not breathe the same air? Are they not covered by the same sky? Are they not warmed by the same sun?"[15] Less than a decade after his arrival in Brazil, the colonists had heard enough; Vieira and a handful of his Jesuit colleagues were deported.

While Jesuits charted a path that European society rejected, not even they themselves were bold enough to track that path to its logical endpoint. True, it was largely at Jesuit instigation that freedoms for indigenous people were legislated and in some measure protected in Brazil. Yet not even Vieira was courageous enough to call for the end of African slavery, despite proclaiming its victims equally "the children of Adam and Eve, . . . warmed by the same sun." The most he and other Jesuit activists ever called for was more humane treatment of African slaves. That was radical enough in the seventeenth-century Americas—but a far cry from uncompromising Jesuit battles for indigenous rights that were to come in Paraguay. Presumably, Vieira was shrewd enough to realize that African slaves formed the alternate labor pool that floated the Brazilian economy after Jesuits helped cut off the steady flow of native slave labor. He may have reasoned that liberties for indigenous people were as much as a resentful colonial population would bear; advocating eradication of African slavery might ignite a backlash, inciting colonial populations to renege on their begrudging acceptance of indigenous liberties.

Still, unimpeachable though such tactical logic might have been, it somehow doesn't sit well with the spirit of those Jesuits in Paraguay who freed indigenous people from *encomienda* without considering *any* compromise to placate the colonials. Perhaps the issue of African slavery hit too close to home for the Jesuits; after all, in New World colonies, the Jesuits' extensive network of schools and houses was supported by patronage of large estates and thus, by extension, by one of the largest African slave corps in Latin America.

The Jesuits had not even stretched their courageous defense of the rights of indigenous people in South America to its logical endpoint. True, Jesuit efforts helped the Guaraní reach levels of cultural achievement and establish living standards that, albeit still deficient, vastly exceeded those of other Latin American indigenous populations exposed to European colonialism. Yet while the Guaraní made themselves successful musicians, artists, builders, and writers, at least one career path eluded them: Jesuit priesthood. The Jesuits, like virtually every major religious order, erected what amounted to color bars throughout the New World. The Jesuits reasoned that the Guaraní were too young in the faith for priestly ordination. It was logical reasoning: early reduction settlers were not only the first Guaraní generations to encounter Christianity, but also the first to attain basic literacy. They weren't likely candidates to survive the rigorous intellectual formation to which Jesuits subjected their recruits. But that logic wore thin as the generations rolled by.

The underlying point is not that the early Jesuits fell short of perfection but that heroic leadership is never-ending, challenging work. It involves the willingness to continue questioning and probing one's approach, tactics, values, and culture. In the Jesuits' case, that heroic approach often set them apart from mainstream European culture. They wrangled with provincially minded, nationalistic Spanish and Portuguese crowns reluctant to allow multinational Jesuit teams into their overseas colonies. They wrangled with papal authorities unhappy with their radical departures from the monastic tradition. Latin American colonists resented Jesuit defense of the rights of indigenous people. And across Asia, progressive Jesuit missionary strategies rankled non-Jesuit missioners.

Leadership often is a swim against the current. And as hard as it is to swim upstream, it becomes all the more difficult once the seductive opportunity to turn around and drift with the flow presents itself. Heroic, out-in-front leadership became a less compelling choice as the Jesuit company had more and more to lose. It was no different then than it is today: risk taking comes easier to

> Heroic, out-in-front leadership became a less compelling choice as the Jesuit company had more and more to lose.

the edgy, nothing-to-lose start-up than to the well-established, everything-to-lose mainstream player.

The phenomenon is as old as eighteenth-century Jesuits and as new as late-twentieth-century Xerox, AT&T, and IBM. Technology aficionados will recall when the personal computer was an exotic novelty, hardly a threat to an information management industry structured around big-box mainframes. Xerox, AT&T, and IBM technologists had all engineered early breakthroughs that proved critical to the personal computer's development. And all three companies had the financial resources to exploit their innovations and dominate the nascent industry—yet none of them did (or none did as early or as well as they might have). Why not?

The reasons are complex, but it's safe to say that the management of each of these three companies decided to stick with what was working rather than pounce aggressively on untested, high-risk ventures—even though all three companies had first vaulted to prominence precisely by innovating and taking risks. Like the Jesuit company—grown a bit too big, complacent, and risk averse for its own good—all three had slipped away from a core value critical to their continued success. While these mainstream behemoths slowly marched forward, poorly capitalized start-ups like Apple and Microsoft surged forward to carve out niches in the evolving business.

Throughout their history, the early Jesuits occasionally gave up the heroic, countercultural course. When they did so, a prophetic voice from the aging founding generation was often there to excoriate them. Loyola himself challenged the company's reluctance to welcome Asian recruits as candidates for full Jesuit membership, encouraging Jesuit managers in India to take more risk: "of the boys who are being educated in the college, . . . those who are more talented and stronger in the faith, better behaved and more presentable, could be admitted [to the Jesuits]."[16] His colleagues never quite summoned up the courage to do so, and Loyola was long dead by the time their reluctance had hardened into policy.

Succeeding generations, caving in to political pressure, back-tracked on other commitments assumed by the founders. Loyola and his colleagues had taken on more than a few political battles to admit New Christians into the order, but a half-century after Loyola's death, the company imposed crippling restrictions on New Christian candidates. After all, every other major religious organization had had the same restrictions in place for generations; by remaining the odd man out, the company was losing political support across Europe. With most of the founding generation deceased, it remained to Pedro Ribadeneira, himself nearing seventy, to castigate colleagues for selling out the early Jesuit vision.

The challenge of clinging to heroism

The Jesuit education network best illustrates the difficult struggle that faces maturing companies trying to cling to whatever heroic impulses led to their greatness. The early schools thrived by taking utmost advantage of the Jesuit *modo de proceder*: be mobile, open to new ideas, blind to national borders, mutually supportive, and restlessly disposed to continuous improvement. Superbly educated in core disciplines yet driven through indifference to seize new intellectual currents, Jesuits married traditional scholastic disciplines and the best ideas of progressive humanism in their schools. At Clavius's insistence, even a marginal, up-and-coming discipline such as mathematics found its way into the Jesuit core curriculum—at the time a unique innovation in classical education. (Obviously, it caught on.) Like the very best learning organizations, headquarters institutionalized the exchange of ideas through their *Ratio studiorum* (plan of studies). Suggestions and best practices flowed into Rome from Jesuit educators all over the world and were circulated back to the field in revised plans of studies.

For a company dedicated to living with one foot raised, red flags should have gone up as soon as Jesuits at headquarters began talking about *completing* and *finalizing* the *Ratio studiorum*. The completed document instructed Jesuit theologians to hew definitively to the teachings of the great St. Thomas Aquinas. Not that any Jesuit in the late sixteenth century would have nominated a different authority, but the *finality* of it contradicted the founders' world-embracing, wide-open vision. At least so it seemed to the last surviving cofounder, septuagenarian Alfonso Salmeron. Most companies expect curmudgeonly dissent from the elder generation, but not the rebuke that the youngsters are becoming too conservative! Salmeron argued that instead of definitively endorsing any one theological authority, the company should maintain the open, optimistic stance that one of their own might someday devise an even better approach than that of Aquinas, "which Blessed Ignatius of happy memory expected."[17]

Even as the curriculum became more rigid, the school network experienced runaway success, which in turn threatened other Jesuit leadership principles. At first just one of many Jesuit operations, the network soon absorbed nearly three-quarters of all available manpower. School system culture inevitably started to clash with broader Jesuit culture. Schools weren't very compatible, for example, with Loyola's cherished mobility, flexibility, and adaptability. High-quality schools flourish in part because of staffing continuity from one year to another. Yet Loyola had envisioned a team ready to "leave unfinished any letter" in order to respond to new and urgent opportunities, and it simply wasn't feasible to dash out of a classroom lecture or interrupt an academic semester to journey to India on forty-eight hours' notice, as Xavier had done.

Schools required school buildings. Jesuits became increasingly saddled with property holdings and the mundane preoccupations that came with them. Their mission poised them to respond innovatively to unfolding opportunities, but Jesuit managers were forced to reserve at least some creative energy for keeping the boiler running and the school roof from collapsing. Their mindset and risk appetite must have been affected by the nitty-gritty of school life: maintaining the physical plant, retaining a stable staff, and keeping up with labor-intensive work. The earliest Jesuits behaved like light infantry. Abiding by Loyola's counsel not to become committed to mobility-inhibiting jobs, they easily packed up and decamped for new opportunities. But disengagement was more challenging for a team running a school; there were implicit commitments to the student community, not to mention to the physical plant itself.

Loyola, model of Jesuit indifference, claimed he would have little trouble reconciling himself were the Jesuits ever dissolved: "If I recollected myself in prayer for a quarter of an hour, I would be happy, and even happier than before."[18] How easy was it for Jesuit managers to maintain this vital mindset once they found themselves presiding over hundreds of schools that were fabulously successful? It's much easier to risk everything on ambitious new ventures when you have nothing to lose than when you have lots to lose. The same struggle presented itself on a person-by-person level: could Jesuits working in well-established institutions maintain the same change readiness and risk appetite that colleagues who didn't have institutional affiliations possessed?

Bad things happen—and heroism evaporates—when leadership becomes confused with surviving, getting ahead, or watching one's back. A New York Times profile of one rising organizational star will sound depressingly familiar to too many employees at major corporations. The Times portrayed a "bright and effective organizer" who "never upstages his boss." He engineered a relentless rise up the ladder by "working tirelessly" through a succession of increasingly responsible assignments, "building alliances and leaving no imprints." Unsurprisingly, one insider complained that "he's certainly smart and adept at protecting himself, but we have no idea where he stands on most crucial issues."[19]

Yet it's probably unfair to smear the subject of the profile. After all, he was merely following the conventional, well-established trail that leads to the top of almost any organizational hierarchy. It would be counterproductive for an ambitious would-be leader to manage his or her ascent differently. The problem is that while no organization wants "go along to get along" leaders, it becomes difficult to weed out such a culture once it has taken root. When corporations do break out of this cycle, it is often thanks to the inspired heroics of those who focus on genuine leadership values rather than on managing their careers or on how they appear to others. It usually takes heroes to save companies from themselves.

Who was the subject of the *Times* profile? A rising political star in China's Communist Party. It's disheartening to realize that the profile of a Communist Party bureaucrat could easily describe a rising star in corporate America.

For years the Jesuits pulled off a heroic feat that no other government or private institution was foolish enough to even consider. Providing secondary education to the poor was well beyond the pale to the majority of sixteenth-century Europeans (and seventeenth-century Europeans, and much of eighteenth- and nineteenth-century Europeans, for that matter). Early in the endeavor, Juan Polanco prepared a fifteen-point treatise outlining the Jesuit rationale for entering the education business. It reduced to utterly matter-of-fact terms an unprecedented, remarkably ambitious aspiration: "The poor, who could not possibly pay for teachers, much less for private tutors, will [make progress in learning]." Talk about a BHAG.

Almost from the outset, though, this vision of providing quality education to the poor came under severe stress. It was all well and good that the Jesuits were offering a free secondary education, but primary education still wasn't free. The cost of a tutor to teach their young children how to read and write outstripped the means of most poor families, and consequently many illiterate, poor children landed on the doorsteps of the Jesuit secondary schools. Two difficulties ensued as Jesuits mounted remedial reading and writing classes to bring these illiterate children up to speed. However effective the remedial training was, most of these students never completely caught up with the more privileged students who were beneficiaries of primary schooling. And *no* child benefited when newly literate "graduates" of remedial lessons were eventually streamed into classrooms with far more advanced students. And then there was the challenge of staffing the remedial classes, yet another demand on the already stretched company.

It became clear even within Loyola's lifetime that the demands of the welcome-all-comers approach were sapping company resources. The Jesuits came up with a logical if fateful solution: restricting enrollment to literate students. The Jesuit curriculum was the most demanding in Europe. Youngsters could hardly hope to master that curriculum from an illiterate starting point. But because only the well-to-do had the means to secure primary education for their children, generally only well-off children cleared the literacy hurdle to qualify for enrollment. Jesuit schools increasingly (if unintentionally) became institutions catering primarily to the well-off. The trend assumed a life of its own. The rigorous curriculum and well-qualified faculty sealed the Jesuits' reputation as educators of choice for the noble and wealthy. Of course, influencing the influential was a core company strategy, and Polanco's treatise had also argued that "those who are now only students will grow up to be . . . civic officials . . . and will fill other important posts to everybody's profit and advantage."[20] By the early 1600s, admission to the Jesuit school at Parma, for example, was restricted to boys of verifiable noble lineage. Molded to fit these young men's station and destiny in life, the Parma curriculum supplemented traditional academic studies with courses in horsemanship and in designing defensive fortifications.[21]

Nothing had gone *wrong.* It was the world's finest school system, and it continued to be. It was serving customers who were essential to the company's top-down strategic approach.

Magis-driven heroic leadership, though, has something to do with pulling off what seems impossible to everyone else. The Jesuits built a school system that *was* impossible for any European to have conceived at the time. But an *even more* impossible school system eluded them. Maybe more *magis* would have made it possible.

Magis-driven heroic leadership involves bold imagination and the desire to take bold chances. Jesuits freed themselves from the European mindset in order to see the world through a very different lens. And so heroes in India and in Paraguay ventured far out on limbs, not pausing to worry whether those limbs would support them. How could they not take the chance? They were involved in the "greatest enterprise in the world today." And those limbs held while Paraguay Jesuits pushed a progressive agenda for indigenous rights that few of their contemporaries would have dared imagine, much less approve or attempt. Those limbs held while de Nobili in India, Ricci in China, and others like them fashioned new modes of expressing the Christian message.

But over time there came moments when the end of a limb seemed too precarious a perch. Jesuits took more compromising positions on African slavery and on who could be admitted to their ranks. Oddly enough, Jesuits prospered most when they mustered all the heroism and ingenuity they could to continue their high-wire acts. It was only once they looked down and began retreating to safer-looking perches that their corporate balance became suddenly wobbly.

CHAPTER 10

"Exceptional Daring Was Essential"

How the End of Risk Taking Almost Ended the Jesuits

Few companies maintain the leadership edge necessary for success from generation to generation—let alone across centuries. Consider that only sixteen of the top hundred U.S. companies of the year 1900 were still around at century's end. Why do so few successful companies survive? Success breeds complacency. Or market leaders turn defensive, conservatively glancing back rather than looking forward for new opportunities or threats on the horizon. *Magis*-driven leadership, the continued focus on what lies ahead and on what more ambitious goals can be achieved, remains the only reliable way to ensure that important parts of the vision and mission remain vital and aren't overlooked—or discarded altogether.

The Jesuits might have shifted gears, but they didn't reverse course or abandon their leadership principles. They didn't go from being a change-ready, world-embracing, and *magis*-driven company to a stodgy, risk-averse bureaucracy. Even while restrictions on New Christian candidates were being refined in Rome, de Nobili was daubing sandal paste on his forehead with General Acquaviva's support. Even while Jesuit instructors were building toy fortifications with noble students in Parma, Jesuits were building real cities and fortifications alongside the Guaraní in Paraguay. The leadership principles that had helped them achieve tremendous growth and success were very much in evidence as the company neared its two hundredth anniversary.

But perhaps those principles didn't as thoroughly grip this company that now had a lot to lose. The mid–eighteenth century saw the Jesuits pitched by what their official historian at the time called "violently tossing waves." True to both his namesake and the Jesuit heroic tradition, that same commentator, Giulio Cesare Cordara, argued that his company could have avoided the shipwreck that befell them: "I believed that to handle misfortunes of an uncommon nature uncommon means should be employed. . . . I was convinced that exceptional daring was essential and that not an inch of ground should be yielded."[1] Unfortunately, the exceptional daring that characterized Loyola, Xavier, Goes, Ricci, de Nobili, and dozens of others was badly lacking at their Rome headquarters when the Jesuits needed it most.

THE BYPRODUCT OF UNPRECEDENTED SUCCESS: A LONG LIST OF ENEMIES

No neatly ordered textbook-style list would do justice to the complex crosscurrents battering mid–eighteenth-century Jesuits. European enemies of the Jesuits were everywhere: conservatives and progressives, politicians and priests, devoutly loyal Catholics and inveterate enemies of organized religion. It was an unlikely coalition drawn together by one platform alone: wanting the Jesuits to go. It is easy to explain the detractors' motivations but much harder to understand how their antipathy gradually overcame the Jesuit company. It is difficult, even now, to find the "tipping point" at which this company at its zenith turned suddenly vulnerable.

Enlightenment thinkers took aim from one end of the ideological spectrum. Advances in the sciences helped spur a broader movement dedicated to "rational man's" search for universal laws governing nature and society. Enlightenment philosophers, determined to honor only truths demonstrated through reason or experience, ascribed little value to revealed religion. Nor did they think much of pronouncements grounded on what they deemed arbitrary papal authority. If liberating Europe from dominance by the Catholic Church and its superstitious rites represented total victory, Voltaire saw defeating the Jesuits as the first step toward that triumph. "Once we have destroyed the Jesuits we shall hold a good hand against the detestable thing [i.e., the Catholic Church in France]."[2] He knew firsthand what he was talking about: the Jesuits had educated him. Toppling them would not only be a visible, symbolic blow to the church, but it would also conveniently sideline those most capable of refuting Enlightenment arguments. The first volume of Denis Diderot's *Encyclopédie* had been hailed, including by its less-than-modest chief editor, as a triumph of the new, enlightened approach to intellectual enterprise. Jesuit commentators had rained on the self-congratulatory parade by noting that many of the volume's articles had been cribbed wholesale—including from Jesuit authors. Any wonder why Diderot and others thought their movement would be better off without Jesuit input?

Anti-Jesuit salvos flew from the opposite flank as well. Jesuit theologians had vigorously opposed a Catholic reform movement known as Jansenism. As fierce defenders of the doctrine of human free will, Jesuits detected a defense of predestination in the Jansenists' stress on divine grace. In response, Jesuits engineered various papal condemnations of Jansenism. But they didn't count on Jansenism's Rasputin-like staying power or on the movement's politically powerful sympathizers in the French church and government. Bested by the Jesuits in the niceties of theological debate as early as the mid-1600s, Jansenists a full century later were still publishing pamphlets that leveled indiscriminate, unsubstantiated, scudlike attacks on the hated Jesuits:

> Always giving free rein to their limitless ambition to increase their power and domination, they [the Jesuits] have piled up funds and immense riches by any means available, either by gifts which they have begged from unsuspecting kings, or by goods which they have extorted from towns and cities, or by invading the ranks of merchants of every nation with a sordid kind of commerce which is unlawful to priests and religious, or by stripping families of their inheritances either violently or seductively.[3]

Both the Enlightenment thinkers and the Jansenists considered the Jesuits their most powerful ideological opponent—but for different reasons. Enlightenment champions of reason and free will attacked the Jesuits as the most visible and prominent defenders of the Catholic Church. On the other side, the Jansenists were attacking the Jesuits' ardent adherence to the doctrine of free will. By the mid-1700s the Jesuits were too deeply embattled to appreciate the irony of their predicament.

But there was another problem. Jesuits inordinately relished these high-profile polemical battles. Loyola had been prescient nearly two centuries earlier in warning one of his team to tone down the rhetoric: "We [already] have a reputation among some persons who do not trouble to find out the truth, especially here in Rome, that we would like to rule the world."[4] Perhaps this tendency to look for a fight was a corporate Achilles' heel.

More crucially, one wonders whether creeping intellectual arrogance hadn't clouded the change-ready, world-embracing vision that was instrumental to their early success. Perhaps the earlier, "exceptionally daring" Jesuit teams could have more constructively

engaged Enlightenment thinkers. Whether Clavius with
Galileo, de Nobili with his
Brahmin converts, or Ricci's
successors with the Chinese
emperor, imaginative Jesuits
had managed to find common
ground with those who had
radically different viewpoints

Whether Clavius with Galileo, de Nobili
with his Brahmin converts, or Ricci's
successors with the Chinese emperor,
imaginative Jesuits had managed to find
common ground with those who had
radically different viewpoints.

from their own. Odd that this open disposition had deserted them
with the Enlightenment thinkers, many of whom had been educated in Jesuit schools and trumpeted at least one theme dear to the
Jesuits themselves: belief in the dignity, potential, and exalted
nature of the human person.

THE GREATEST RISK IS
NOT TO TAKE RISKS AT ALL

Jansenists and Enlightenment thinkers were far from the only ones
throwing stones. Jesuit advocacy of indigenous people's liberties
might have pleased indigenous communities, but it hadn't quite
enhanced Jesuit popularity with colonials. And the colonials had
other compelling gripes. Jesuits in Latin America, Asia, and Africa
had operated plantation estates to support their mission colleges
and churches. They considered themselves to be on equal footing
with their competitors in the export business, but the playing field
looked anything but level to their commercial competitors. The
Spanish crown exempted religious orders in Spain's New World
colonies from paying sales taxes on their revenue-producing
plantation activities, an advantage that enabled Jesuits to under-
price competing merchants in sugar, wine, cattle, and other produce. What's more, while colonists ran small, fragmented, and
isolated farms, the Jesuits operated on a vastly larger scale, and

their network of houses and communities—in the interior, in Latin American port towns, and in major European cities—helped them surmount the inevitable hiccups that afflict export businesses. Whatever animosity merchants felt toward Jesuits for their advocacy work was amplified by what they saw as unfair business advantages.

Irritated colonists soon added their own fabulous rumors to those circulated by the Jansenists and others: that the Jesuits operated vast gold mines; that they monopolized exports in cacao, Madeira wine, and other goods; that they were masterminding a vast global trading empire.

The rumors, the innuendoes, and the slights real and imagined crescendoed at a most unfortunate moment for the Jesuits. European states were looking for ways to assert power against an ever more vulnerable-looking Vatican. The Jesuits were an easy target. The Parliament of Paris decried the unpatriotic spectacle of French Jesuits pledging allegiance to their foreign general in Rome and proposed that French Jesuits instead govern themselves. Embarrassed French Jesuits of course rejected the idea, and their opponents had a field day vilifying the ultramontane Jesuits' allegiance to a foreign authority.

In Lisbon, foreign minister and card-carrying Enlightenment disciple Sebastião de Carvalho itched to bring to his native Portugal the same subsidiary relationship of church to state that he admired while serving as ambassador in England. The Jesuits became a convenient target in Carvalho's struggle to assert state power, and the Guaraní War was the perfect opportunity to smear the Jesuits as obstructionist enemies of Portugal. A propaganda pamphlet sponsored by the Portuguese foreign minister summed up the state of affairs across Europe: "The Jesuits are on the brink of being driven from this Kingdom. Other Powers may well follow the example of Portugal. These Gentlemen have carried their ambition and their dissembling spirit too far. They wished to dominate all consciences and invade the Empire of the Universe."[5]

Yet where "Julius Caesar" Cordara would have counseled fellow Jesuits to use "uncommon means" and "exceptional daring" to ensure that "not an inch of ground" be yielded, Jesuit generals backed away from confrontation and hoped for the best. It was an uncharacteristic strategy for a company so accustomed to its well-placed members engineering high-level coups on an as-needed basis. Something seemed wrong with the previous chapter's snapshot of Paraguay Jesuits standing by as the Guaraní republic was dismantled, but the picture now falls into focus within the larger European context. Paraguay Jesuits had expected their general and colleagues in Madrid and Lisbon to lobby on their behalf. Instead, they were ordered to stand down: "I impose on every member of the Province a precept in virtue of holy obedience and under pain of mortal sin that [no Jesuit] impedes or resists directly or indirectly the transfer of the seven Reductions . . . and [to use] influence and efforts to get the Indians to obey without resistance, contradiction or excuse."[6] Appeasement rarely proves an effective strategy; risk-averse Jesuit managers only emboldened their enemies to probe for further vulnerability.

The dismantling of the Jesuits occurred in slow motion. First expelled from Portugal in 1759, the Jesuits were later eradicated from France and Spain, and what happened in Loyola's own homeland illustrates what later took place all over Europe. Jesuits across Spain were summoned to their community meeting rooms by military troops at midnight on April 3, 1767. By the end of that day, with only the clothes they were wearing and the personal possessions they could carry, Jesuits from dozens of houses were herded under armed guard to designated deportation sites. Like exiles anywhere else in the world in any other era, six hundred Jesuits were forced onto a thirteen-ship flotilla to travel the world in search of a willing host country. The pope's backyard might have seemed a reasonable destination for the pope's own shock troops, but the flotilla was rebuffed by the papal states with the kind of logic that only a logician could love: by permitting the Jesuits to disembark, the papal office would be implicitly acknowledging the Spanish government's authority to expel them. There was another, more practical reason to refuse entry to the Spanish Jesuits. Rome was already overrun with hundreds of Jesuits who had been expelled from Portugal eight years earlier, and the problem was taxing Jesuit and Vatican resources. The outcasts anchored off the Corsican coast, some cooped up on stinking ships for months before they were able to secure government permission to settle there. But they didn't stay long. They were on the move again within a year when the French government finalized its purchase of Corsica and Jesuits fell subject to the same expulsion edict already in effect in France. The Jesuit refugee population more than doubled as hundreds expelled from the Guaraní missions and all over Latin America joined their Spanish colleagues. Some filtered into Genoa, Ferrara, and other Italian cities. Hundreds gave up, straggling back to Spain to take up teaching jobs or enter other professions. Hundreds more died.

A COMPANY IS DISSOLVED—AND NEW FIELDS ARE OPENED

Pope Clement XIV didn't think it in his or his church's best interest to stand up to Portuguese, Spanish, and French states intent on global Jesuit eradication. His 1773 brief had a "they made me do it" quality that is more seemly in repentant teenagers than in a pontiff:

> But these same Kings [i.e., of France, Spain, Portugal, and Sicily], our most dear sons in Jesus Christ, believed that this remedy [i.e., expelling the Jesuits only from their own countries] could not have a lasting effect and be sufficient to establish tranquility in the Christian world unless the Society itself were wholly suppressed and abolished. . . . After ripe reflection . . . we suppress and we abolish the Society of Jesus; we liquidate and abrogate each and every one of its offices.[7]

Jesuit trainees were dismissed from religious life and sent home. Jesuit priests were allowed to join other religious orders. In a cinematic if wholly unnecessary touch, the Jesuit general was jailed in Rome until his death. Jesuit possessions were carved up country by country. Contrary to rumor, there were no gold mines, fortune, or global trading empire. Still, looters contented themselves with what riches there were, and remnants from Jesuit libraries turned up in the British Museum, in the Bibliothèque Nationale de France, on the auction block at Sotheby's, and in countless personal collections.

> Jesuit possessions were carved up country by country. Contrary to rumor, there were no gold mines, fortune, or global trading empire.

Twenty-first-century Enron—just like the eighteenth-century Jesuits—had long been the class of its industry. Both organizations attracted individuals committed to performance excellence in a creative, visionary environment. Somewhere along the line both companies' managements lost sight of principles that spurred their greatness: Jesuit managers lost the appetite for risk-taking heroism that had invigorated Loyola and his cofounders; Enron managers lost sight of more fundamental principles of honesty and fair dealing. In both cases the "employees," talented individuals still committed to core company principles, were left holding the bag. Paraguay reduction Jesuits wondered why their managers in Rome left them stranded while diplomats negotiated over their heads; Enron's rank and file were left suddenly impoverished and jobless when the company collapsed. Thus the weightier mantle of the manager-leader: steward not only of vital company principles but also of the trust of team members attempting to live by those principles.

Whatever the next chapter in Enron's odyssey may be, it is unlikely to parallel the odd turn of Jesuit fortunes not long after the company was disbanded. Only a year before their company's suppression, two hundred Jesuits had gone to sleep one night in Poland and had awakened the next morning in Russia. They hadn't gone anywhere, but the political ground had shifted beneath them. Prussia, Austria, and Russia had each helped themselves to a chunk of what had been Poland (needless to say, Polish diplomats had not been invited to the negotiations that carved up their state). Two hundred Jesuits and their four colleges came with the slice that Catherine the Great took for Russia, not that Catherine knew or much cared at the time.

But the Russian Orthodox Catherine took an interest when the Roman Catholic pope's brief on the suppression of the Jesuits found its way to St. Petersburg little more than a year later. Not that she preoccupied herself with debates over supposedly unfair Jesuit trading practices, the rights of indigenous people in Latin America, alleged Jesuit wealth, conflicts between Jesuits and Jansenists over grace and free will, nonstandard baptismal rites administered by Jesuits in China and India, or the proper authority of the Roman Catholic Church in the modern European states. Catherine's interests were simpler and more provincial: Jesuits were running four great schools in her empire. There were few schools like them in Russia. She wanted them to continue. She did not allow the papal edict suppressing the Jesuits to be promulgated within her empire.

Catherine was an unlikely defender in an unlikely locale. The two hundred Jesuits were the first to work in Russia in decades, but they weren't the first *ever*. Jesuits had worked in Russia intermittently over the years and had been kicked out of the country on two separate occasions. Peter the Great had expelled a small Jesuit team in 1689, incited by advisers who

> Paraguay reduction Jesuits wondered why their managers in Rome left them stranded while diplomats negotiated over their heads; Enron's rank and file were left suddenly impoverished and jobless when the company collapsed.

accused the Jesuits of subverting Russian Orthodoxy in order to implant Roman Catholicism. A few months later, Peter expelled the Jesuits again, in anger over their role as translators supporting Chinese negotiators in a China-Russia border dispute; Peter blamed the Jesuits when his ambassadors were bested at the negotiating table.

Now, almost a century later, two hundred Jesuits, most of them ethnic Poles stripped of their national identity by the First Partition of Poland, ended up through the strangest combination of circumstances safely sheltered in a Russia well-known for expelling Jesuits long before the rest of the world caught on to the craze. Had the monarchs of Russia, Austria, and Prussia not carved up Poland, the extermination of the Jesuit company would have been entirely completed. As it was, although the two hundred could no longer formally call themselves Poles, only they could formally call themselves Jesuits. After a while, they elected a general. With Catherine's blessing, they constructed a novitiate so they could replenish their ranks with new recruits. Outraged European ambassadors protested to the Vatican. Catherine was amused *and* had good schools.

A decade after the pope's suppression of the Jesuits, John Carroll, an ex-Jesuit living in Maryland, wrote to his British friend and ex-Jesuit Charles Plowden: "An immense field is opened to the zeal of apostolic men. Universal toleration throughout this immense country, and innumerable Roman Catholics going and ready to go into the new regions bordering on the Mississippi Valley, perhaps the finest in the world, and impatiently clamorous for clergymen to attend them."[8]

Too bad the *magis*-driven Jesuit company no longer existed, when the newly independent United States offered such enormous opportunities for their leadership. But news of the several hundred Jesuits tucked away in Catherine's Russia traveled fast. John Carroll wrote Plowden again in 1800, wondering whether the Englishman had accurate intelligence concerning a fantastic rumor that had found its way to the United States: "[Have] heard tidings relative to a revival of the Society. I beg you to send me, as early as possible, all the authentic information on this subject."[9] As it turned out, Carroll himself was by then bishop of Baltimore, one of forty-six ex-Jesuits named bishops throughout the world following the suppression edict. Curiously enough, the same Vatican authorities who had deemed the Jesuit company unfit to exist hadn't been shy to scoop up ex-Jesuit talent for their own purposes.

Communications between St. Petersburg, Russia, and Baltimore, Maryland, left something to be desired. Leonard Neale, yet another ex-Jesuit turned bishop, contacted his own sources to track down information, adding that he and his ex-Jesuit colleagues had started a small college on the outskirts of Washington, D.C., and were desperately in need of faculty reinforcements: "If we could get members of the Society, they would be objects of our wishes. Anything genuine from our ancient body would be highly gratifying . . . assistance to our poor George Town college."[10]

The Jesuit general Gabriel Gruber posted a letter from his St. Petersburg headquarters in March 1804 confirming both the company's continued existence and his authority to enlist former and new members in the United States and elsewhere: "This *viva voce* concession [from the pope] empowers us to affiliate members to the Society in any place whatsoever, provided it be done quietly and without ostentation."[11] He later dispatched three missionaries from his Russia team to assist the recently reaffiliated U.S. Jesuits struggling to keep George Town college afloat.

Quietly and *without ostentation* were the key words. Papal authorities and no few state princes had begun to regret the Jesuit suppression. It may not have bothered them when Jesuit missions in Asia, Africa, and the Americas went dark, but the loss hit home when they looked around their own backyards and saw empty or poorly managed schools, church pulpits that once featured talented Jesuit preachers, and academic circles absent once powerful scholarly voices. Some rulers decided to jump on the opportunity presented by the spared Jesuits in Russia. The duke of Parma went looking for Jesuit help from Russia. Pope Pius VI approved it, distancing himself from his predecessor's suppression edict: "We have never said nor thought that it was a good thing to disband a body of men which served the Church well . . . and whose absence today has led to the disastrous consequences which we can plainly see."[12] Still, it wasn't as if Pius VI could be counted on to take any heat should European potentates bridle at the Jesuits' creeping reemergence: "But if some of the great Catholic princes take umbrage, . . . we will be forced to disapprove the determination of Your Highness [i.e., the duke of Parma], which we are pleased to ignore at the moment although we are quite well aware of it."[13]

Politics are politics, in whatever era. And thus the pope allowed the reemergence of the Jesuits by ignoring it officially.

A COMPANY IS REBORN: THE JESUITS' PHOENIXLIKE RESURGENCE

Handfuls of Jesuits continued to crawl out of the woodwork a good thirty years after the company's dissolution, perhaps emboldened by the same "nothing to lose" spirit that energized the company's founders. The next pontiff, Pope Pius VII, might have caught a touch of that spirit as well. Pope Clement XIV had caved in to bullying from Portugal, France, and Spain, perhaps reasoning that sacrificing the Jesuits could buy some papal breathing room. But the humiliations later suffered by Pope Pius VII made plain the weak hand the Vatican was playing. Summoned ignominiously to Paris to crown Napoleon emperor, Pius VII later found himself imprisoned at Fontainebleau after Napoleon seized the Papal States. Upon his release and return to Rome, and perhaps driven by that "nothing to lose" attitude, Pius composed *Sollicitudo Omnium Ecclesiarum:*

> With one voice the Catholic world demands the reestablishment of the Company of Jesus. We would believe ourselves guilty before God of great error if, . . . rocked and assailed by continual storms, we refused to make use of vigorous and tested branches which offer themselves up spontaneously to break the force of a sea that threatens us at every moment with shipwreck and death. . . . We have decided to do today what we would have wished to do at the beginning of our Pontificate.[14]

Few people can even *name* a company that went out of business forty years ago. What other company ever reemerged after forty years of suspended animation—with its leadership principles intact?

Within a year of restoration, there were a thousand Jesuits. Within a generation, more than five thousand Jesuits were working all over the world. Over time, the company easily surpassed its presuppression scale.

Few people can even *name* a company that went out of business forty years ago. What other company ever reemerged after forty years of suspended animation, with its leadership principles intact, no less?

HEROIC LEADERSHIP IS A DAILY PERSONAL PURSUIT

Most people wonder about their capacity to act heroically should a momentous opportunity suddenly present itself. Loyola's Spiritual Exercises forced recruits to consider instead their capacity for heroism on a daily basis. Jesuit heroism is not just a response to a crisis but a consciously chosen *approach to life;* it is judged not by the scale of the opportunity but by the quality of the response to the opportunity at hand. For the Jesuit teacher, every day presented a choice, summed up by Ribadeneira: either another day spent with brats, "so frivolous, so restless, so talkative, and so unwilling to work, that even their parents cannot keep them at home" *or* another day devoted to a business so vital that "all the well-being of Christianity and of the whole world" depended on it. Every pursuit offers its own version of the same choice. How one chooses profoundly affects personal satisfaction and performance quality; after all, how can you not be motivated when the "well-being of the whole world" depends on what you do?

This mindset wasn't a mental trick they played on themselves. They were consciously committed to extracting every kernel of potential from every moment and had the foresight to see what could happen when that commitment was multiplied many times over. So one teacher at a time, one student at a time, one year at a time, one school at a time, they created the world's most extensive and highest-quality education network. If all politics is local, as Jesuit-educated Tip O'Neill once observed, so too is all heroic leadership. Great results emerge one motivated individual at a time.

Magis-driven leadership inevitably leads to heroism. Heroism begins with each person considering, internalizing, and shaping his or her mission. Whether one works within a large organization or alone, no mission is motivating until it is personal. And it is sustainable only when one makes the search for *magis* a reflexive, daily habit. A *magis*-driven leader is not content to go through the motions or settle for the status quo but is restlessly inclined to look for something more, something greater. Instead of wishing circumstances were different, *magis*-driven leaders either make them different or make

> A *magis*-driven leader
> is not content to go through the motions
> or settle for the status quo but is
> restlessly inclined to look for something
> more, something greater.

the most of them. Instead of waiting for golden opportunities, they find the gold in the opportunities at hand.

Heroes lift themselves up and make themselves greater by pursuing something greater than their own self-interest. Our classic heroic role models often do so through extraordinary bravery at uniquely critical moments. But heroism is not limited to these rare and privileged opportunities. They are also heroes who demonstrate the courage, nobility, and greatness of heart to pursue a personal sense of *magis*, to keep themselves pointed toward goals that enhance them as people.

CHAPTER 11

"The Way We Do Things"

*Four Core Values, but
One Integrated Life*

The elements of a leader's life "fit together." A leader's life makes sense—first and most important to the leader, but to others as well. By figuring out what he or she is good at, stands for, and wants in life, the leader positions him- or herself to choose a career and a lifestyle that draw on those strengths, values, and goals.

Moreover, the leader understands that his or her values and ways of working must form an integrated, self-reinforcing whole, or as Jesuits called it, a *modo de proceder*. In the Jesuits' case, their work and their life values of self-awareness, ingenuity, love, and heroism reinforced one another in a virtuous circle: better self-awareness made for greater ingenuity, and so on around the circle. In the end, the leader's values keep his or her life feeling "pulled together" in a complex world. The leader is recognizable to self and to others as the same person, animated by the same principles, at home and at work. Personal leadership is not a grab bag full of 101 discrete tricks and tactics. Rather, leadership is a way of living in which basic life strategies and principles reinforce one another.

This is easy to say but harder to practice. For most people, each day brings new crises calling for new and different solutions. How can a person possibly feel "pulled together" when everyday stresses and work demands pull him or her in so many different directions?

Nothing better illustrates the power of self-reinforcing principles than the reality of intense, constant change. Ingenuity-driven Jesuits embraced change. But they would have drifted aimlessly without anchoring self-awareness. The link between self-awareness and ingenuity, stability and change, epitomizes self-reinforcing principles in action. Two recent academic research efforts have highlighted not only the link but also the payoff for organizations that get it right.

PRINCIPLES THAT
REINFORCE ONE ANOTHER

Harvard Business School professors John Kotter and James Heskett mounted a four-year research project to dissect the commonly held but often flimsy assumption that "strong" corporate cultures breed performance success. If corporate culture is defined as an identifiable set of shared values and practices, do strong-culture companies outperform others? Well, yes and no. The researchers noted in *Corporate Culture and Performance* that strong cultures sometimes *damage* company performance by causing employees to reject new ideas and approaches: "A culture can blind people to facts that don't match its assumptions . . . and . . . an entrenched culture can make implementing new and different strategies very difficult."[1]

But a strong corporate culture can also spur outstanding results, when three key characteristics fall into place:

- The culture is strong not just on paper but in a *tangible* way that guides day-to-day employee behavior. When a retailer successfully instills in his or her company a customer service culture, employees instinctively go the extra mile to meet customer requests.

- The culture is *strategically appropriate*. A detail-oriented culture emphasizing operational controls is better suited to a low-margin precision manufacturer than an advertising agency.

- Most critically, the culture promotes *adaptability*. The culture doesn't block change; it promotes it.

Kotter and Heskett describe the organizations that got it right: "The leaders got their managers to buy into a timeless philosophy or set of values that stressed both meeting constituency needs and leadership or some other engine for change—values that cynics would liken to motherhood, but that when followed can be very powerful."[2]

They adhered to a "timeless philosophy or set of values" that incorporated some "engine for change." Say, for example, something like "*traveling through the various regions of the world* at the order of the [pope] or of the superior of the Society itself, to preach, hear confessions, and use *all the other means it can . . . to help souls*" (emphasis added).[3] Successful cultures tap the motivating power of deeply held beliefs—in the Jesuit case, personal commitment to helping souls. But they also encourage change and innovation—the willingness to do whatever and go wherever. Kotter and Heskett found that strong cultures succeed only when both values come together. And companies that successfully embedded both attributes in their corporate culture outperformed those that didn't by a huge margin: "Over an eleven-year period, the former . . . grew their stock prices by 901 percent versus 74 percent [for the latter], and improved their net incomes by 756 percent versus 1 percent."[4]

Two Stanford academics applied very different methodology only to uncover strikingly consistent findings. James Collins and Jerry Porras culled a sample set of what they called visionary companies, distinguished by their track records and identified by direct competitors as industry leaders. The research questions were simple: What made these companies visionary? And were

> The paradox is that the energizing power lies precisely in the combination of nonnegotiable core beliefs *and* a willing embrace of change.

there success factors common to great companies across a wide range of industries? Unlike the Harvard researchers, they didn't go out looking for the effects of corporate culture. But corporate culture is what they found. The distinguishing mark of the visionaries was not great product ideas, financial controls, or even superior management; rather, it was the same package of cultural traits identified by Kotter and Heskett. Collins and Porras concluded that above all else, visionary companies linked an identifiable ideology with an unrelenting drive for progress: "In building and managing an organization, the single most important point to take . . . is the critical importance of creating tangible mechanisms aligned to *preserve the core and stimulate progress*" (emphasis added).[5]

The paradox is that the energizing power lies precisely in the combination of nonnegotiable core beliefs *and* a willing embrace of change. These would seem to be opposing impulses that could lead only to contradictory, confused behavior. Strong, deeply held values and beliefs might suggest a conservative instinct to shrink from change, while a change-ready attitude might imply a willingness to abandon any belief in the relentless drive to stay ahead of the curve. It would seem that melding the two instincts, whether in an organization or in a person, would court disaster.

But the Harvard and Stanford researchers discovered exactly the opposite: outstanding performance occurs *only* when both traits are merged. Neither impulse alone generates the positive energy that results when the two are conjoined. There is a complementarity, a creative tension generated by the cohesion of the opposing tendencies. Collins and Porras portray "preserving the core" and "stimulating progress" as the two halves of the ancient yin-yang symbol. In the Jesuit case, both values are woven into the core mission: help souls by remaining flexibile, mobile, and innovative as well as consistently dedicated to the mission. The values don't conflict; they reinforce each other.

Why it works is no great mystery. In *Leaders,* Warren Bennis explains how vision and core beliefs spur innovation and creativity. Against the assumption that organizations with strong cultures become cultlike places peopled with zombies incapable of original thought, Bennis argues that a clear vision is the compass that enables confident risk taking, autonomy, and creativity:

> A shared vision of the future . . . helps individuals distinguish between what's good and what's bad for the organization, and what it's worthwhile to want to achieve. And most important, it makes it possible to distribute decision making widely. People can make difficult decisions without having to appeal to higher levels in the organization each time because they know what end results are desired.[6]

The same is equally true of *self*-leadership. Well-defined anchoring goals and values enable ambitious, even drastic innovation and adaptability. De Nobili pursued a more thorough acculturation strategy than his contemporaries would have dared, but not because he was less cognizant of core Christian beliefs. It was exactly the opposite. By clearly demarcating the boundaries he wouldn't cross, de Nobili understood the playing field within which he could experiment with confidence.

HOW IT ALL COMES TOGETHER

Four earlier chapters each explored a strand of the unified Jesuit culture, their *modo de proceder.* This chapter weaves them into their one cultural fabric. Warren Bennis and the Harvard and Stanford academics help by providing concrete, bottom-line support for what might otherwise feel mysterious and quicksilver.

Key to attaining self-awareness is identifying motivating core values and beliefs. But ingenuity encourages the embrace of new approaches, strategies, ideas, and cultures. While they may seem contradictory, these two leadership pillars of self-awareness and ingenuity are intimately linked. Energy is created when they fuse. They are not two appealing entrees plucked from a menu of leadership tactics but two dimensions of one integrated, self-reinforcing way of living.

This can sound like so much New Age gobbledygook. It even sounds like gobbledygook when leading business scholars toss around notions like *a timeless philosophy or set of values that incorporates an engine for change* or the yin-yangish, Zen-like advice to preserve the core and stimulate progress. But it becomes decidedly less like gobbledygook as soon as one focuses on the payoff: growing stock prices "by 901 percent versus 74 percent."

Whatever the equivalent of 901 percent total financial return was for a sixteenth-century religious company, the early Jesuit team surely reached it—precisely because their leadership values fit together in a self-reinforcing *modo de proceder*.

Self-awareness facilitates ingenuity

Those who know where they're going and what's nonnegotiable liberate themselves for confident, even radical, experimentation. Consider de Nobili's dramatic but focused innovation. In contrast, those who don't know their nonnegotiable goals and values become loose cannons—they have plenty of firepower but no clear target. Or, paralyzed by indecision at each fork in the road, they shun risk, tread only well-beaten paths, and fall short of their potential.

Ingenuity enhances self-awareness

As self-awareness enabled Jesuit ingenuity, ingenuity and living through change deepened self-understanding. Deeply rooted in the rhythm of Jesuit life was the belief that personal growth and development were possible, that those attempting to "run at full speed towards perfection" were not stuck on a treadmill but moving forward. Not only did self-awareness dispose a Jesuit to ingenuity, but new ideas, cultures, and personal challenges presented never-ending opportunities to refine self-understanding. It's safe to bet that Xavier and the thousands more who left Europe's cultural homogeneity for unfamiliar environments a world away learned as much about themselves as they did about foreign cultures.

Jesuit recruits first inventoried personal weaknesses and change-blocking "inordinate attachments" during the meditative Spiritual Exercises. But the self-learning continued with real-life experiences. Doing dangerous work, failing in an important assignment, struggling alongside irritating colleagues, brainstorming solutions to seemingly insoluble work challenges: all are prize opportunities to learn one's fears, attachments, and personal resources. It's not surprising that Loyola went ballistic when told that Spanish Jesuits were prolonging their daily meditations. Not only were they giving short shrift to the company mission of helping souls, but they were also depriving themselves of the rich self-knowledge that came with being contemplative in action—learning by doing, reflecting daily on life, and learning from change.

Heroism inspires ingenuity

When Loyola informed Portuguese Jesuits that "no commonplace achievement will satisfy the great obligations you have of excelling," he created heroic expectations that could be met only through change and innovation on a dramatic scale. By way of illustration, imagine any modern corporate setting. The manager who sets an expense reduction target of 10 percent gets his team wondering where to buy cheaper pencils: 10 percent means safe, mainstream thinking. An expense reduction target of 40 percent, however, is "no commonplace achievement" but a *heroically* ambitious target that requires outside-the-box thinking. With this goal, no one is thinking about cheaper pencils anymore; it's time to conceive radically new ways of doing things. The heroism that gripped Jesuits led to the same radical thought patterns. So it wasn't enough for Jesuit teams in Paraguay to advocate marginally better treatment of indigenous people within the *encomienda* system; they rejected the whole system to establish the radically new reduction model. The tradition of thinking outside the box began when Loyola himself jettisoned the centuries-old model of religious life to invent a completely new kind of religious company.

Self-awareness gives rise to love and heroism

Xavier—and the Paraguay teams, and thousands of teachers— knew themselves through the Spiritual Exercises to be talented and uniquely dignified persons: they had self-love. Knowing *themselves* as loved transformed the way they looked at *others*. They were no longer driven by the sterile dogma that everyone was created by the same God; it became personal. Because they were anchored by an appreciation of their own dignity, they developed an appreciation of the aspirations, potential, and dignity of others. And so self-awareness gave rise to the love that spurred the heroic efforts of the Paraguay teams. And supportive colleagues helped them sustain that heroism.

When we explore just a few permutations of how the four pillars reinforce one another, their power becomes clear. It becomes increasingly difficult to see where one principle gives way to another, where, for example, self-awareness ends and ingenuity begins. It's easy enough to detect a color spectrum with a prism, but without the prism, one is left only with light. So too with the Jesuit *modo de proceder.* One can freeze-frame momentarily this way of doing things in order to analyze its key parts—self-awareness, ingenuity, love, and heroism—but at the speed of life these four separate principles dissolve into one integrated approach.

How Leadership Shaped a Life despite Dramatic Circumstances

This model may seem a bit too pat and neatly packaged. Here are four reinforcing principles—adhere to them, and presto!: an integrated, fulfilling, carefree life.

Loyola and every Jesuit surely knew that this was not how things worked in reality. The most fitting exemplar of this integrated, four-pillared approach to life is, ironically, the Jesuit hero who sometimes seemed to lose track of those principles. As the early Jesuits navigated life's rapidly flowing, uncharted, winding waters, even sound navigational principles couldn't help them solve every problem. Insoluble problems emerged, as did dilemmas that had no attractive solutions. Johann Adam Schall von Bell lived in that real world where complicated life choices are compounded by human weakness. At his best, he paced the Jesuits in China to wins that not even the imaginative Ricci could have contemplated. Yet Schall made missteps as well. In that respect, he's the ideal subject for our closing leadership lesson learned from the Jesuit team: no one will successfully honor life principles during every moment of a life lived in vigorous pursuit of those principles. The challenge is to honor those principles over the course of one's life (if not during its every moment), buttressed by mechanisms that refocus one on core principles after the inevitable human stumbles.

Jesuit astronomers in China

"The news of Mr. Terrentius has displeased me for the loss to our society as much as, on the other hand, it has pleased me for his holy resolution and for the gain to the other society, to which I owe so much."[7] Galileo could afford such a generous sentiment. It was 1611, and he was riding high, thanks in no small part to the society to which he owed so much. That is, the Jesuits.

The society that "lost" Mr. Terrentius was the Academy of the Lincei, a selective society for top scientists. Much as Loyola prided himself on making the already highly selective Jesuit entrance standards ever more stringent, even he couldn't match the Lincei Academy's candidate filter. Galileo was admitted to the academy in its eighth year as only its *sixth* member. A week later the academy accepted the Swiss mathematician Johann Terrenz Schreck, also known by the Latinized Terrentius. The controversial Galileo had been doubly vindicated: on top of his own admission, the newly admitted Terrenz just happened to be one of his star pupils.

The society that "won" Terrenz was the Jesuits. Only six months after his induction into the academy, he entered a Jesuit novitiate, one of very few ever entitled to boast that the Jesuits were *not* the most selective club he had ever joined.

Few could have predicted just how dramatically the lives of colleagues Galileo and Terrenz would diverge. In China, Terrenz opened doors for his Jesuit colleagues with his astronomical prowess; Galileo unintentionally *closed* doors with his scientific genius, eventually sealing off hope of rapprochement with church bureaucrats. As the Catholic Church's mounting hostility toward Galileo soured his feelings for his once beloved Jesuits, his former pupil turned to a famed Protestant astronomer to form one of Europe's odder partnerships. And by the time the almost seventy-year-old Galileo escaped the Roman Inquisition by abjuring belief that the earth orbited the sun, the much younger Terrenz had already been dead for three years.

That a talented mathematician and astronomer like Terrenz ended up in China had much to do with the strategic vision of Matteo Ricci. Before Terrenz ever entered the door of a Jesuit novitiate, Ricci had already begun clamoring for just such talent for the China mission:

> Nothing could be more advantageous than to send to Peking [Beijing] a father or brother who is a good astronomer. I say astronomer, because as far as geometry, horology, and astrolabes are concerned, I know them well enough and have all the books I need on these subjects. But [the Chinese] do not make so much of these things as they do of planetary phenomena, the calculation of eclipses, and especially of one who can make up a calendar. The emperor maintains, I think, more than two hundred persons at great expense to prepare the calendar each year. . . . This would enhance our reputation, give us freer entry into China, and assure us greater security and liberty.[8]

Despite the Jesuits' vaunted reputation for mobility and rapid response to opportunities, Ricci's appeal for an astronomer went unaddressed. He waited. No one came. He died without ever seeing his goal realized. And his successor as superior of the handful of Jesuits then working in China likely would have died waiting as well had he not resorted to more aggressive measures.

The French Jesuit Nicolas Trigault was freed from his duties and dispatched to Rome by his Jesuit superior to plead the China team's case in person. It was a long trip, almost as long as his wish list. For years Jesuit reinforcements had trickled into China at a pace reminiscent of Lincei Academy inductions: fewer than two a year on average. In Rome, Trigault straight-facedly pressed a resource-strapped Jesuit general for two dozen or more recruits. Rather than dismissing the request outright, the general allowed Trigault to barnstorm Jesuit Europe soliciting interest.

Ricci's request for a good astronomer had been ignored in Rome for more than a decade; all at once it was answered in spades. Galileo's protégé Terrenz volunteered. So did the German mathematician Johann Adam Schall von Bell, a man destined to lend new meaning to the word *polymath*. As Trigault's pitch made the rounds, it became increasingly clear that Jesuit Europe might be emptied of mathematical and scientific talent if every change-ready, *magis*-driven volunteer was allowed to enlist. While Terrenz, Schall, and others were included in the mission team, one of the most prominent of the post-Clavius generation, Christopher Scheiner, instead received the following letter from the Jesuit general: "Your Reverence in your letter has explained your inclination towards the mission in China. . . . Finally, I have decided that for the greater glory of God and for the good of the Society it is preferable for Your Reverence to stay in Europe, and energetically promote mathematical studies. Thus, you will be able to do by means of your disciples in China what you will not be able to do yourself."[9]

Even without Scheiner, Trigault's haul was an enormous coup for Jesuit China: he recruited twenty-two men, enough to increase Jesuit manpower in China by 50 percent. But any self-congratulatory glee would be short-lived. He left Europe with his twenty-two recruits; he would arrive in Asia with far fewer.

Trigault and his recruits left Europe in 1618, five years after he had departed China. He reentered the Chinese mainland in 1621 with Johann Terrenz Schreck, Adam Schall, and two others—four of the original twenty-two, one recruit for every one and a half years of his grueling six-year roundtrip. The horrific journey had taken a crushing toll. Dutch pirates scuttled a quarter of the convoy; a contagious fever raced through another ship, claiming a couple of the Jesuits and dozens of the other passengers and crew. Other Jesuits were held back in the transit port of Goa, too ill to travel further or diverted to more pressing needs. Trigault's recruiting triumph turned into a personal, poignant tragedy: the Jesuit dead included his brother and his cousin.

And what of Christopher Scheiner, whose request to join the China mission had been refused by the Jesuit general? To his credit, he became a Clavius-like mentor to a next generation of "brilliant and eminent" Jesuit mathematicians and scientists; he also joined the roster of Jesuit innovators by helping invent the pantograph, a map-duplicating tool. But Scheiner also made short work of the friendship Clavius and Terrenz had forged with Galileo. Tangling with Galileo over interpretations of sunspots, comets, and other phenomena, an overmatched Scheiner and his Jesuit colleague Orazio Grassi—writing under the dashing pseudonym Lothario Sarsi—were routed by Galileo in an angry exchange of academic publications. For Galileo it was a Pyrrhic victory. He was already a controversial, suspect character to church bureaucrats; the last thing he needed was a very public, hostile food fight with two prominent, church-affiliated astronomers.

It was the last thing the Jesuits needed as well. Once Terrenz set to work in China it was abundantly clear why Ricci had called so urgently for skilled astronomers. A large, high-profile imperial bureau struggled each year to produce a workable calendar—no great feat today but nightmarishly complex in Ming dynasty China. The Chinese calendar required not the quadrennial extra day but a full extra *month* approximately every twenty years. Mailing in Clavius's reformed Gregorian calendar was not an acceptable solution. Cumbersome and flawed though it was, the Chinese calendar, reckoned in an unbroken line from 2697 B.C., symbolized a rich, proud history. And it assumed great importance in a culture deeply rooted in a vision of integral harmony of heaven and earth. As *Tian Zi* (son of heaven), the emperor incarnated that harmony. An accurate calendar helped signify that heaven's mandate remained intact, and with every eclipse it became more obvious that the calendar was anything but accurate.

That Terrenz had such a clear opportunity to make a high-profile impact must have made it all the more painful and nerve-wracking that his letters to his mentor Galileo requesting advice went unanswered. Terrenz in faraway China couldn't have known how thoroughly the disputes with Scheiner and Grassi had alienated Galileo. Galileo's stubborn silence ultimately pushed the Jesuit Terrenz to the near unthinkable: collaboration with a Protestant. Through a Jesuit intermediary, Terrenz wrote Johannes Kepler, the other giant of early-seventeenth-century astronomy. To Kepler's great benefit, as a Protestant he was *already* a heretic to Catholic Church bureaucrats. So while a harried Galileo squirmed, Kepler promoted the same heliocentric theories without the same worries about church condemnation.

Unlike the alienated Galileo, Kepler responded promptly to Terrenz's request for help with a long document outlining calculation approaches for him to try. He closed with fond wishes for the Jesuit effort in China. Terrenz's forging of a multinational, warm-hearted, ecumenical partnership so that he could leverage one discipline (astronomy) in order to achieve a totally unrelated result (conversion of China) wasn't business as usual in seventeenth-century Europe. But it was Jesuit ingenuity at its best: an outside-the-box approach that opened the door to future progress in a way that "business as usual" solutions never could have.

Ricci had called for scientific reinforcements in 1605. It seems somewhat of an overstatement to claim that Kepler's 1627 letter arrived just in time. Yet in a sense that's exactly what happened. The post-Ricci years had seen Jesuits marginalized if not treated with open hostility in China. The almost three-hundred-year-old Ming dynasty was suffering prolonged death throes. Whatever forward momentum had once energized the dynasty had long since given way to unproductive internal jockeying for influence among court eunuchs and mandarins. Jesuit fortunes rose and fell as the influence of their mandarin supporters waxed and waned. Even if Terrenz had arrived in China a decade earlier he would have been blocked from any meaningful participation in scientific debate. But in the late 1620s, the Jesuits' stars aligned for the first time in years. A Christian mandarin was appointed vice president of the Board of Rites and was charged with calendar maintenance and

The emperor's confidant

This rendering of Jesuit astronomer and cannon manufacturer Johann Adam Schall von Bell was published the year after his death by his Jesuit colleague Athanasius Kircher. Schall's garment is emblazoned with the golden crane, a sign reserved for those who had attained the status of first-rank mandarin at China's imperial court. Schall was the first, and likely the only, westerner to be so honored.

reform. The talented Johann Terrenz Schreck had done his homework, ably coached from afar by the Protestant Kepler. And, conveniently, an eclipse was expected in the summer of 1629. Terrenz's accurate prediction of that June 21, 1629, eclipse in a contest against Chinese astronomers definitively demonstrated the superiority of Jesuit astronomical methods and won the Jesuits a mandate to reform the Chinese calendar.

It came just in time. Terrenz died within a year of the 1629 eclipse. So did Kepler. Galileo might well have joined them three years later—and not by natural means—had he not knelt before Vatican inquisitors to forswear belief in heliocentricity.

Schall, the calendar reformer

It had taken seventeen years from Ricci's first letter requesting a qualified Jesuit astronomer for Terrenz to reach China. Trigault's European recruiting trip secured not only the talent needed to

achieve a great Jesuit breakthrough but also the backup to fill the
breach created by Terrenz's untimely death. His shipmate, Johann
Adam Schall von Bell, immediately assumed the vacated role on
the calendar-reform commission.

Over the next thirty-five years, Schall propelled the Jesuits to the
peak of their prominence in China. Xavier never reached the Chinese
mainland. Ricci never made it past the emperor's outer courtyard.
Schall was to entertain the emperor as a regular houseguest.

Schall, the cannon maker

Not long after Schall assumed the role of calendar reformer, he was
diverted to a more pressing operation—a more far-fetched opportunity than he, Xavier, or even the imaginative Ricci could ever
have anticipated: manufacturing cannons to defend a dynasty.
Imperial bureaucrats had decades earlier seen the weapon demonstrated by the Dutch and had accordingly dubbed it *Hung-I p'ao*
(cannon of the red-haired barbarians). But arrogance had pre-
vented them from adopting the technology and mounting an
armaments program until threatening Manchu armies made the
need for cannons as obvious as the need for calendar reform. And
as cannon manufacture was a European craft, it struck his Chinese
hosts that the same Schall who fashioned western astronomical
equipment could construct western cannons as well. Schall's pro-
testations about what did and didn't constitute a priestly occupation were undermined, ironically, by the very strategy that had
fueled the Jesuits' ascent in the first place. It might have been
clear to *Jesuits* that astronomy fit their broad vision of helping
souls while manufacturing cannons didn't; Schall's hosts didn't
appreciate the distinction.

Oddly enough, and probably unknown to his royal Chinese
employers, it wasn't Schall's first experience with cannons—or
with red-haired barbarians, for that matter. In 1622, his Chinese

language studies in Macao had been rudely interrupted by a Dutch
fleet scattering the island's small Portuguese garrison to put ashore
a landing party and secure the island. With Portuguese military
resistance all but nonexistent, Jesuit scholars postponed class to
save the day. Manning a few old cannons deployed long ago on the
grounds now occupied by their college, the Jesuit "soldiers," Schall
included, managed not only to fire a cannon but by sheer luck to
hit something—an enemy target, no less. In the ensuing confusion
the Portuguese rallied to drive the Dutch back to their boats. The
implications of the victory were all out of proportion to the size of
the skirmish. Had the Dutch—who were also Calvinist—taken
and held Macao, they would certainly have ended Jesuit efforts in
China. Moreover, while Chinese authorities had long refused
Portuguese requests to fortify a trading post so close to their mainland, the Portuguese scuffle with the Dutch changed Chinese
thinking. Indeed, even as the Dutch and British slowly squeezed
Portuguese power from the Pacific, the fortified Macao remained
safely in Portuguese hands until its negotiated return to China
nearly four hundred years later. And it was all thanks to the Jesuits
(sort of).

The incident apparently provided Schall with all the training
he ever needed in cannon technology. He not only supervised the
manufacture of nearly five hundred cannons, but in a fit of
unpriestly zeal he also drafted a defensive plan for the imperial
capital and published a Chinese-language treatise on the manufacture and use of guns and mines. Unfortunately for the emperor,
Schall's cannon and military strategy were never even tested.
Time had come for rats to desert a sinking Ming regime. While
some troops fled, others defected to the traitorous bandit rebel Li
Tzu-ch'eng. The last Ming emperor committed suicide outside the
imperial precincts while Li proclaimed himself emperor. The pre-
tender's reign was short-lived. Manchu armies, bolstered by yet
more disaffected Ming troops, routed Li within weeks to claim an

imperial city that had been reduced to flames. The six-year-old emperor Shun-chih was enthroned to inaugurate the Qing dynasty in 1644.

And Adam Schall was left to ponder the prospect of presenting himself to the conquering Manchu not as a humble employee of the Calendar Bureau but as artillery manufacturer in chief for the defeated regime.

Schall, the "Master of Universal Mysteries"

But the Qing didn't launch their dynasty with retribution or a ruthless purge of state enemies real and imagined. While Manchu armies fanned out to assert authority over China's sprawling provinces, order was restored in the capital and the imperial bureaucracy was reinvigorated. By most measures it was change for the better after years of moribund Ming rule, even if ethnic Chinese privately resented the edict to adopt the favored Manchu fashion of shaved head and pigtail. Adam Schall adopted the new hairstyle like everyone else. And in a strange twist, he found himself not censured for his military role in Ming dynasty China but *promoted* to head of the Bureau of Astronomy. While Schall and his Jesuit colleagues had long masterminded the bureau's efforts, official oversight and its attendant mandarin status had always been reserved for a Chinese. But the Manchu, perhaps because they were outsiders themselves, suffered no such prejudice.

So after a momentary albeit anxious blip during the dynastic transition, Schall was once again a rising star. Honorifics piled up as he ascended through the nine grades of the mandarin hierarchy. By the time he joined the select inner circle of first-division/first-rank mandarins, he boasted titles ranging from the impressively esoteric "Master of Universal Mysteries" to the simpler but weightier "Imperial Chamberlain." His influence in the empire was unequaled by that of any European before or after him. Imagine the dismay of the Protestant Dutch ambassador ushered into the Chinese Council of State only to find the chief minister accompanied by "a Jesuit, with a long white beard, his head shaved and dressed in Tartar fashion. He is from Cologne on the Rhine, is named Adam Schall, and has been forty-six years in Peking [Beijing], enjoying great esteem with the Emperor of China."[10] Presumably, the Dutch ambassador was spared Schall's fond recollection of last seeing the Dutch in Macao from the friendly end of a cannon barrel.

Schall, the emperor's *mafa*

Ricci's strategic gamble of using astronomy and western technology to win status was vindicated as Terrenz and Schall wedged themselves into courtly positions of influence thanks to their knowledge and expertise. But neither Ricci nor Schall himself could possibly have predicted that Schall's most influential position would not be director of the Astronomy Bureau or "Imperial Chamberlain" but *mafa*. Schall rose through the Chinese hierarchy by prodigious intellectual horsepower and sheer resourcefulness, but when all was said and done it was as a trusted *mafa*, "grandpa," that he was most valued. The emperor Shun-chih was a little boy when Schall first met him, orphaned at an early age and installed by powerful, self-interested regents in a role he could not have understood in unfamiliar surroundings far from his homeland. It was no surprise that such a child would seek a surrogate *mafa*. Who knows why he chose Schall—though as a Jesuit Schall was at least better prepared to play the grandfatherly confidant than to manufacture cannons. Their unique relationship continued even after the emperor shucked his regents to assert some independent authority.

Schall, the architect

Schall's colleagues basked in his glow. "Would that we had a hundred Adams," one wrote, "for despite his distance he is so real a

> With no one more qualified available, Schall the astronomer, mathematician, cannon maker, calendar reformer, and defense strategist became church architect and contractor.

help to us that we need only to say that we are his companions and brothers and no one dares venture a word against us."[11] The Jesuits had always maintained a low profile in China to avoid provoking xenophobic outbursts. Their converts worshiped in inconspicuous chapels sheltered within the walls of Jesuit residences. But Schall's growing renown emboldened them. They decided to construct a hundred-foot-high baroque-style church in the capital, Beijing's first major example of western architecture. With no one more qualified available, Schall the astronomer, mathematician, cannon maker, calendar reformer, and defense strategist became church architect and contractor.

While the emperor relished his relationship with his surrogate *mafa,* many of Schall's colleagues saw Schall's increasing prominence in a different light. Successful though Schall was, and successful though his colleagues became riding on his coattails, he became a lightning rod. Whether out of resentment at his success or genuine concern over his compromised lifestyle (or some combination of both), Schall's colleagues began second-guessing his tactics. Some complained that his lifestyle contradicted Jesuit poverty. Given the perks of mandarin status, they were certainly right, albeit rather shortsighted. Others accused him of implicitly condoning superstitious practices, as Chinese customarily used his bureau's calendar to determine propitious days for weddings, travel, or other significant personal events. Many of the charges were petty, but as Schall became increasingly enmeshed at the imperial court, he gave even his supporters reason to worry. It was one thing for Schall to take the Shun-chih child emperor under his wing or to show up in the Jesuit community sporting brocade robes emblazoned with the golden crane symbol reserved for first-rank mandarins; it was quite something else when the celibate Schall informed his Jesuit colleagues that he had a *grandson*.

Well, it could have been worse; at least it was his *adopted* grandson. Shun-chih, the emperor who had grown close to Schall in his youth, had pushed on the Jesuit the honor of accepting a grandson without obligating Schall to raise or support the child. Refusing would have been an affront to his powerful patron, not that Schall's input was invited. An imperial decree confirmed the adoption—but also gives a rare glimpse into Chinese feelings about the Jesuits. However Schall and his colleagues attempted to blend into the local culture, their lifestyle must have seemed puzzling and sad to their hosts:

> In view of the fact that T'ang Jo-wang [i.e., Schall] has taken a vow of chastity and lifelong celibacy and consequently like an exile must live sad, alone and without help, the emperor desired him to adopt a boy as his grandson. . . . T'ang Jo-wang comes from a foreign land and has for many years served the empire. He is not married. . . . Therefore his adopted grandson may be admitted to the college. We decree it so.[12]

The wounded relations between Schall and a few of his colleagues festered, distracting them from fully exploiting their most promising opportunity in China. However narrow-minded his detractors, Schall's temperament didn't exactly promote a warm and speedy reconciliation. Schall was a man who didn't suffer fools, and from his lofty perch even talented colleagues sometimes seemed fools. A Jesuit investigating the charges against Schall reported that his personality exacerbated otherwise simple disagreements: "On the exterior a rather harsh man, very irascible and morose after the German fashion."[13] As the discord created an undercurrent of friction among the China team, the question of whether a Jesuit could accept leadership of the Calendar Bureau wound its way to the Vatican. Perhaps it was easier for the pope to assess the matter dispassionately. After all, he didn't have to eat dinner every night with the harsh, irascible, and morose Schall. In any event, papal authorities completely vindicated him: "In view of the manifest advantages for the propagation of the faith afforded by the post of official astronomer, the Holy Father grants all dispensations that may be required in order that members of the Society may accept it."[14]

Schall, the accused

Whatever minor loss of momentum the Jesuits suffered from the intramural squabble was nothing compared to the fallout from the emperor Shun-chih's premature death at age twenty-four in 1661. It was the cue for Schall's court enemies to crawl out of the wood-work. Marginalized bureaucrats and court eunuchs, former Calendar Bureau members, xenophobes, and anti-Christians all rallied around the mandarin Yang Kuan-Hsien, who made himself the point person for the anti-Christian faction by publishing the diatribe "Refutation of the Noxious Doctrine."

Unfortunately for the Jesuits, Schall, already more than seventy years old, suffered a paralyzing stroke as the controversy escalated. It further encouraged his enemies to press their attacks. Schall and three colleagues were paraded before the Board of Rites and jailed on a long list of charges, chief among them spreading false teach-ings and beliefs through China. As head of the Calendar Bureau, Schall was tagged with indirectly bringing about the emperor's pre-mature passing—as they saw it, only inauspicious scheduling of the emperor's affairs and formal rituals could have caused such an untimely death, and Schall's calendar must have been the basis for such unfortunate scheduling. For their lesser offenses, Schall's three companions were caned and the full Jesuit company was banished from China. Schall's initial sentence of death by strangulation was overturned by magistrates who decided that the enormity of his crimes against the state merited the more exquisitely torturous *ling ch'ih*: piecemeal dismemberment, each new wound cauterized with a hot iron to minimize the blood loss—and prolong the torture.

A violent earthquake rocked Beijing the day Schall's death warrant was presented to the emperor. What sign could be clearer?

Schall had devoted a good part of his career—and had derived much of his success—from studying the heavens. Now in one final, dramatic twist the heavenly portents intervened on Schall's behalf. A violent earthquake rocked Beijing the day Schall's death warrant was presented to the emperor. What sign could be clearer? Spooked and shaken (literally), magistrates and prosecutors quickly reconsidered his death sentence. Leniency suddenly seemed a better idea, and Schall was allowed to return to his residence.

Stripped of all duties and titles, personally broken and suffering near total paralysis, Schall died within a year. The author of *Divergences of European Astronomy from Chinese Astronomy*, *Treatise on the Telescope*, *History of Occidental Astronomers*, and a handful of other Chinese-language treatises composed one last work before dying. This one was for a more limited audience. Schall dictated it to a Jesuit protégé, and it was read to Schall's Jesuit colleagues in his presence:

> I present myself . . . before this Community which represents for me the whole Society of Jesus. I am not going to defend myself as I did a few months ago in the courts, but rather to charge myself in full honesty and candour. . . . In adopting my servant's son I was guilty of imprudence. I have caused scandal, and offended against brotherly love by word and by pen, especially among my colleagues in this city.[15]

He cited other personal lapses before continuing:

> Lastly, I beg that no one takes this confession as an afterthought or
> as having been extorted by adversity; it was not indeed the fruit of
> my own thought but of the will of the merciful God who touches
> the hearts of men with gentleness and power at the times and in
> the manner which his providence and grace ordain.[16]

He died soon after.

A WHOLE LIFE, LIVED BY PRINCIPLES

It may seem an odd final image of Jesuit leadership: Adam Schall
on his deathbed, his fame and influence completely gone.

Or perhaps it is a fitting image.

Schall's deathbed reflections returned him to the Spiritual
Exercises, which first molded his leadership vision. Loyola, their
author, could not have envisioned Schall's unlikely life or the succession of impossible choices that tested him. But Loyola had
understood that Jesuits immersed in a complex world would find
themselves confronted with difficult choices. And so the Exercises
buttressed each recruit's judgment with methods "of making a
sound and good election"—that is, any important life choice—
including a series of mental role-plays:

> I will imagine a person whom I have never seen or known.
> Desiring all perfection for him or her, I will consider what I
> would say in order to bring such a one to act and elect for the
> greater glory of God . . . and the greater perfection of his or her
> soul. Then, doing the same for myself, I will keep the rule which
> I set up for another. . . .

> I will consider, as if I were at the point of death, what proce-
> dure and norm I will at that time wish I had used in the manner
> of making the present election. Then, guiding myself by that
> norm, I should make my decision on the whole matter. [17]

The role-plays were grounded in the belief that any important decision merits a thoughtful investment of time, imagination, and energy. Loyola wanted recruits to mull a decision over from different angles, including from the sobering perspective of one's deathbed: how would you decide if you were at death's door? What values and personal objectives would guide you at that moment?

Schall returned to these meditations during his final days, but this time he *was* at

From when he entered Jesuit training at nineteen up to his final moments, Schall's routine included the twice-daily habit of reflecting on his actions, reassessing his goals, learning from his mistakes, and adjusting his course.

the point of death—it was no imaginative exercise. From when he entered Jesuit training at nineteen up to his final moments, his routine included the twice-daily habit of reflecting on his actions, reassessing his goals, learning from his mistakes, and adjusting his course. And after more than forty thousand such *examens* in his Jesuit lifetime, he confessed the realization that he still didn't have everything right.

Not that he could have—and not that any human being ever will. It's precisely in his flawed humanity that Schall epitomizes an integrated life of leadership. Conventional wisdom would find leadership in Schall's attaining inner-circle power in the world's largest empire. But his whole life was an example of leadership, whether he was succeeding or failing. The leader was not only Schall the first-rank mandarin, but also Schall the powerless prisoner. It was not only Schall when colleagues wished they had a hundred more like him, but also Schall the "rather harsh man, very irascible and morose." It was not only Schall the *mafa* and the "Master of Universal Mysteries," but also Schall the man who did the best he could to chart a heroic, risky path through a complicated world fraught with more no-win dilemmas than easy choices.

Ironically, the best example of how well Schall served his leadership principles—and how well they served him—can be found not at the pinnacle of his glory and influence but on his deathbed, where he was still taking the risk to lead, still upholding his integrity by standing by his principles, still leading at age seventy-six, and still persevering.

The first act of heroism is taking the risk to lead

The dying Schall catalogued his missteps: adopting his servant's son, pursuing a lifestyle that offended holy poverty, and so on. Of course, there was at least one way Schall could have avoided those mistakes: he could have never accepted the risk of leading. With personal risk comes missteps, but not to take risks is to shrink from leadership and dissipate one's potential. Not taking risks would mean fewer missteps to contemplate at life's end, perhaps, but also more "might have beens" and less significant achievements.

> No depth of self-awareness would have saved him from every misjudgment, nor is that a realistic goal of self-reflection.

Had Schall been more self-aware, more effective in his twice-daily self-examinations, might he have made decisions he would not have regretted at life's end? Perhaps. But no depth of self-awareness would have saved him from every misjudgment, nor is that a realistic goal of self-reflection. Instead, the pursuit of self-awareness is grounded in the reality that humans make mistakes—lots of them. But leaders go steps further: they reflect on mistakes, learn from them, and move on.

Schall's final leadership risk? Being the first to back down. Jesuits looked at the world and others through the lens of love, but those lenses were sometimes clouded. No love-driven Jesuit team ever managed to exempt itself from the human condition; in this case Schall and his colleagues wasted energy pointing fingers at one another rather than making the most of the opportunities created by Schall's successes. It was the dying Schall who took the risk to effect the reconciliation that had eluded them: "I have . . . offended against brotherly love."

A life utterly changed
is still the same life

What gave Schall's life its integrity, its wholeness? Superficially, nothing. His life *seemed* fragmented, what with his ever mutating portrait. His changes in appearance—from European priestly dress to the long hair and beard of Ming China to the shaved head and pigtail of a Manchu—caricature his profound personal transformation. This transformation took place over a lifetime: from youth through old age, through changes in occupation, changes in relationships, and changes in life circumstances. What ties a life together, making it recognizable as one life?

What gave Schall's constantly changing life wholeness and integrity was his lifelong commitment to a set of goals and values. They were the only things in his life that hadn't changed, yet he needed nothing else. In Schall's case those motivating principles had begun to take shape when he became a Jesuit at age nineteen; Loyola hadn't articulated the same principles for himself until he was almost forty—well more than halfway through a typical sixteenth-century lifetime. More important than *when* each person discovers defining life principles is *making the commitment to pursue them*. Whether these life principles are discovered early or late in life, the commitment to measure life choices against them is crucial. By this process life is transformed from a succession of random episodes to something whole, a life with integrity.

Everyone leads, and everyone is leading all the time

Although Schall was stripped of his duties and titles, his ability to lead had not been taken from him. Schall the "Master of Universal Mysteries" was no greater or no less a leader than the elderly, dying Schall stripped of his power and influence. His leadership opportunities didn't end with his fall from grace. Even as he neared death he had opportunities to lead: to continue to reflect on his life, to learn, to live by the principles he valued—and to make peace with his colleagues and with himself, then die with dignity and integrity.

Leaders persevere

The "one defining moment" leadership theory misses by definition a critical hallmark of leadership. By focusing only on a leader's decisive engagement on the world's center stage, it diverts us from the years of preparation, the life habits, the values, and the self-knowledge gained through stumbles that contributed to the defining moment.

Leaders persevere. Leaders have the courage and the will to keep going. Schall's final wish, long after his glory and influence had vanished, will seem odd to any but those who share his vision that one's leadership opportunities continue as long as one's life does: "Since the compassionate God has in his patience enabled me to live even till now in the society, . . . so I have full trust that, won account of your prayers and blessed works, he will grant me perseverance to the end."[18] Perseverance for *what*? For his last leadership project—completing what he started by dying true to his principles—which he saw as no less crucial than earlier, more glamorous leadership opportunities.

Perseverance is a core element of Jesuit leadership, by no means unique to Schall. The same spirit of perseverance motivated Benedetto de Goes through a long, disappointing journey that ended with his death in remote Xuzhou.

And the same drive to persevere inflamed a Jesuit team that forty years *after* Schall's death—and a century after that of Goes—paced China's Great Wall to its terminus overlooking barren plains not far from Xuzhou.

Leaders persevere not only out of pride, integrity, and commitment to their values. They persevere because they are all at once trusting, optimistic, foolish, and humble enough to hope and expect that the seeds of their efforts will blossom in times, ways, and places that they can neither predict nor control. It is an attitude that inspired thousands of teachers in the world's most successful school system and that animates teachers and parents today. And it infected Schall and his colleagues. After decades of crawling back from each reversal in China, Schall's humiliation and death, together with the banishment of thirty colleagues, definitively signaled the Jesuits' utter defeat in China—except to the handful of *magis*-driven Jesuits foolish enough to believe that they could once again resurrect their fortunes there.

It didn't take long for them to do so. Freed from jail but in danger of expulsion, Ferdinand Verbiest stayed in China, kept a low profile, and waited. His colleagues throughout the country were summarily deported to Canton, but no officials arrived to enforce the expulsion edict in the capital. It soon became clear at the court of Emperor K'ang-hsi that Schall's archpersecutor and successor as head of the Calendar Bureau, Yang Kuan-Hsien, was far from a master of universal mysteries. When Verbiest was finally summoned by imperial bureaucrats, it was not to arrange for his deportation but to solicit his input on how to salvage Yang's error-plagued excuse for a calendar. Verbiest was well prepared for this moment, having been mentored by Schall, as Schall had been by Terrenz and as Ricci had been by Clavius. "Jesuits learn best by teaching others," Polanco had said—and that included teaching one another. Within three years of Schall's death and the banishment of his colleagues, Jesuits began trickling back to the mainland, and Verbiest was in charge of the Calendar Bureau. A succession of Jesuits headed the bureau for nearly another century, and Jesuit dominance of the position was ultimately interrupted not by another reversal in China but by the pope's 1773 edict dismantling the entire Jesuit company.

Matteo Ricci's world map had aroused the curiosity of his learned Chinese friends and had led to initial Jesuit success in China. A century after his death, maps once again figured in Jesuit success. French Jesuits, new members of the Academie Royale des Sciences after an apprenticeship at Louis XIV's observatory in Paris, reached China at a fortuitous moment. Thanks to Verbiest, the company was back in favor. And the emperor, K'ang-hsi, was eager to learn more about his vast empire. The French Jesuits proposed to win his confidence in their skills by mapping the Great Wall. Three of them left Beijing in June of 1708 and returned seven months later, having traced the Wall toward its western terminus near the Tarim Basin once crossed by Goes. The emperor was apparently pleased with their product, a fifteen-foot-long map noting rivers, forts, and some three hundred gates. He commissioned a complete atlas of his empire. Three Jesuit teams fanned out and spent the better part of a decade conducting survey work for the first comprehensive atlas of China, a work that remained a key reference for European maps of China until well into the nineteenth century. Their imperial safe-conduct guaranteed a positive reception from provincial bureaucrats, even in the remote wilderness and vast expanse of northern Mongolia, which they reduced to a single map: "Tho' [the map of Mongolia] was empty enough, . . . the emperor was pleased with it."[19] Most of the officials they met in their travels had never before seen a westerner, though some were aware of the reputations of Li Ma-tou (Ricci) and T'ang Jo-wang (Schall) and of the contributions the two had made to China.

From Ricci, innovation and imagination. From Goes, perseverance and risk taking. From Clavius, intellectual rigor and a commitment to excel. From the founder of the Jesuits and countless colleagues living and dead, a way of living and a way of making their lives whole—by integrating the principles of self-awareness, ingenuity, love, and heroism.

CHAPTER **12**

Conclusion

A Google search of the word *leadership* returns more than ten million matches. An online bookseller offers more than ten thousand titles on the theme. It's safe to assume, even without a painstaking review of these titles, that none of them portrays society as awash in leadership. It is almost certainly the opposite. Many of these works will only reinforce what we already intuitively know, that we need more principled and more effective leadership at the helms of major corporations, more confident personal leadership at home and in the workplace, and more visionary and inspired leadership from those who coach, teach, mentor, and advise us.

It's also a pretty safe bet that few to none of those thousands of titles promote as a rich font of leadership wisdom the handful of friends who approximately 469 years ago banded together to start a new company. They seemed entirely unprepared: they had no product, no capital, no company name, no experience, and no business plan. Their odds of succeeding seemed slim.

Yet before long, a thousand-strong Jesuit company was operating on four continents. In little more than a generation the Jesuits became the world's most successful religious company, arguably the era's most successful company *of any kind*. They pioneered strategy for engaging non-European peoples that one historian deemed "one of the few serious alternatives to the otherwise brutal ethno-centrism

277

of the European expansion over the earth."[1] And they literally pioneered: they were the first European explorers to chart the Upper Mississippi River, vast stretches of China's interior, the source of the Blue Nile, Baja California, and areas yet further afield, "regions which neither avarice nor curiosity had tempted any of their countrymen to enter; . . . tongues of which no other native of the West understood a word."[2]

The signature of their conquest? Not boatloads of booty, usurped hegemony, or flags planted for distant European kingdoms but *knowledge*. Europe was soon overflowing with maps, natural histories, wisdom literature, grammars and dictionaries, and comparative studies of theology churned out by Jesuits all over the world—Ricci's Italian rendering of the Confucian Four Books; Marquette's charts of the Upper Mississippi; Asian missionaries' translating dictionaries of Japanese, Tamil, Vietnamese, and a handful of other languages; celestial readings by Jesuit astronomers on opposite ends of the world (Beijing and deep in the South American interior). Europe learned from the Jesuits, and so did host countries beyond. Immanuel C. Y. Hsü's *The Rise of Modern China* inventoried Jesuit cultural and technological contributions: "From them the Chinese learned the Western methods of cannon-casting, calendar-making, cartography, mathematics, astronomy, algebra, geometry, geography, art, architecture, and music. At the same time, the Jesuits introduced Chinese civilization to Europe. It was the initial meeting of China and the West in modern times, and provided China with the chance to modernize itself."[3]

Yet their most visionary and influential innovation seems in retrospect so plain, so obvious, and almost inevitable. Some great ideas are so widely embraced and imitated that we eventually forget they were once new and exotic: automobiles, telephones, . . . school systems. To be sure, schools and primitive school networks predated Jesuit efforts, but no other organization had ever launched a system of such great scale and imagination. Leading global companies *still* struggle to incorporate certain business practices that marked the Jesuit school system four full centuries ago: building a multinational staff, managing across borders, relentlessly surfacing and circulating best practices, and differentiating oneself from competitors by one's commitment to a "total quality" product. Where Jesuits went, colleges followed—in Prague, Vienna, Lisbon, Paris, Goa, Ingolstadt, and two dozen other cities during the first generation of their efforts alone.

FOUR PRINCIPLES THAT MADE ALL THE DIFFERENCE

Infinitely more valuable than the plan, product, and capital the Jesuits so obviously lacked was what the founders did have: uncompromising commitment to a unique way of working and living, to a life that integrated four leadership principles—self-awareness, ingenuity, love, and heroism.

Neither Loyola nor his cofounders understood these as four leadership pillars any more than they would have considered them *leadership* skills, as we use the term today. Rather, taken together and reinforced over a lifetime of practice, these four principles became for them a way of doing things, an integrated approach to life. They responded to opportunities and crises not by grasping at flavor-of-the-month tactics. Instead, they operated the same "way" today as they had yesterday and would tomorrow, at home and at work, through successes and failures. The dying septuagenarian Schall relied on the same methods he had relied on as a twenty-year-old fresh recruit in Rome. The astronomer Clavius in Rome profited from the same self-reflective discipline practiced by the musician Antonio Sepp in the Yapeyú reduction. And the same love energized Antonio Vieira whether he was facing down slavers in Brazil or mentoring younger Jesuit colleagues in Portugal.

Companies aren't self-aware; people are. And organizations don't love; only humans do. Leadership is a personal choice.

Whatever missteps Jesuit managers made, none ever forgot that leaders are developed one at a time. And none ever skimped on the process that turned Jesuits into leaders. Generation after generation, every recruit undertook the Spiritual Exercises, rooted in Loyola's own tortuous journey toward effective personal leadership. Loyola had attracted some of Europe's finest talent not through his superior intellect or stunning accomplishments and certainly not with a compelling business plan—or *any* business plan, for that matter. His magnetic appeal lay in his ability to help others become leaders. Loyola's approach to mentoring his cofounders became the company model: everyone has leadership potential, and true leaders unlock that potential in others.

Heroism revisited

Magis-driven heroism encourages people to aim high and keeps them restlessly pointed toward something more, something greater. Loyola urged Jesuit trainees in Italy to "conceive great resolves and elicit equally great desires." He reminded another team that "no commonplace achievement" should satisfy their ambitions to excel. His lieutenant Nadal barnstormed Jesuit Europe exhorting recruits that whatever occupation they pursued, they should "not be satisfied with doing it half-way." The astronomer Clavius, from his Collegio Romano perch, envisioned churning out "brilliant and most eminent men, who . . . are distributed in various nations and kingdoms like sparkling gems."[4]

It could sound like so much fancy rhetoric from the bosses, except for the fact that the bosses believed and lived it themselves. And they didn't just live *magis*-driven lives or tell recruits about the *magis*—they invited each recruit to consider and commit to it. Recruits accepted the invitation, and *magis*-driven Jesuits all over the world started believing and acting as if whatever they were doing was somehow "the greatest enterprise in the world today." And when enough team members feel that way, it becomes a self-fulfilling prophecy. *Magis*-driven heroes bring energy, imagination, ambition, and motivation to their work; the results take care of themselves.

Heroism makes a person equal parts dreamer and indefatigable pragmatist. Xavier was sent to India but concocted the utterly unrealistic scheme of taking on all of Asia instead (utterly unrealistic *except* that his later colleagues pulled it off). Jesuit high school teachers operated within the more limited confines of classroom walls—but with no less heroism. Their heroism was measured not by the scale of their opportunities but by the quality of their responses to the opportunities at hand. Heroic leaders don't bide their time until the big moment comes along; they grasp the opportunities within reach and extract as much richness from them as possible. Herosim lies in the nobility of committing to a way of life that focuses on goals that are greater than oneself.

Ingenuity revisited

Ingenuity disposes people not just to think outside the box but to live outside the box. Confident that most challenges had solutions, men like Ricci and de Nobili explored tactics and strategies that transcended the narrow mindset of their European contemporaries. It wasn't just that Ricci and de Nobili were smart or hardworking but that they had cultivated the vital attitude of indifference—the lack of inordinate attachments—and the inspiring spirit that the whole world would become their house.

Indifference leads people to root out provincialism, fear of the unknown, attachment to their own status or possessions, prejudice, aversion to risk, and the attitude that "we've always done it this way." And when people see the whole world as their home, they can turn a hopeful, interested, and optimistic gaze toward new ideas, cultures, places, and opportunities. By freeing themselves from inordinate attachments that could inhibit risk taking or innovation, they become poised to pounce imaginatively on new opportunities. And by looking at the future with optimism, they become more likely to find those opportunities and solutions. Loyola called it "living with one foot raised."

Love revisited

Love lends purpose and passion to ingenuity and heroism. The Jesuit company mission to help souls remained a sterile abstraction until love made it personal. Love transformed that mission and how the Jesuits went about it. Loyola's colleague Jerónimo Nadal remarked that, "Our Father [i.e., Loyola] used to say that we should not help our neighbor coldly or in slow motion. And by this simple dictum he expressed the end of our Society: namely, to run fervently to the salvation and perfection of our fellow men."[5] Love gave them the passion and courage to take on Spain's most powerful courtiers and the whole societal mindset they represented. "I am told that Your Lordship is displeased that we admit so many 'New Christians' to our company. The company may and must not exclude anyone. . . . It may refuse no talent, nor any man of quality, whether he be 'New Christian' or noble knight or another."[6]

It's easy enough to understand how a loving outlook could benefit a company dedicated to helping souls. But love makes *all* companies stronger. How? Love allows a company to embrace all talent, regardless of creed, color, social status, or credentials. Love is the passion to see team members excel, "to run at full speed towards perfection." And love is the glue that binds individuals into loyal, supportive teams.

Love-driven leaders see a world of uniquely dignified humans, not "fearful, greedy deceivers." They live by the premise that people perform their best when working with and for people who offer genuine support and affection.

Self-awareness revisited

Self-awareness roots and nourishes the other leadership virtues. The person who figures out what he or she wants and stands for has taken the first step toward heroic leadership. Those who have pinpointed and begun to root out their weaknesses and unhealthy attachments are building the indifference essential to ingenuity.

Early Jesuit recruits discovered the power of explicitly naming their values: This is who I am, this is what I stand for, this is what I want. That naming process has two consequences. First, most are pleasantly surprised at how much they *already* stand for, and they become more energetically committed to their values simply by articulating them. Second, with the process inevitably comes reassessment: Am I happy with this? Is this the leadership statement I want to make in the world? Is this the legacy I want to leave behind?

Self-awareness is no one-time project. No less essential than the initial assessment of one's strengths, weaknesses, values, and worldview is the ongoing, everyday habit of self-reflection, the *examen.* It's an opportunity to measure life—a little bit at a time—against principles and goals. Did I teach the last class with loving interest in my students, or did I go through the motions? Did I engage my imagination at work today or settle for a "good enough to get by" effort? It is an opportunity to ensure that one remains balanced on the fine line walked by de Nobili and others: adventurous yet committed to core beliefs. The *examen* is grounded in the assumptions that even leaders make mistakes, that we can learn from our mistakes, and that each of us has a limitless capacity for growth and development.

Although the concept of self-reflection may conjure up images of withdrawing from the world, those who get it right find themselves better equipped for energetic engagement with the world. The three daily mental pit stops—"upon arising," "after the noon meal," and "after supper"—help one achieve the focused, re-collected lifestyle that early Jesuits called *simul in actione contemplativus*, "contemplative even in action." As a colleague said of Loyola, "It is unbelievable with what ease our Father recollected himself in the midst of a tide of business."[7] Getting to that point was no unique saintly trick; it was the fruit of continuous patient investment in self-awareness—the initial commitment to discovering one's resources, weaknesses, and goals, followed by the daily habit of self-reflection.

How Today's Managers Can Lead Leaders

We're all leaders, and we're all leading all the time, often in small, unintended ways. The hundreds of casual encounters with fellow humanity that one experiences each day—buying one's morning coffee, jostling onto trains, dealing with subordinates—are all opportunities to convey respect (or not). Innumerable fifteen-second transactions with one's assistant, colleagues, or spouse and children turn into hours of interaction over a month. Few stop to consider the message they're sending in these passing encounters, which add up to most of one's waking life. The leader embracing the "one great moment" theory drifts through them, searching out instead the defining dramatic opportunity that will qualify as capital-L leadership. But let's be frank. More attitudes have probably been shaped for good or ill by a chief executive's manner toward employees sharing an elevator ride than by his or her eloquently worded pronouncement intended to make a profound and lasting impression on thousands of lives for generations to come.

Heroic leadership invites people to assess their daily impact, to refocus if necessary, and to articulate the leadership mark they want to make. It invites them too to replace accidental leadership with purposeful leadership, of self and others. In Loyola's leadership-greedy vision, even those elevator moments are opportunities to lead. It's a humble yet optimistic approach. Humble because it acknowledges that leaders ultimately don't control results, only their own actions—their input, as it were. Yet optimistic because it recognizes that one's actions can be profoundly influential not only in the present moment but years later as a model for future teachers, parents, employees, and managers.

In the case of the Jesuits, the four-pillared approach to leadership was not something "done to" them by their managers; it was what each Jesuit chose for himself. It's no accident that their greatest leadership feats were accomplished by inspired leaders in the field, not by managers at headquarters. Ricci, de Nobili, Schall, the reductions Jesuits, and thousands of high school and college teachers all sought out opportunities. And personal leadership transformed these opportunities into heroic achievements.

So if everyone leads, and if leadership flows bottom up, what role remains for corporate and organizational Pooh-Bahs? It's commonly assumed that leaders are those in charge: the generals, captains, managers, team leaders, and chief executives. But the Jesuit vision spins that notion on its head. If those once considered followers are in fact leaders, what becomes of those we once considered leaders? How can those traditionally considered leaders, managers, or bosses apply the wisdom of the Jesuits?

First of all, they stop behaving as if they're leading followers and start acting as if they're leading leaders by doing what helps others lead.

Lead yourself—and others by example

If you want your team to perform heroically, be a hero yourself. If you want your employees to support one another, support them with the encouragement, loyalty, and honest coaching that helps each "run at full speed towards perfection."

No leadership tool is as effective as the example of the leader's own life: what he or she does, what values his or her actions reflect, and how well the "walk" matches the "talk." Personal example makes the difference between deep, long-lasting influence on others and "just a piece of paper" nonleadership that breeds cynicism.

Develop the brightest and best talent

Quamplurimi et quam aptissimi. The Jesuit founders built their company by finding and developing "as many as possible of the very best." When developing *aptissimi* required diverting already scarce resources into educating recruits, they didn't hesitate. They understood that well-developed talent drives company success. Shuffling other priorities in order to develop that talent was not *altering* the company strategy; it *was* the company strategy.

Every annual report boasts some version of the now tired cliché "Our people are our most important asset." But are the managers of these companies actively involved in finding and developing *aptissimi*—not just saying that their people are their most important asset but committing time, insight, and energy to unlocking the total potential of those most important assets? Do teams see their managers—including the chief executive and top management—still working to turn *themselves* into *aptissimi*? Or do they see Pooh-Bahs whose commitment to their own development ended once they reached a certain rung on the corporate ladder?

Point to the vein in the mine

It would be convenient—and save a lot of time—if managers could concoct magic words to unleash motivated performance on a mass scale. It doesn't happen, never has, and never will. The corporate mission will likely fire up only those who drafted it, precisely because the process of shaping it made it personally important to those involved. So leader-managers must find ways to help their subordinates make it personal—the key to self-motivation.

As Jesuit directors of the Exercises were reminded, "it is a lesson of experience that all men are more delighted and more moved by what they find out for themselves. Hence it will suffice just to point, as with the finger, to the vein in the mine, and let each one dig for himself."[8]

Loyola and his colleagues would have been pleased to find their approach validated in research conducted four centuries after them by management consultants McKinsey and Company. Pursuing strategies to help companies attract and retain scarce talent, McKinsey asked top executives what motivated their best talent. Following is an excerpt from their findings:

Percentage of top 200 executives rating factor absolutely essential [to motivating talent]:

Values and culture	58%
Freedom and autonomy	56%
Job has exciting challenges	51%
Well managed	50%
High total compensation	23%
Inspiring mission	16%[9]

What do *aptissimi* want? They want to exercise initiative ("freedom and autonomy") and make a meaningful contribution ("job has exciting challenges"). And they care about the values and culture of a workplace: what colleagues stand for, how they treat one another, and how they approach opportunities and ideas. In a phrase, they care about the *modo de proceder*. What they don't much care about is the piece of paper, judging by the meager 16 percent who identified "inspiring mission" as a key motivator. In Jesuit terms, what excites *aptissimi* is working in an environment where people understand that everyone is a leader and everyone leads all the time.

Support and trust the leaders you lead

"Olivier, cut your suit according to your cloth; only let us know how you have acted."[10] Once a manager has molded leaders, he or she must support them. Most managers encourage subordinates to show more initiative—until it actually happens. Then things become a bit uncomfortable. Subordinates actually make decisions, and they don't always do things as their manager would. Sometimes—God forbid—they even make mistakes. Then managers start trumpeting a different song, to the tune of micromanagement.

The leader-manager instead follows Loyola's instinct that those "who are on the ground will see better what should be done."[11] What's more, the leader-manager has the courage, trust, and patience to support subordinates through mistakes, understanding that the most effective leaders are often fired in the kiln of their early missteps—developing resilience, the ability to learn from mistakes, and the wisdom to accept oneself and one's teammates as imperfect.

When subordinates are courageous enough to venture out on a limb for the company, leader-managers are courageous enough to back them in their risk taking. When de Nobili and Schall needed support from Rome, they got support, not a brushoff from risk-averse Jesuit generals suddenly more interested in covering their own backsides. Conversely, it was a bad sign for Jesuit heroism when Paraguay Jesuits received instructions to stand down from their cause instead of assurances that their general was wading into diplomatic battle behind them.

Don't lead unless you're ready for adventure

When leadership is working, it hurts—the good news is the bad news. The leader who finds and develops *aptissimi*, gives them opportunities to lead, and supports their risk taking will almost inevitably find him- or herself with the same staffing and prioritizing headaches that perennially throbbed throughout Jesuit headquarters. It's a great problem: fired-up teams constantly uncovering new opportunities, all convinced that they're working on "the greatest enterprise in the world today"—and all clamoring for reinforcements. The time to worry is the day the headache stops. When bottom-up leadership ends, it gets nice and quiet at the top. But those who want peace will do better with a monastic lifestyle, not with the world-immersed lifestyle of four-pillared leadership.

In a world of bottom-up leadership, leader-managers

- lead themselves, inspiring others by their own example and creating environments of greater love than fear

- find and develop *aptissimi*

- help subordinates locate their inner switches for motivated performance

- trust and support those who are "on the ground"

A thirty-hour investment per employee

Loyola is a model of the leader-manager. He himself coached many first-generation Jesuits through the Spiritual Exercises, guiding these future leaders through a self-assessment of strengths, weaknesses, values, and worldview. It was a significant commitment: they met once a day for thirty days for as much as an hour each visit. How many years would it take most managers nowadays to chalk up thirty hours of unadulterated one-on-one developmental discussion? Most would squeal that the many pressing demands of their high office would prevent them from coaching individual subordinates so extensively (never mind that Loyola himself presided over a multinational company that doubled in size every few months).

Perhaps they would be right. Or perhaps shortsighted. The thirty-hour coaching session should be thought of as an investment.

Loyola's paid off handsomely in enormous operating leverage. While managers today frequently waste time second-guessing subordinates' decisions, Loyola took a hands-off approach: "Whatever means you shall judge to be better in our Lord, I fully approve. . . . In this matter we have but one will, but you are in closer touch with affairs where you are."[12] While executives today typically trust only themselves and their inner circle to handle top-level sales or diplomatic contacts, Loyola confidently dispatched a long parade of Jesuits to face off with world leaders—from the king of Portugal to the Mughal emperor. Not a bad return for a thirty-hour investment per Jesuit. And the investments had a huge multiplier effect. Loyola got to know and trust his future leaders through Exercises that also prepared each one to represent the company as a focused, confident, self-aware Jesuit. What's more, each inherited from Loyola the tradition of investing oneself in developing the next generation.

Leader-managers today commit to making similar investments in their subordinates, not out of duty or some vague desire to be nice, but out of what might be called enlightened love: a personal desire and commitment to unlocking each person's potential combined with an understanding that the return on a well-developed leader far outstrips that of countless other investment opportunities.

STRONG LEADERS QUESTION THE STATUS QUO

Jesuits embraced four self-reinforcing leadership principles and were grounded in the tradition that each generation would mold its successors to live those same core principles. The perfect leadership machine? Well, not quite. It was only as perfect as each Jesuit, which is to say not very. *Aptissimi* or no, they were still human. Once their self-reinforcing, self-replicating leadership contraption was flying, Jesuits could hardly afford to flip on the autopilot and enjoy the ride. It was exactly the opposite. As their successes mounted, the Jesuits found that remaining committed to their principles grew not easier but harder. Why? Ingenuity, *magis*-driven heroism, and self-reflection inevitably forced them to question the status quo—their own behaviors, the work they were doing, and the cultures in which they operated.

The Jesuits were soon faced with the challenge that confronts every successful company: to keep reinventing themselves instead of resting on their laurels. Once they had "arrived," the motivation to keep reinventing themselves was less obvious—it's little wonder that they avoided agonizing over their wildly successful school system and whether it was eroding their prized mobility and flexibility.

That Jesuits fell short of their own leadership principles is no indication that their model was flawed. There is no sure-fire leadership formula, because no formula is humanproof. It's not a tragedy to fall; the tragedy is not accepting and understanding one's missteps, learning from them, picking oneself up, and moving forward again a wiser, better leader. Effective leaders stick to their countercultural, inquiring, *magis*-driven approach, knowing that trouble will likely arise when they stop asking questions and challenging themselves and others. The modern-day leader who maintains a self-reflective instinct, like the Jesuits who did so nearly five centuries ago, avoids the worst leadership tragedy of all: waking up one morning plagued by the distressing question "What have I been doing with my life for the last year, last five, last thirty?"

LEADERS, BUT NOT ALWAYS SAINTS

The Jesuit leadership principles don't guarantee worldly success, nor, for what it's worth, do they guarantee outstanding holiness for those living them. Almost two hundred Jesuits—including Ignatius Loyola and Francis Xavier—have been canonized or beatified by the Catholic Church.[13] No Jesuit church seems complete without some ornate, triumphant depiction of these twin towers of heroic Jesuit sanctity. But precious few of the other Jesuit leaders profiled here have achieved the same saintly distinction— not Ricci, Goes, Schall, de Nobili, Clavius, or Laínez. Perhaps we should take this as small reassurance that the Jesuit leadership way is not a Trojan horse harboring a particular set of religious beliefs.

Still, then as now, it *was* a religious calling that inspired Jesuits—both saintly and stumbling—to embrace those leadership principles. In fact, *every* Jesuit would insist that following Jesus is the primary, and ultimately the only, nonnegotiable of the "way." Heroism, love, and ingenuity become meaningful to them as a path to living that religious faith.

But it was not their religious beliefs that made them leaders. Nor, given the apparently weak correlation between stellar Jesuit leadership and eventual sanctity, did leadership necessarily make them better, holier, more grace-filled Christians. The four principles are not "for" any belief system, and they "work" independent of any belief system. Though for the Jesuits—as for anyone—a clear sense of their purpose in life undoubtedly brought greater energy, commitment, and desire to lead.

The Jesuit leadership way might not be a Trojan horse for Christianity, but a powerful vision shared by many of the world's great religious traditions nonetheless flows just beneath the surface of these principles. Real leaders—real heroes—find fulfillment, meaning, and even success by shifting their gaze beyond self-interest and serving others. And they become greater— enhanced as persons—by focusing on something greater than self-interest alone.

The notion may have a quaintly idealistic, out-of-touch ring in the rough-and-tumble modern world. It's easy enough to accept Polanco's claim that "Jesuits learn best by teaching others." Most would agree that teaching others is in itself a learning process for the teacher, in regard to both the subject matter and oneself. But what might be called "Polanco's paradox"—that serving others benefits oneself—is by no means a phenomenon limited to the teaching profession alone. It plays itself out in other, unlikely arenas. John Kotter and James Heskett, the authors of *Corporate Culture and Performance*, surveying the relentlessly Darwinian corporate battlefield, found that leaders at outstanding companies were distinguished by their ability to transcend narrow self-interest to focus broadly on shareholders, customers, and employees. In sharp contrast is the dominant culture at mediocre, also-ran companies: "If the managers at the lower-performing firms do not value highly their customers, their stockholders, or their employees, what do they care about? When asked, our interviewees most often said: 'Themselves.'"[14]

An earlier chapter quoted Harvard Business School professor John Kotter's discouraging judgment: "I am completely convinced that most organizations today lack the leadership they need. And the shortfall is often large. I'm not talking about a deficit of 10% but of 200%, 400% or more in positions up and down the hierarchy."[15] Kotter was right, and the leadership deficit he discussed is much broader than a mere corporate problem. That gap won't be closed by a few Pooh-Bahs atop large organizations clinging to "one great man" or "one great moment" leadership theories.

Instead, the gap is filled one person at a time, one day at a time—in families, classrooms, offices, firehouses, nursing homes, playing fields, and libraries. It's filled by all who refuse to drift through life simply going through the motions and instead commit to purposeful leadership. The world's most successful school system "just kind of happened," one teacher at a time, one day at a time, one school at a time. So too, our society's leadership gap—even one as great as 400 percent—evaporates as parents, teachers, managers, and others seize, one by one, the opportunity to make a leadership statement with their lives.

How Do You Grasp
Your Own Leadership Role?

How do you become a leader who makes the kind of impact on the world that Ignatius Loyola did?

- You appreciate your own dignity and rich potential.

- You recognize weaknesses and attachments that block that potential.

- You articulate the values you stand for.

- You establish personal goals.

- You form a point of view on the world— where you stand, what you want, and how you will relate to others.

- You see the wisdom and value in the *examen* and commit to it—the daily, self-reflective habit of refocusing on priorities and extracting lessons from successes and failures.

Self-awareness is the prelude to fulfilled, committed engagement with the world—and to greater, more heroic leadership. Leaders choose the impact they want to make when they mold a personal *modo de proceder*. Whatever their chosen mission, be it "helping souls," raising the next generation, writing a symphony, or selling insurance, those living the Jesuit leadership way champion four values:

- understanding their strengths, weaknesses, values, and worldview

- confidently innovating and adapting to embrace a changing world

- engaging others with a positive, loving attitude

- energizing themselves and others by
  heroic ambitions

This way—like all genuine leadership—focuses on the possible, the future. Love-driven leaders seek out and honor the potential in self and others. Heroic leaders seek to shape the future rather than passively endure whatever unfolds. And ingenuity-driven leaders uncover ways to turn human potential into achievement and a vision of the future into a reality.

For the first Jesuits, adopting Loyola's way meant taking a chance on an unproven leader and his untested vision. But those embracing that way today have a bit more to go on. The formula has since been tested across generations, across continents, and across cultures. It has served explorers, mapmakers, linguists, astronomers, theologians, sannyasis, musicians, social activists, writers of children's stories, lobbyists, preachers—even school teachers and cannon manufacturers. It is the integration of four essential pillars:

- self-awareness

- ingenuity

- love

- heroism

Acknowledgments

I t's my pleasure to thank some of those who read parts of the manuscript or provided other valuable support: Christina Best, Klecius Borges, Laurel Brien, Thomas Cahill, Vin DeCola, S.J., Laura Dillon, Cristina Garcia, Barbara Hack, Pat Hammond, Jim Higgins, S.J., Rev. Paul Keenan, Paul Kiernan, Charlie McGovern, Monica Neal, Pedro Prieto, Bernadette Prigorac, Ray Schroth, S.J., Justo Tarrio, S.J., and Georgina Turnbull.

Lou Jerome's astute comments and ingenuity helped frame a key section of this work. Jim Loughran, S.J., was a perceptive reader who also provided encouragement throughout the project. Mary Anne Myers's comments on the proposal were a great writing tutorial. Jesuit John O'Malley's vision of early Jesuit history influenced my thinking even more profoundly than the liberal sprinkling of his works throughout the endnotes would suggest. I was honored to have him read the manuscript and I greatly benefited from his insightful comments. Gerry Cameron, Gail Elia, Peter Honchaurk, John Law, Chris Lynch, and George Simon all offered helpful suggestions.

Thanks to my agent, Jim Fitzgerald, for chancing a first-time author's unsolicited proposal and successfully shepherding it to a publisher. Jim Manney brought this work to Loyola Press and offered steady encouragement while I finished it. My editor, Vinita Wright, made this a better book; her astute suggestions came with tangible support (and were delivered with kid gloves when necessary). Heidi Hill, Terry Locke, Melissa Crane, and Heidi Toboni were advocates for the book's themes, always looking for ways to make its message more powerful. Many more of their Loyola colleagues may go unmentioned due to space constraints, but none go unappreciated.

My friends and one-time managers, Walter Gubert and Nancy Harwood, championed my request for a leave of absence from J. P. Morgan, enabling me to launch this project.

Before I ever scribbled notes about leadership, I saw it modeled all around me—first by my parents, of course, and in my early years by those who endowed a church, school, and apartment building on 93rd Street with more leaders per block than any other street in Queens. My mother, sister, and brother continue to manifest the kind of love and loyalty that the Jesuit heroes surely envisioned for their team.

It was my great privilege at J. P. Morgan to be surrounded by a number of great leaders—those who managed me in New York, Tokyo, Singapore, and London; others who worked for me or alongside me as peers.

Finally, but by no means least, I'm profoundly grateful for all the Jesuits have given me: an education, a moral foundation, many laughs, close friends, an informed faith, and the remarkable leadership vision that has guided their *compañía* from its founding.

The support and counsel of all of the above made this a better book and saved me from not a few bloopers. Many inadequacies surely remain; for all of those I take full responsibility.

Notes

The *Spiritual Exercises,* the *Autobiography* of Ignatius Loyola, and the *Constitutions* of the Society of Jesus are cited by the standard paragraph numbers. Quotations from these sources have been taken from:

The Spiritual Exercises of Saint Ignatius: A Translation and Commentary, trans. George E. Ganss (St. Louis: Institute of Jesuit Sources, 1992). Abbreviated *Spiritual Exercises* throughout.

A Pilgrim's Testament: The Memoirs of Ignatius of Loyola, As Faithfully Transcribed by Luís Gonçalves da Câmara, trans. Parmananda R. Divarkar (St. Louis: Institute of Jesuit Sources, 1995). Abbreviated *Autobiography* throughout.

The Constitutions of the Society of Jesus, trans. George E. Ganss (St. Louis: Institute of Jesuit Sources, 1970). Abbreviated *Constitutions* throughout.

Chapter 1: Of Jesuits and J. P. Morgan

1. The maxim is an eloquent paraphrase of a clumsier version recorded by one of Loyola's cofounders, "In all things pertaining to the service of our Lord which [Loyola] undertook he made use of all human means to succeed in them, with as much care and energy as if success depended on these means; and he trusted in God and remained dependent on His divine Providence as if all these other human means which he employed were of no effect at all." Edward C. Phillips, S.J., "St. Ignatius' Doctrine on the Interdependence of Work and Prayer," *Woodstock Letters: A Historical Journal of Jesuit Educational and Missionary Activities* 71, no. 1 (February 1942): 71.

   The interpretation of this famous maxim has been a favored subject of learned squabbling among Jesuit scholars, and there is an alternative rendering that yields exactly the opposite meaning: "Pray as if everything depended on *you;* work as if everything depended on *God.*" William A.

Barry, S.J., a noted authority on Jesuit spirituality, argues for this interpretation in a recently published monograph, "Jesuit Spirituality for the Whole of Life," *Studies in the Spirituality of Jesuits* 35, no. 1 (January 2003): 11. I continue to be persuaded by Fr. Phillips's version, however, based on his analysis of source material for the maxim: Pedro Ribadeneira's firsthand accounts of Loyola as recorded in the *Monumenta Historica Societatis Iesu*.

2. Joseph H. Fichter, S.J., *James Laynez: Jesuit* (St. Louis: B. Herder Book Co., 1944), 77–78.

3. Strictly speaking, there are more followers of the Franciscan tradition than there are Jesuits, but the Franciscans are divided into branches, each governed by its own distinct leadership.

4. Matthew Bunson, ed., *2003 Our Sunday Visitor's Catholic Almanac* (Huntington, Ind.: Our Sunday Visitor, 2002), 464.

5. Thomas Hughes, S.J., *History of the Society of Jesus in North America: Colonial and Federal* (London: Longmans, Green, 1917), Text 2:604.

Chapter 2: What Leaders Do

1. Adapted from John P. Kotter, *Leading Change* (Boston: Harvard Business School Press, 1996), 26.

2. John P. Kotter, *John P. Kotter on What Leaders Really Do* (Boston: Harvard Business School Press, 1999), 1.

3. Niccolò Machiavelli, *The Prince*, ed. and trans. Robert M. Adams, 2d ed. (New York: Norton, 1992), 23, #7.

4. Ibid., 46, #17.

5. Ibid., 47, #18.

6. Ibid., 48, #18.

7. Strictly speaking, the term *Vatican*—as a synonym for the papal bureaucracy—is not appropriately used for the period before 1870. It is used throughout this work—admittedly anachronistically—as an informal, shorthand reference for the papal bureaucracy.

8. John J. O'Malley, S.J., "To Travel to Any Part of the World: Jerónimo Nadal and the Jesuit Vocation," *Studies in the Spirituality of Jesuits* 16, no. 2 (March 1984): 7.

9. *Constitutions*, #667.

10. Georg Schurhammer, S.J., *Francis Xavier: His Life, His Times*, trans. M. Joseph Costelloe, S.J. (Rome: Jesuit Historical Institute, 1973–82), 4:438.

11. William J. Young, S.J., ed. and trans., *Letters of St. Ignatius of Loyola* (Chicago: Loyola Press, 1959), 245.

Chapter 3: The Jesuits

1. Joseph H. Fichter, S.J., *James Laynez: Jesuit* (St. Louis: B. Herder Book Co., 1944), 271.

2. Joseph de Guibert, S.J., *The Jesuits: Their Spiritual Doctrine and Practice, a Historical Study*, ed. George E. Ganss, S.J., trans. William J. Young, S.J. (Chicago: Institute of Jesuit Sources, 1964), 70.

3. Abraham Zaleznik, *The Managerial Mystique: Restoring Leadership in Business* (New York: Harper and Row, 1989), 5.

4. de Guibert, *Jesuits*, 23.

5. W. W. Meissner, S.J., *Ignatius of Loyola: The Psychology of a Saint* (New Haven, Conn.: Yale University Press, 1992), 31.

6. *Autobiography*, #8. Note: Throughout his autobiography, Loyola refers to himself in the third person.

7. Ibid., #12.

8. Ibid., #19.

9. Ibid., #41.

10. Ibid., #50.

11. Ibid., #30.

12. Dominic Maruca, S.J., trans., "Deliberation of Our First Fathers," *Woodstock Letters: A Historical Journal of Jesuit Educational and Missionary Activities* 95 (1966): 328.

13. Ibid., 331.

14. Jules J. Toner, S.J., "The Deliberation That Started the Jesuits," *Studies in the Spirituality of Jesuits* 6, no. 4 (June 1974): 204.

15. Dauril Alden, *The Making of an Enterprise: The Society of Jesus in Portugal, Its Empire, and Beyond, 1540–1750* (Stanford, Calif.: Stanford University Press, 1996), 26.

16. Matthew Bunson, ed., *2003 Our Sunday Visitor's Catholic Almanac* (Huntington, Ind.: Our Sunday Visitor, 2002), 340.

17. See introduction, endnote 3.

18. Thomas M. Lucas, S.J., *Landmarking: City, Church and Jesuit Urban Strategy* (Chicago: Loyola Press, 1997), 149.

Chapter 4: Leadership Role Models

1. Jonathan D. Spence, *The Memory Palace of Matteo Ricci* (New York: Penguin Books, 1985), 126.

2. M. Joseph Costelloe, S.J., trans., *The Letters and Instructions of Francis Xavier* (St. Louis: Institute of Jesuit Sources, 1992), 180.

3. Spence, *Memory Palace of Matteo Ricci*, 66.

4. Cornelius J. Wessels, S.J., *Early Jesuit Travellers in Central Asia, 1603–1721* (The Hague: Martinus Nijhoff, 1924), 17.

5. Ibid., 21.

6. Ibid., 37.

7. Manfred Barthel, *The Jesuits: History and Legend of the Society of Jesus*, trans. and adapt. Mark Howson (New York: William Morrow, 1984), 141.

8. Jean Lacouture, *Jesuits: A Multibiography*, trans. Jeremy Leggatt (Washington, D.C.: Counterpoint, 1995), 186.

9. George H. Dunne, S.J., *Generation of Giants: The Story of the Jesuits in China in the Last Decades of the Ming Dynasty* (Notre Dame, Ind.: University of Notre Dame Press, 1962), 44.

10. Spence, *Memory Palace of Matteo Ricci*, 115.

11. Lacouture, *Jesuits*, 192.

12. Spence, *Memory Palace of Matteo Ricci*, 97.

13. Dunne, *Generation of Giants*, 79.

14. Michael John Gorman, "Consuming Jesuit Science, 1600–1665," in *The Jesuits: Cultures, Sciences, and the Arts, 1540–1773*, ed. John W. O'Malley, S.J., Gauvin Alexander Bailey, Steven J. Harris, and T. Frank Kennedy, S.J. (Toronto: University of Toronto Press, 1999), 172.

15. James M. Lattis, *Between Copernicus and Galileo: Christoph Clavius and the Collapse of Ptolemaic Cosmology* (Chicago: University of Chicago Press, 1994), 198.

16. Ibid., 181.

Chapter 5: "To Order One's Life"

1. Joseph L. Badaracco Jr., "The Discipline of Building Character," *Harvard Business Review* (March/April 1998): 116.

2. W. W. Meissner, "Psychological Notes on the Spiritual Exercises," *Woodstock Letters: A Historical Journal of Jesuit Educational and Missionary Activities* 92, no. 4 (November 1963): 355.

3. William V. Bangert, S.J., *A History of the Society of Jesus*, 2d ed. (St. Louis: Institute of Jesuit Sources, 1986), 22.

4. William J. Young, S.J., *Letters of St. Ignatius of Loyola* (Chicago: Loyola Press, 1959), 320.

5. James Brodrick, *Saint Peter Canisius, S.J., 1521–1597* (London: Sheed and Ward, 1935), 451–52.

6. Antonio M. de Aldama, S.J., *An Introductory Commentary on the Constitutions,* trans. Aloysius J. Owen, S.J. (St. Louis: Institute of Jesuit Sources, 1989), 81.

7. Ibid., 82.

8. Peter F. Drucker, "Managing Oneself," *Harvard Business Review* (March/April 1999): 70.

9. Ibid, 66.

10. Daniel Goleman, "What Makes a Leader?" *Harvard Business Review* (November/December 1998): 94.

11. Adapted from ibid., 95.

Chapter 6: The Spiritual Exercises

1. *Spiritual Exercises,* #1.

2. Ibid., #15.

3. W. W. Meissner, "Psychological Notes on the Spiritual Exercises," *Woodstock Letters: A Historical Journal of Jesuit Educational and Missionary Activities* 92, no. 4 (November 1963): 355.

4. *Spiritual Exercises,* #21.

5. Ibid., #63.

6. Ibid., #66–68.

7. Ibid., #23.

8. E. Edward Kinerk, S.J., "Eliciting Great Desires: Their Place in the Spirituality of the Society of Jesus," *Studies in the Spirituality of Jesuits* 16, no. 5 (November 1984): 9.

9. *Spiritual Exercises,* #155.

10. Joseph de Guibert, S.J., *The Jesuits: Their Spiritual Doctrine and Practice, a Historical Study,* ed. George E. Ganss, S.J., trans. William J. Young, S.J. (Chicago: Institute of Jesuit Sources, 1964), 100.

11. *Spiritual Exercises,* #93.

12. Ibid., #96.

13. Ibid., #97.

14. Ibid., #233.

15. John A. Hardon, S.J., *All My Liberty: Theology of the Spiritual Exercises* (Westminster, Md.: Newman Press, 1959), 71.

16. *Spiritual Exercises*, #230–231, 235, 236.

17. Ibid., #43.

18. Ibid., #25.

Chapter 7: "The Whole World Becomes Our House"

1. Georg Schurhammer, S.J., *Francis Xavier: His Life, His Times*, trans. M. Joseph Costelloe, S.J. (Rome: Jesuit Historical Institute, 1973–82), 1:554.

2. Ibid., 1:543.

3. Ibid., 1:549.

4. Ibid., 2:17.

5. John W. Padberg, S.J., "The Three Forgotten Founders of the Society of Jesus: Paschase Broët (1500–1562), Jean Codure (1508–1541), Claude Jay (1504–1552)," *Studies in the Spirituality of Jesuits* 29, no. 2 (March 1997): 34.

6. Ibid., 35.

7. Jean Lacouture, *Jesuits: A Multibiography*, trans. Jeremy Leggatt (Washington, D.C.: Counterpoint, 1995), 133.

8. William J. Young, S.J., *Letters of St. Ignatius of Loyola* (Chicago: Loyola Press, 1959), 299.

9. David Mitchell, *The Jesuits: A History* (New York: Franklin Watts, 1981), 81.

10. St. Benedict, *Rule for Monasteries*, trans. Leonard J. Doyle (Collegeville, Minn.: St. John's Abbey Press, 1948), 29, #8.

11. Ibid., 7, #1.

12. *Constitutions*, #308.

13. Ibid., #588.

14. Ibid., #603.

15. John J. O'Malley, S.J., "To Travel to Any Part of the World: Jerónimo Nadal and the Jesuit Vocation," *Studies in the Spirituality of Jesuits* 16, no. 2 (March 1984): 8.

16. Ibid, 6.

17. Robert McNally, S.J., "St. Ignatius, Prayer and the Early Society of Jesus," *Woodstock Letters: A Historical Journal of Jesuit Educational and Missionary Activities* 94, no. 2 (Spring 1965): 121.

18. Ibid.

19. Joseph de Guibert, S.J., *The Jesuits: Their Spiritual Doctrine and Practice, a Historical Study*, ed. George E. Ganss, S.J., trans. William J. Young, S.J. (Chicago: Institute of Jesuit Sources, 1964), 45.

20. Friedrich Wulf, S.J., et al., *Ignatius of Loyola, His Personality and Spiritual Heritage, 1556–1956: Studies on the 400th Anniversary of His Death* (St. Louis: Institute of Jesuit Sources, 1977), 151.

21. *Constitutions*, #577.

22. John W. Padberg, S.J., Martin D. O'Keefe, S.J., and John L. McCarthy, S.J., *For Matters of Greater Moment: The First Thirty Jesuit General Congregations, a Brief History and a Translation of the Decrees* (St. Louis: Institute of Jesuit Sources, 1994), 9.

23. Roberto de Nobili, "The Report on Certain Customs of the Indian Nation," in *Preaching Wisdom to the Wise: Three Treatises*, trans. Anand Amaladass, S.J., and Francis X. Clooney, S.J. (St. Louis: Institute of Jesuit Sources, 2000), 63.

24. Ibid., 220.

25. Ibid., 179.

26. Ibid., 226.

27. Francis X. Clooney, S.J., a noted scholar of the Hindu faith, eloquently elaborates on this tension between "interreligious dialogue" and "proclaiming the gospel" in his recent monograph, "A Charism for Dialog: Advice from the Early Jesuit Missionaries in Our World of Religious Pluralism," *Studies in the Spirituality of Jesuits* 34, no. 2 (March 2002). Readers of his essay will be able to appreciate the current state of discussion on this question and will also be reminded how much Jesuits such as Xavier, de Nobili, and others can still teach their modern successors.

    Many of the stories in this book are drawn from an age when the prevalent mindset among Christian missioners was driven by "making conversions," plain and simple. No Jesuit today—and certainly not this author—would condone what we now understand to be a simplistic (and sometimes disrespectful) approach to dialogue with those of the Jewish, Hindu, and Muslim faiths, or those of any other religious faiths. Rather, inherent in any Christian's mandate to "proclaim the gospel" is a genuine, deep respect for other humans, their free will, their beliefs, and what we have to learn from those beliefs even as we share our own.

28. George H. Dunne, S.J., *Generation of Giants: The Story of the Jesuits in China in the Last Decades of the Ming Dynasty* (Notre Dame, Ind.: University of Notre Dame Press, 1962), 272.

29. Ibid., 273.

30. Vincent Cronin, *A Pearl to India: The Life of Roberto de Nobili* (London: Rupert Hart-Davis, 1959), 226.

31. Ibid., 229.

32. *Constitutions*, #547.

33. Ibid.

34. de Guibert, *Jesuits*, 100.

35. Young, *Letters of St. Ignatius of Loyola*, 401.

36. Ibid., 59.

37. de Guibert, *Jesuits*, 102.

38. Ibid.

Chapter 8: "Refuse No Talent, Nor Any Man of Quality"

1. Joseph H. Fichter, S.J., *James Laynez: Jesuit* (St. Louis: B. Herder Book Co., 1944), 282.

2. James J. Reites, S.J., "St. Ignatius of Loyola and the Jews," *Studies of the Spirituality of Jesuits* 13, no. 4 (September 1981): 17.

3. Charles W. Reinhardt, S.J., "An Apostle of Europe," *Woodstock Letters: A Historical Journal of Jesuit Educational and Missionary Activities* 71, no. 2 (June 1942): 151.

4. William J. Young, S.J., *Letters of St. Ignatius of Loyola* (Chicago: Loyola Press, 1959), 270–71.

5. Ibid., 272–73.

6. Jean Lacouture, *Jesuits: A Multibiography*, trans. Jeremy Leggatt (Washington, D.C.: Counterpoint, 1995), 168.

7. Reites, "St. Ignatius of Loyola and the Jews," 23.

8. Lacouture, *Jesuits*, 166.

9. *Spiritual Exercises*, #230.

10. Joseph de Guibert, S.J., *The Jesuits: Their Spiritual Doctrine and Practice, a Historical Study*, ed. George E. Ganss, S.J., trans. William J. Young, S.J. (Chicago: Institute of Jesuit Sources, 1964), 93.

11. Ibid.

12. Young, *Letters of St. Ignatius of Loyola*, 242.

13. *Constitutions*, #667.

14. Niccolò Machiavelli, *The Prince*, ed. and trans. Robert M. Adams, 2d ed. (New York: Norton, 1992), 46, #17.

15. Edgar H. Schein, *Organizational Culture and Leadership*, 2d ed. (San Francisco: Jossey-Bass, 1992), 125.

16. Ibid.

17. Louis Uchitelle, "These Days, Layoffs Compete with Loyalty," *New York Times*, 19 August 2001, sec. 3, p. 4.

18. Frederick J. Reiter, *They Built Utopia: The Jesuit Missions in Paraguay, 1610–1768* (Potomac, Md.: Scripta Humanistica, 1995), 24.

19. Ibid.

20. Ibid., 29.

21. C. J. McNaspy, S.J., *Conquistador without Sword: The Life of Roque González, S.J.* (Chicago: Loyola Press, 1984), 137.

22. Ibid, 138.

23. Reiter, *They Built Utopia*, 87.

24. Ibid., 37.

25. Philip Caraman, *The Lost Paradise: The Jesuit Republic in South America* (New York: Seabury Press, 1976), 141.

26. Ibid., 153.

27. Antonio Ruiz de Montoya, S.J., *The Spiritual Conquest: Accomplished by the Religious of the Society of Jesus in the Provinces of Paraguay, Paraná, Uruguay, and Tape*, trans. C. J. McNaspy, S.J., John P. Leonard, S.J., Martin E. Palmer, S.J. (St. Louis: Institute of Jesuit Sources, 1993), 17.

28. Joel S. Panzer, *The Popes and Slavery* (New York: Alba House, 1996), 34.

29. Caraman, *Lost Paradise*, 237.

30. Ibid., 250.

31. Ibid., 137.

32. Panzer, *Popes and Slavery*, 20.

33. David Maraniss, *When Pride Still Mattered: A Life of Vince Lombardi* (New York: Simon and Schuster, 1999), 405.

34. Ibid., 374.

35. M. Joseph Costelloe, S.J., trans., *The Letters and Instructions of Francis Xavier* (St. Louis: Institute of Jesuit Sources, 1992), 312.

36. Georg Schurhammer, S.J., *Francis Xavier: His Life, His Times*, trans. M. Joseph Costelloe, S.J. (Rome: Jesuit Historical Institute, 1973–82), 4:438.

37. *Constitutions*, #134.

38. C. R. Boxer, *Race Relations in the Portuguese Colonial Empire, 1415–1825* (Oxford: Clarendon Press, 1963), 96.

Chapter 9: "An Uninterrupted Life of Heroic Deeds"

1. Jeffrey L. Seglin, "The Values Statement vs. Corporate Reality," *New York Times*, 17 September 2000, sec. 3, p. 4.

2. William J. Young, S.J., *Letters of St. Ignatius of Loyola* (Chicago: Loyola Press, 1959), 122.

3. John W. O'Malley, S.J., *The First Jesuits* (Cambridge: Harvard University Press, 1993), 61.

4. Frederick Herzberg, *The Managerial Choice: To Be Efficient and to Be Human* (Homewood, Ill.: Dow Jones-Irwin, 1976), 107.

5. William V. Bangert, S.J., *A History of the Society of Jesus*, 2d ed. (St. Louis: Institute of Jesuit Sources, 1986), 349.

6. John W. Padberg, S.J., "Development of the Ratio Studiorum," in *The Jesuit Ratio Studiorum: 400th Anniversary Perspectives*, ed. Vincent J. Duminuco, S.J. (New York: Fordham University Press, 2000), 98.

7. J. F. Moran, *The Japanese and the Jesuits: Alessandro Valignano in Sixteenth-Century Japan* (New York: Routledge, 1993), 51.

8. C. R. Boxer, *Race Relations in the Portuguese Colonial Empire, 1415–1825* (Oxford: Clarendon Press, 1963), 87.

9. Two sources have particularly guided the Jesuit education story presented in this chapter. John W. O'Malley, S.J., in *The First Jesuits*, discusses the Jesuit entry into the field of education. Paul F. Grendler, in *Schooling in Renaissance Italy: Literacy and Learning, 1300–1600* (Baltimore: Johns Hopkins University Press, 1989), discusses the European educational environment into which the Jesuits launched their effort.

10. For the Jesuits' urban strategy, see Thomas M. Lucas, S.J., *Landmarking: City, Church and Jesuit Urban Strategy* (Chicago: Loyola Press, 1997).

11. O'Malley, *First Jesuits*, 55.

12. James C. Collins and Jerry I. Porras, *Built to Last: Successful Habits of Visionary Companies* (New York: HarperBusiness, 1994), 91 n.

13. Dauril Alden, *The Making of an Enterprise: The Society of Jesus in Portugal, Its Empire, and Beyond, 1540–1750* (Stanford, Calif.: Stanford University Press, 1996), 488–89.

14. Robin Blackburn, *The Making of New World Slavery: From the Baroque to the Modern, 1492–1800* (London: Verso, 1997), 209.

15. Ibid.

16. Alden, *Making of an Enterprise*, 262.

17. Padberg, "Development of the Ratio Studiorum," 87.

18. E. Edward Kinerk, S.J., "Eliciting Great Desires: Their Place in the Spirituality of the Society of Jesus," *Studies in the Spirituality of Jesuits* 16, no. 5 (November 1984): 9.

19. Erik Eckholm, "China's Man to Watch Steps into the U.S. Spotlight," *New York Times*, 27 April 2002, sec. A, p. 3.

20. O'Malley, *First Jesuits*, 213.

21. Paul F. Grendler, *Schooling in Renaissance Italy*, 375–76.

Chapter 10: "Exceptional Daring Was Essential"

1. William V. Bangert, S.J., *A History of the Society of Jesus*, 2d ed. (St. Louis: Institute of Jesuit Sources, 1986), 365.

2. Ibid., 298.

3. Thomas H. Clancy, S.J., *An Introduction to Jesuit Life: The Constitutions and History through 435 Years* (St. Louis: Institute of Jesuit Sources, 1976), 174.

4. Thomas M. Lucas, S.J. *Landmarking: City, Church and Jesuit Urban Strategy* (Chicago: Loyola Press, 1997), 149.

5. Jean Lacouture, *Jesuits: A Multibiography*, trans. Jeremy Leggatt (Washington, D.C.: Counterpoint, 1995), 267.

6. Philip Caraman, *The Lost Paradise: The Jesuit Republic in South America* (New York: Seabury Press, 1976), 242.

7. Lacouture, *Jesuits*, 294.

8. Edward I. Devitt, S.J., "The Suppression and Restoration of the Society in Maryland," *Woodstock Letters: A Historical Journal of Jesuit Educational and Missionary Activities* 34, no. 2 (1905): 204.

9. Ibid., 208.

10. Ibid., 209.

11. Ibid., 216.

12. Paul Dudon, S.J., "The Resurrection of the Society of Jesus," trans. Gerald McCool, S.J., *Woodstock Letters: A Historical Journal of Jesuit Educational and Missionary Activities* 81, no. 4 (November 1952): 330.

13. Ibid.

14. Lacouture, *Jesuits*, 328.

Chapter 11: "The Way We Do Things"

1. John P. Kotter and James L. Heskett, *Corporate Culture and Performance* (New York: Free Press, 1992), 41.

2. Ibid, 55.

3. *Constitutions*, #308.

4. Kotter and Heskett, *Corporate Culture and Performance*, 11.

5. James C. Collins and Jerry I. Porras, *Built to Last: Successful Habits of Visionary Companies* (New York: HarperBusiness, 1994), 89.

6. Warren Bennis and Burt Nanus, *Leaders: The Strategies for Taking Charge* (New York: Harper and Row, 1985), 92.

7. Pasquale M. D'Elia, S.J., *Galileo in China: Relations through the Roman College between Galileo and the Jesuit Scientist-Missionaries (1610–1640)*, trans. Rufus Suter and Matthew Sciascia (Cambridge: Harvard University Press, 1960), 15.

8. George H. Dunne, S.J., *Generation of Giants: The Story of the Jesuits in China in the Last Decades of the Ming Dynasty* (Notre Dame, Ind.: University of Notre Dame Press, 1962), 210.

9. D'Elia, *Galileo in China*, 24–25.

10. Dunne, *Generation of Giants*, 347.

11. Ibid., 325.

12. Ibid., 330.

13. Ibid., 333.

14. Rachel Attwater, *Adam Schall: A Jesuit at the Court of China, 1592–1666* (Milwaukee: Bruce, 1963), 142.

15. Ibid., 154.

16. Ibid.

17. *Spiritual Exercises*, #185–86.

18. Attwater, *Adam Schall*, 154.

19. Theodore N. Foss, "A Western Intepretation of China," in *East Meets West: The Jesuits in China, 1582–1773*, ed. Charles E. Ronan, S.J., and Bonnie B. C. Oh (Chicago: Loyola Press, 1988), 226.

Chapter 12: Conclusion

1. Charles E. Ronan, S.J., and Bonnie B. C. Oh, eds., *East Meets West: The Jesuits in China, 1582–1773* (Chicago: Loyola Press, 1988), xxxiii.

2. T. Babington Macaulay, "Ranke's History of the Popes," in *Critical and Miscellaneous Essays*, vol. 1 of The Modern British Essayists (Philadelphia: Carey and Hart, 1846), 407.

3. Immanuel Chung-Yueh Hsü, *The Rise of Modern China*, 4th ed. (New York: Oxford University Press, 1990), 103.

4. Michael John Gorman, "Consuming Jesuit Science, 1600–1665," in *The Jesuits: Cultures, Sciences, and the Arts, 1540–1773*, ed. John W. O'Malley, S.J., Gauvin Alexander Bailey, Steven J. Harris, and T. Frank Kennedy, S.J. (Toronto: University of Toronto Press, 1999), 172.

5. Thomas H. Clancy, S.J., *An Introduction to Jesuit Life: The Constitutions and History through 435 Years* (St. Louis: Institute of Jesuit Sources, 1976), 111.

6. Jean Lacouture, *Jesuits: A Multibiography*, trans. Jeremy Leggatt (Washington, D.C.: Counterpoint, 1995), 166.

7. Joseph de Guibert, S.J., *The Jesuits: Their Spiritual Doctrine and Practice, a Historical Study*, ed. George E. Ganss, S.J., trans. William J. Young, S.J. (Chicago: Institute of Jesuit Sources, 1964), 45.

8. W. W. Meissner, "Psychological Notes on the Spiritual Exercises," *Woodstock Letters: A Historical Journal of Jesuit Educational and Missionary Activities* 92, no. 4 (November 1963): 355.

9. Adapted from Elizabeth G. Chambers, et al., "The War for Talent," *McKinsey Quarterly*, no. 3 (1998): 50.

10. de Guibert, *Jesuits*, 102.

11. Ibid., 100.

12. William J. Young, S.J., *Letters of St. Ignatius of Loyola* (Chicago: Loyola Press, 1959), 401.

13. Joseph N. Tylenda, S.J., *Jesuit Saints and Martyrs* (Chicago: Loyola Press, 1998), xvi.

14. John P. Kotter and James L. Heskett, *Corporate Culture and Performance* (New York: Free Press, 1992), 50.

15. John P. Kotter, *John P. Kotter on What Leaders Really Do* (Boston: Harvard Business School Press, 1999), 1.

Suggestions for
Further Reading

A comprehensive bibliography of the works dedicated to any of the broad topics touched on in this book would run to many pages; the following focuses instead on select English-language works that helped mold my picture of Jesuit leadership values and Jesuit history. Readers should consult the notes for references to some of the many other valuable sources not highlighted in the following but nonetheless instrumental to my research and preparation of this book.

General Histories of the Jesuits

In *The First Jesuits* (Cambridge: Harvard University Press, 1993), author John W. O'Malley, S.J., traces Jesuit prehistory and the Jesuits' early years. Readable yet scholarly, it is a masterpiece. *A History of the Society of Jesus,* 2d ed. (St. Louis: Institute of Jesuit Sources, 1986), by William V. Bangert, S.J., is a comprehensive, carefully researched history of the company from its founding through the early 1980s. It's probably the most comprehensive one-volume effort of its kind in English. Jean Lacouture's *Jesuits: A Multibiography* (Washington, D.C.: Counterpoint, 1995), translated by Jeremy Leggatt, traces the same period explored in Fr. Bangert's work, but in a more colorful and less comprehensive fashion. He bends his selection of anecdotes slightly to accommodate his original French audience. Dauril Alden's *The Making of an Enterprise: The Society of Jesus in Portugal, Its Empire, and Beyond, 1540–1750* (Stanford, Calif.: Stanford University Press, 1996) is a seven-hundred-page scholarly work focusing on Jesuit operations in the Portuguese empire. Because Portuguese domains figured so prominently in early Jesuit history, Alden ranges across all major aspects of Jesuit operations, and he does so effectively. Malachi Martin's *The Jesuits: The Society of Jesus and the Betrayal of the Roman Catholic Church* (New York: Simon and Schuster, 1987), verging on the sensationalistic, will sate those compelled to search out a "dark" interpretation of Jesuit history by an author with a definite point of view.

More specialized surveys: *The Jesuits: Cultures, Sciences, and the Arts, 1540–1773* (Toronto: University of Toronto Press, 1999), edited by John W. O'Malley, S.J., Gauvin Alexander Bailey, Steven J. Harris, and T. Frank Kennedy, S.J., is a fascinating, wide-ranging collection of papers. Gauvin A. Bailey's *Art on the Jesuit Missions in Asia and Latin America, 1542–1773* (Toronto: University of Toronto Press, 2001) is a well-illustrated treatment of the topic; the art of the Paraguay reductions receives substantial attention. *The Jesuits: Their Spiritual Doctrine and Practice, a Historical Study* (Chicago: Institute of Jesuit Sources, 1964), written by Joseph de Guibert, S.J., translated by William J. Young, S.J., and edited by George E. Ganss, S.J., is a classic technical study of the Jesuits' distinctive spirituality.

Biographies of Ignatius Loyola: Unfortunately, none of the many biographies of Ignatius Loyola does full justice to this remarkable, inspiring figure. *Ignatius of Loyola, Founder of the Jesuits: His Life and Work,* by Cándido de Dalmases, S.J., and translated by Jerome Aixalá, S.J. (St. Louis: Institute of Jesuit Sources, 1985), gives a very reliable, factual account. *Ignatius of Loyola: The Psychology of a Saint* (New Haven: Yale University Press, 1992), by W. W. Meissner, S.J., will appeal to those interested in a psychoanalytic interpretation of Loyola's life.

A Bibliographical Essay on the History of the Society of Jesus: Books in English (St. Louis: Institute of Jesuit Sources, 1976), by William V. Bangert, S.J., is limited only—but importantly—by its publication date. A similar resource on Ignatian spirituality is "A Bibliography on St. Ignatius' Spiritual Exercises," by Paul Begheyn and Kenneth Bogart, in *Studies in the Spirituality of Jesuits,* volume 23, issue 3 (May 1991). More generally, *Studies in the Spirituality of Jesuits* offers journal-length treatments of Jesuit history, spirituality, and lifestyle. It is indexed annually.

Primary Sources on the Jesuits

Ignatius Loyola's short *Autobiography* is the most rewarding primary work for general readers. One of many editions is *A Pilgrim's Testament: The Memoirs of Ignatius of Loyola,* translated by Parmananda R. Divarkar (St. Louis: Institute of Jesuit Sources, 1995). Readers wishing to tap into Loyola's wisdom by reading his *Spiritual Exercises* (*The Spiritual Exercises of Saint Ignatius: A Translation and Commentary,* by George E. Ganss, S.J. [St. Louis, Institute of Jesuit Sources, 1992]) may be disappointed. True to Loyola's word, they are Exercises to be *done,* not read; the book doesn't come across as a flowing work of wisdom literature or a collection of aphorisms. More readable are Loyola's letters. One excellent collection is *Letters of St. Ignatius of Loyola,* edited and translated by William J. Young, S.J. (Chicago: Loyola Press, 1959). The Jesuit *Constitutions* (*The Constitutions of the Society of Jesus,* translated by George E. Ganss [St. Louis: Institute of Jesuit Sources, 1970]) encapsulates many of the themes discussed throughout this book. But structured as a "rule book," it does not make for stimulating reading. The early Jesuits were prolific writers and diligent archivists: the multivolume *Monumenta Historica Societatis Iesu* includes letters of St. Ignatius, letters of his early colleagues, and various documents relating to early Jesuit history throughout the world. Knowledge of Latin is essential to make much headway.

General Works on Leadership

New works on leadership—scholarly, semischolarly, and outright playful—appear almost daily. Among the important contributions, in my opinion, to this broad field are listed here.

John Kotter has written many readable yet academically grounded works on leadership. Two good starting points are *Leading Change* (Boston: Harvard Business School Press, 1996) and, with James L. Heskett, *Corporate Culture and Performance* (New York: Free Press, 1992). The short length of Warren Bennis and Burt Nanus's work *Leaders: The Strategies for Taking Charge* (New York: Harper and Row, 1997) belies its deep value. Daniel Goleman has helped spearhead the emerging emphasis on emotional intelligence in the workplace with *Emotional Intelligence* (New York: Bantam Books, 1995), *Working with*

Emotional Intelligence (New York: Bantam Books, 1998), and most recently, *Primal Leadership: Realizing the Power of Emotional Intelligence* (Boston: Harvard Business School Press, 2002). Abraham Zaleznik's *The Managerial Mystique: Restoring Leadership in Business* (New York: Harper and Row, 1989) illuminates some of the personal character traits of successful leaders. James C. Collins and Jerry I. Porras's *Built to Last: Successful Habits of Visionary Companies* (New York: HarperBusiness, 1994) is a creative, well-researched classic. Collins recently extended some of its themes in *Good to Great: Why Some Companies Make the Leap—and Others Don't* (New York: HarperBusiness, 2001).

The History of Religious Orders

David Knowles's *From Pachomius to Ignatius: A Study in the Constitutional History of the Religious Orders* (Oxford: Clarendon Press, 1966) is a concise yet sweeping vision of the evolution of religious orders in the West.

Matteo Ricci and Jesuits in China

Early Jesuit Travellers in Central Asia, 1603–1721 (The Hague: Martinus Nijhoff, 1998), by Cornelius J. Wessels, S.J., covers Goes's journey and other epic early Jesuit journeys into Tibet and elsewhere. Ricci's reflections on China, including his chronicle of Goes's trek, can be found in *China in the Sixteenth Century: The Journals of Matthew Ricci, 1583–1610,* translated by Louis J. Gallagher, S.J. (New York: Random House, 1953). There are various Ricci biographies. Jonathan D. Spence's *The Memory Palace of Matteo Ricci* (New York: Penguin Books, 1985) is a thoroughly engaging, meticulously researched, and fascinating account by a renowned scholar of Chinese history. The sometimes cumbersome *Generation of Giants: The Story of the Jesuits in China in the Last Decades of the Ming Dynasty* (Notre Dame, Ind.: University of Notre Dame Press, 1962), by George H. Dunne, S.J., is a comprehensive account of Jesuit activity in China roughly from Ricci through the death of Adam Schall.

Francis Xavier

Francis Xavier: His Life, His Times (Rome: Jesuit Historical Institute, 1973–82), written by Georg Schurhammer, S.J., and translated by M. Joseph Costelloe, S.J., is a scholarly marathon sprawling across four volumes. Few will want to read it in full, but dipping into it will provide rich detail both on Xavier's life and his sixteenth-century European and Asian work environments. *The Letters and Instructions of Francis Xavier,* translated by M. Joseph Costelloe, S.J. (St. Louis: Institute of Jesuit Sources, 1992), collects many of Xavier's more important letters.

Roberto de Nobili

Vincent Cronin's *A Pearl to India: The Life of Roberto de Nobili* (London: Rupert Hart-Davis, 1959) remains one of the better accounts of de Nobili's life. Anand Amaladass, S.J., and Francis X. Clooney, S.J., translated and wrote the introduction to Roberto de Nobili's *Preaching Wisdom to the Wise: Three Treatises* (St. Louis: Institute of Jesuit Sources, 2000), which includes de Nobili's defense of his acculturation approach.

Diego Laínez

There are virtually no English-language standalone accounts of Laínez's life other than *James Laynez: Jesuit* (St. Louis: B. Herder Book Co., 1944), by Joseph H. Fichter, S.J., which does not make for the easiest reading. "St. Ignatius of Loyola and the Jews," by James J. Reites, S.J., in *Studies in the Spirituality of Jesuits,* volume 13, issue 4 (September 1981), outlines sixteenth-century attitudes toward the Jewish people and how those attitudes were reflected (or not) by the early Jesuits.

The Paraguay Reductions

The Paraguay reductions are regularly the subject of scholarly and popular treatments, by no means all of them complimentary to the Jesuits. Philip Caraman's *The Lost Paradise: The Jesuit Republic in South America* (New York: Seabury Press, 1976), though already more than twenty-five years old, remains a well-researched, reliable discourse. Sélim Abou's *The Jesuit "Republic" of the Guaranís (1609–1768) and Its Heritage,* translated by Lawrence J. Johnson (New York: Crossroad Publishing Company, 1997), combines beautiful photos and a very general overview. C. R. Boxer's works, always masterfully researched and written, treat various topics in Jesuit history. Among his works is *Race Relations in the Portuguese Colonial Empire, 1415–1825* (Oxford: Clarendon Press, 1985). *The Christian Century in Japan* covers a fascinating period in Jesuit history that is unfortunately treated only in passing in this book. Robin Blackburn's *The Making of New World Slavery: From the Baroque to the Modern, 1492–1800* (London: Verso, 1997) is a scholarly treatment of both the roots and the economic conditions of New World slavery.

Jesuit Secondary Schools and Education

Saint Ignatius' Idea of a Jesuit University (Milwaukee: Marquette University Press, 1954), translated by George E. Ganss, S.J., traces the evolution of Jesuit involvement in schooling. Paul F. Grendler's *Schooling in Renaissance Italy: Literacy and Learning, 1300–1600* (Baltimore: Johns Hopkins University Press, 1989) treats Jesuit schools as part of a broader scholarly investigation.

The Jesuit Suppression

The Jesuit suppression has been the subject of very few standalone treatises. In *The Expulsion of the Jesuits from Latin America* (New York: Knopf, 1965), editor Magnus Mörner gathers essays from a range of perspectives. "The Second Centenary of the Suppression of the Jesuits," by William V. Bangert, S.J., in *Thought* 48 (1973), traces the roots of the Jesuit suppression in a clear, article-length treatment.

Galileo, Adam Schall, and Jesuit Scientist-Missionaries

Galileo in China: Relations through the Roman College between Galileo and the Jesuit Scientist-Missionaries (1610–1640), written by Pasquale M. D'Elia, S.J., and translated by Rufus Suter and Matthew Sciascia (Cambridge: Harvard

University Press, 1960), is as excellently researched and presented as it is concise. Dava Sobel's *Galileo's Daughter: A Historical Memoir of Science, Faith, and Love* (New York: Walker and Co., 1999) primarily covers the astronomer's relationship with his daughter but also weaves Galileo's troubles with the church and his relationships with various Jesuits into a wonderfully readable account. *East Meets West: The Jesuits in China, 1582–1773,* edited by Charles E. Ronan, S.J., and Bonnie B. C. Oh (Chicago: Loyola Press, 1988), is a collection of essays covering, among other topics, the Jesuit mapping projects in China. Rachel Attwater's *Adam Schall: A Jesuit at the Court of China, 1592–1666,* (Milwaukee: Bruce, 1963), adapted from French Jesuit Joseph Duhr's book, is a concise and easy-to-read, though somewhat superficial, account of Adam Schall's life. George Dunne's wider ranging *Generation of Giants* incorporates a better-documented but less readable account of the same material.

Index